MIND AND MATTER

Book One in the Mind and Matter series

MIND AND MATTER

A HEALING
APPROACH TO
CHRONIC ILLNESS

Lewis E. Mehl, MD,PhD

Mindbody Press
Berkeley, California

Acknowledgements

Cover Design by Richard Stodart
Photography by George Ward
Production Coordination by Marianne Morgan
Typesetting by Barlow Typesetting, Inc., and Berkeley Graphics
Printing by McNaughton & Gunn, Saline, MI
Typing by Mary Strads
Copyediting by Barbara Dalton and Eric Billitzer

ISBN 0-939508-14-1

Library of Congress Catalog Number: 86-80090

Printed in the United States of America.

Mindbody Press   **Berkeley, California**

Dedication

This book is dedicated first and foremost to my wife — my closest friend, mother of my children, constant source of inspiration and growth, the person who introduced me to dance, a beautiful woman, and my lover. It is also dedicated to my children, whom I deeply love, and to Archie and Hazel Price, my grandparents, who mean more to me than I can ever tell them.

Acknowledgements

I wish to acknowledge the help of several important people. Dr. C.J. Singh Wallia, Dr. Karl Knobler, and Ms. Lester Hazell critically read this book several times, providing important criticism and ideas. I wish to thank my students at Stanford University and at the Psychological Studies Institute, Palo Alto, for facilitating an ever deeper probing of the nature of human health and disease. I cannot conclude without thanking my parents and my Cherokee ancestors for giving me a way of "seeing" that has helped so much.

Table of Contents

Preface

It has been 150 years since it first dawned on our culture that almost everything which physicians did was either worthless or downright harmful. But today we pride ourselves that the situation has changed. Unlike our naïve but well-meaning predecessors in the profession, we have *science*, with the stupendous panoply of interventions that the term implies. Yet an awareness has dawned on our *own* culture at century's end, just as that earlier awareness settled on our society in the past century: medicine, in our time, has lost its mind.

If this observation seems hyperbolic, we have only to observe the almost total exclusion of mind from the concerns of most of bioscience. We have fallen into a habit of thinking about the mental domain that suggests that, unbelievably, the mind does not exist. We are reminded, e.g., by Carl Sagan, that the workings of the brain — what we sometimes call mind — are a result of its anatomy, its physiology, and nothing more. One would think that the absurdity of this position would have been recognized by those who are shrewd enough to pursue scientific research, but such is not the case. How, we are forced to ask, are we to take seriously a comment that mind has no meaning, when the researcher issuing the statement wishes to hang onto, at the very least, the meaningfulness of his *own* mentation? The *reductio ad absurdum* that is implied by this position once led Schopenhauer to conclude that the materialists who advance it believe that it should be applied to everybody except themselves.

What is perhaps oddest, in a quick scan of the dominant positions regarding the mind that are taken by various authorities in medical science today, is that of the specialists of the mind — psychiatrists and neurologists. Their fanatical rush toward materialistic approaches to the human illnesses which fall in their domain is difficult to deny. Everywhere the hope is that new drugs will be developed that will be specific antidotes for each particular psychological aberration, much as lithium carbonate has proved useful in the treatment of manic depression. Surgery, brain tissue implantation, and genetic recombination are also seen as promising future approaches. Amid all this enthusiasm the mind — to say nothing of concepts that were once honored in medicine, such as "soul" and "spirit" — is a pariah in its own land.

Thus it is, at this stage of our culture's attitude to medical approaches, that Lewis E. Mehl's *Mind and Matter* seems so refreshing. It is at once set apart from many of the pop treatises on self-help and positive thinking. Mehl has put together an approach that is based both on good science and good philosophy, overlaid with the most important element of all: the clinical application. Do his ideas *work?* This question is answered affirmatively in the rich clinical material that confronts us throughout the book.

The materialistic philosophy that still reigns in modern bioscience is profoundly limited and ultimately unsatisfying, even for those who espouse it. Mehl's book points to a solution. It reminds us that a conceptual pluralism is emerging in many areas of science, ways of thinking that ask us to go beyond the either-or choices that we have supposed we must make. Is it "mind" or is it "matter?" Is it all chemistry and anatomy, or does consciousness make a difference? These mutually exclusive points of view seem increasingly artificial in terms of evolving knowledge, bringing us back to Wittgenstein's observation: When we are asked to make choices between such contradictory elements, we should not feel forced to do so: for these eternal questions are likely to be unanswerable as being true or false, but are in fact nonsensical.

Thus the title of Mehl's book is Mind AND Matter, not Mind OR Matter. The difference demonstrates his complementary approach. It is an approach that hinges on an emerging body of knowledge that comes from many quarters of science today. But the best reasons for taking a complementary approach — the "both/and" instead of the "either/or" view — come not from the bubble chambers of the physicists, where the modern scientific notion of complementarity originated, but from the physician's own data. In the end it is our patients' stories and life experiences that must inform us, not information drawn from more distant quarters.

Lewis Mehl's book is a happy reminder that medicine, having lost its mind in our time, is now in the process of finding it. In this process of rediscovering our sanity in medicine, Dr. Mehl has made an important contribution.

Larry Dossey, M.D.
Dallas, Texas
January, 1986

Introduction

In writing *Mind and Matter*, I wanted to communicate hope that healing can occur. Within the confines of the medical care most people receive in the 1980s, healing is discouraged. Healing does not occur. Occasionally there is spontaneous remission, but nothing we can hope or plan for.

In my medical training at Stanford University, I learned no exceptions to this perspective. I remember a world famous professor of internal medicine who announced to our class that the job of the physician was merely to slow and make less painful the "inexorable and inevitable progression of the patient toward death and decay." I had not come to medical school for this purpose. I had come to learn about healing.

I had one advantage over some of my classmates. I came from a mixed Cherokee/Kentucky hillbilly background. I had witnessed healing as a child. I knew that miracles were possible. And I was religious. I had grown up within both the Christian and the Cherokee religious traditions. I had known of miraculous healings attributed to God or to the power of the Great Spirit moving among us. By the time I was in medical school, I was struggling to define my individual spirituality. I could not call myself any particular religion, but I knew on a cellular level that the world of the unseen existed.

Since medical school I have become even bolder, saying that healing is spiritual. Such spirituality is non-denominational. It is spiritual in the sense that healing involves communication and relationship between more than one person. In the doctor-client relationship, emotion and dialogue is created from which healing evolves. In this dialogue, we transcend our individuality. We use our words to emerge from ourselves and create emotion between us. Through the power of emotion and relationship, miracles are created.

Mind and Matter is about my experiences with clients who have physical disorders — chronic illness. It is about the process through which some of these clients — in relationship with me — discovered healing. It is about mundane miracles, the process of the human body becoming whole again.

Throughout the book, the process of relationship is emphasized. In my practice, I rely on many modalities. These include acupuncture, acupressure, homeopathy, natural remedies, hypnosis, visualization, bodywork, applied kinesiology, nutrition, and others. I emphasize that it is not the technique that heals the patient, but the relationship. Technique provides me with a vehicle for relationship. Nutrition does not heal. It can be very helpful for the healing process. Good food can nourish the spirit and the body. But healing is something more subtle than just nutrition or acupuncture.

If technique healed people, then all people would respond to the same technique. This is the basis for the rejection by modern medicine of non-pharmaceutical, non-surgical healing. Acupuncture does not help every person with arthritis. Every person with cancer does not get well after making dietary changes. Therefore, these modalities are not scientific.

Neither does every person with arthritis heal with drugs. Nor does every cancer patient respond to chemotherapy. But these modalities are considered scientific. They can be studied easily by giving half of the patients a particular drug and not giving the other half any drugs. Drugs will usually win out over no treatment. This is not the point, however. Pharmacological medicine is as non-scientific as acupuncture or naturopathy. Not all patients are cured by a particular drug.

In our society we are afraid to study the so-called placebo effect. We are afraid of the more subtle aspects of healing. We are afraid of emotions and relationship. It is so much easier to give a substance and wait for the results.

In *Mind and Matter*, I present the argument that relationship is crucial to healing. To me, holistic medicine is the concern with all aspects of the client's being in the process of relationship and with respect to the power of relationship. Many modalities may support that relationship — even drugs and surgery. I emphasize that the word holistic refers to the wholeness of the person and not to a treatment modality considered alternative by the American Medical Association. A surgeon can be just as holistic as an herbologist or a homeopath.

Dr. Bernie Siegel, a surgeon at Yale University Medical School, illustrates this. Dr. Siegel is very concerned with mobilizing the clients resources to promote healing. He plays music that he finds healing during surgery and respects the messages that the staff may communicate to even the unconscious patient. Dr. Siegel believes that 15-20% of patients are able to choose to put all their resources to bear on the prospects of getting well. Another 60% are unable to do so, and perhaps 20% want to die.

In my work, I conceptualize the person as part of a larger system — a family, or a community. Some patients are in a position within their larger context such as to be able to direct resources and energy toward healing; others are so enmeshed in a context that requires or supports illness that they are unable to move toward wellness. I work to catalyze change in that system so that the client has more resources to move toward wellness. Dr. John Harrison expresses this well in his book, *Love*

Your Disease. We should love our disease because it is keeping us healthy. Without the disease we have, we might have a worse illness. Disease is always a creative attempt to solve problems. When we accept this, we can move toward wellness by thanking our disease and discovering in relationship with other people — a group or our doctor — other ways to solve the problems which the disease is addressing.

Disease is sometimes a side effect of family interaction. In my family of origin, we never expressed feelings toward each other. My mother, most of all, kept her frustrations inside, and she eventually suffered a stroke two hours after telling my sister that she would rather die than see my sister marry her fiancé. My own personal journey has been to move toward wellness by learning more life-affirming patterns of relating than those I learned in my family. That continues to be a creative struggle that brings me closer to wholeness as I continue to probe and change my reactions and responses.

Spirit is what moves therapy and healing. Spirit is not easy to define. Christians call it soul. Spirit is that part of us that we sense on a mountain top. It belongs both to our bodies and the world of the unseen. Spirit is what we sense in a 1000 year old church or in a religious site of an early Indian tribe. Spirit is the part of us that we most innerly identify with.

We live in a materialistic world which is high on technology and low on spirit. It is no wonder that we turn to technology when we are sick. We want to be scientific. We want something solid to trust. How can we trust in relationship?

This is why psychology and psychiatry are not sciences of healing. Psychology and psychiatry concern themselves with the objectification of emotion. Many therapists are as scared of emotion as their clients. Many psychiatrists turn to drugs when the emotions become too powerful (in the form of alcohol for themselves and major tranquilizers and anti-depressants for their clients). Psychologists will often turn to testing or will refer the client to a psychiatrist for medication. Therapy as it is practiced in the world today cannot necessarily lead us toward wholeness.

Mind and Matter is about therapy for physical illness. This is not insight therapy in which feelings are objectified and people are made into objects (as in object relations theory). This is experiential therapy in which emotions interplay and develop and interweave and people have experiences that change their lives and their perceptions of themselves and other people.

My style of therapy requires that the therapist be willing to be aware of his or her own emotions. This is not always easy for me either, but the process requires an ongoing committment to emotional honesty. Our bodies are always communicating our emotions. To hide these emotions is harmful to the body. Honesty opens the body for expression. Dishonest communication contributes to body distress. Some therapists do not express their emotions, but mirror everything back to the client. These therapists may not even have words for their own feelings, but they have learned in training how to be reflective or interpretative. I have struggled with that problem, too, to learn to do my work.

Not so long ago, I would smile if someone made a cutting remark to me. My wife could insult me to pieces and I would stand there smiling, unconsciously encouraging her to do it more. I had to learn not to smile. I had to learn to reflect my inner feeling in my body language. I had grown up disconnected from that awareness that many people have inately. My kind of therapy is challenging for the therapist, since we must always be looking at ourselves and growing. It is an ongoing quest toward becoming. Never can we be content where we are. Many therapists and doctors would rather settle for a body of knowledge in which competence can be defined and achieved in a relatively short period of time. For that reason, the kind of therapy described in *Mind and Matter* will not be easy to find.

I also agree with Dr. Larry Dossey who argues that the goal of medicine is not perfect health, but rather a process of movement toward health that is emotionally and spiritually satisfying. The process is more important than the outcome. It is through committment to the process of life that a sense of quality of life emerges. Excessive attachment to wellness detracts from the sense of process required to move toward it. Complete wholeness is an ever elusive goal. Being on the path is the best we can achieve. The goal then becomes epiphenomenal, more of a side achievement than the purpose of our quest.

If we train a rat to use its right paw to press a lever, an increase will occur in the number of synapses in the motor area of the brain that controls the right paw. If we then retrain the rat to use its left paw, the number of synapses in the other side of the brain for paw motor control increases while there is a concomitant reduction in the number of synapses on the side of the first training. If we compare ourselves to rats in the negative sense (metaphors of the rat race), why not in the positive sense of the plasticity experiments just cited? People are able to change throughout their lives.

Instead of believing in adaptability and change, medicine takes a defensive, militaristic stance toward the body. We "combat" osteoporosis or "fight off" an infection. We ask that the immune system "remain vigilant against foreign invaders." We do not believe we can retrain ourselves, just as we did the rats, to adapt to being healthier. But we can change the synapses in our brains and move toward healthier behavior.

Fear of death motivates most biomedical behavior. Patients are afraid of dying and present the doctor with total responsibility for their well-being. Doctors are afraid of death. We are afraid to get close to patients with disease for fear they may die. I tell this to the cancer patients with whom I work. I ask them that we make a committment to the process of our work together regardless of the outcome. I want to be with them in death or life. The outcome is not as important as the process in which we work. This is made clear in the example of Xavier in Chapter One.

The movement toward health is a movement toward embracing life in all of its fullness. It is not fearfully asking which calcium supplement is best to prevent osteoporosis, but living in our body so completely that we know what it needs and can give it that. The doctor may have to begin by telling the client what his body needs. The goal of treatment, however, is that the client acknowledge his greater wisdom with respect to his personal body. The patient always knows better than the doctor what is needed, though he may at first be afraid to ask or to look, or may have been trained not to pay attention to that inner voice.

Health is a dynamic process of exchange with the environment. The exchange is of emotions, nutrients, thoughts, and other substances and is all encompassing. When those exchanges are in balance and are harmonized, we quite naturally select the healthiest course for our very unique bodies and circumstances.

In this respect, I do not criticize a particular food and say that all persons who eat, for example, sugar, must become ill. Sugar is fine for some people. Sugar produces devastating effects for others. Caffeine does not affect some; it must be eliminated in others. We are as biochemically unique as we are emotionally and interpersonally unique. True health lies in the freedom to live as we wish. For some, eliminating dairy products creates that freedom. Others who wish to eat dairy find other ways to change their responses to dairy. In all ways, we are moving toward increasing our freedom. My diabetes client of Chapter Two illustrates this graphically. She could have speeded her progress toward lower insulin dosages by changing her diet and exercising more, but she didn't consider those changes as reflecting a move toward increased freedom. She would not make those changes. For her, only inner change would create the freedom she wanted. Other clients are different. Another client I worked with eliminated his need for insulin through a strict regimen of diet and exercise. This was increased freedom for him.

Medical research cannot help us. The results of medical research seem to change every two years. Two years ago smoked fish was discouraged as leading toward heart attacks. Now we know that smoked fish contains a fatty acid that is highly protective. What will we know two more years from now?

Most medical research tries so hard to isolate one factor that it ignores the rest of the world and cannot be applied to people living in an environment of constant change. Through embracing life we can transcend medical research and know for ourselves what we need. This is more reliable than results of studies which change frequently.

Love and the transcendence that love brings can lead us to health quicker than obsessing about minute details of our diets. The pursuit of health follows the path of wholeness rather than the avoidance of disease. Illnesses are sometimes the low points in a road that is, in general, healthy.

Lastly, *Mind and Matter* stresses the need to change the perspective that the individual is the place to study disease. Disease passes through the individual, but the culture and the family must be examined to understand the disease of the individual. This concept will become clear in the case examples of the chapters to follow.

In writing this book, I have used many case examples so the reader will understand what I am doing even when I may not totally understand myself or have missed an important point that my deeper self knew and worked with. At times I reflect upon the physiology of the various disease processes with which I am working. The non-biologist may want to skim these parts of the book and return to the general discussion and the case studies which are the process and which the biological discussions are only meant to amplify. My wish is that this book gives every reader hope for healing chronic illness and that we can all move toward a healthier society; a world in which the movement and dance of love is far more evident than it is now.

Chapter One

Introduction to Holistic Health

The following heading, in a recent edition of the San Francisco
Chronicle,[1] quickly calls forth the issues that prompted *Mind and
Matter*: "Parents Give Credit to God for Healing of Doomed Girl."
Regardless of what or whom is attributed with responsibility for such
healing, its occurrence demands study and explanation. A consideration
of the United Press text of the article provides us with even more
fascinating data:

Grants Pass, Ore.

In November 1979, Ray Wallace was so convinced that
his 1½-year-old daughter was going to die that he contacted a
funeral home about arrangements for her burial.

Today he says the little girl Melynda, just turned 3, is
"totally healed." He and his wife, Pam, credit God, not medical
science.

Soon after her birth, March 2, 1978, Melynda became
critically ill, the victim of a malignant brain tumor. The infant
could not retain food and required constant care.

In August 1979, surgeons at the University of Oregon
Health Sciences Center in Portland removed "about half a
cup" of the tumor, but not all of it because it had invaded the
brain stem.

The doctors said Melynda might live six months or a
year.

The University of California Medical Center in San Francisco offered help, and Melynda spent five weeks there. Her

condition appeared to worsen, however, and her parents took her home to die.

By November 1979, her condition appeared so hopeless that the Wallaces prayed she would die. Her father contacted the funeral home.

The child was taken off her medication in February 1980, because, her parents said, it seemed to increase her suffering, not help it.

"We placed her in the hands of the Lord," Wallace said. Soon, on March 17, 1980, Melynda began eating, and the food stayed down. Soon she was learning to talk, then to walk, and finally was playing with her brothers, Aaron and Daniel.

Now she weighs 27 pounds, and doctors say her development is nearly normal for her age. She can run as well as walk.

A brain scan performed March 3, 1981, at Southern Oregon General Hospital in Grants Pass, showed no sign of the tumor.

"We give the glory to God," Wallace said.

Nothing in the standard textbooks on internal medicine, neurology, or neurosurgery suggests that such healing of a malignant brain tumor could ever be conceivable. Yet it happened. Five years from now a discussion of such healing will probably still not appear in such textbooks, just as similar stories appearing in the newspapers of five years ago are not discussed in today's editions of medical wisdom. Why not? Why are most medical thinkers afraid to consider these phenomena? Perhaps the admission that methods of healing other than those the physicians were trained to use might be successful would result in more anxiety than most could handle. Many doctors need to feel that they know most of what is known in their field. Doctors are trained to believe they hold the ultimate knowledge as learned in current medical technology. The anxiety generated from a challenge to that belief could be tremendous.

Disease seems so simple when conceptualized as a simple mechanical process. The body breaks down, perhaps in a random fashion. The doctor diagnoses it with various scientific tests. Then a drug is given, or surgery performed. If these interventions do not succeed, the problem is hopeless and the doctor prepares the patient and the family to expect the worst. (Perhaps the doctor *conditions* the patient and the family to expect the worst, thereby helping to create a self-fulfilling prophecy of doom.)

If the patient or family approached most doctors with a story such as the one just quoted, or even brought the doctor the newspaper clipping, the report of healing would probably be dismissed as a hoax. The doctor might further discourage the family or patient from considering such possibilities. If we asked such doctors the reason for the discouragement, many would answer that since such healing is not possible, they want to protect their patients from the ravages of possible disappointment. Many doctors frequently discourage women from using natural childbirth methods because of similar fears that the woman cannot succeed and will be disappointed. What if the woman cannot tolerate the pain or has a complication? It is better she not even try than face disappointment. Why are doctors so afraid of their patients' disappointment?

If the universe is entirely rational, then there is no reason to be anxious, because science can always predict what will happen next. The outcome of a disease that cannot be helped with drugs or surgery is always death. Not so with Melynda Wallace. Perhaps doctors are afraid to admit that science does not know everything about how the universe functions. Only within the laboratory does the universe seem rational, and many modern physicists are suggesting that this seeming rationality is all illusion, too.[2] Neither God nor magic has died entirely. But what or who is God? What is magic? Perhaps within our relentless quest for knowledge and understanding, we can begin to understand God and magic in both rational *and* intuitive terms. Not every parent has the faith of Ray and Pam Wallace. Not everyone believes in magic. As health professionals, how can we help our clients to discover their own unique roads to health and personal growth? Atheists can also have "miracle cures." Belief in God is not a necessary precondition to the healing process.

In trying to understand the structure of "miracles," basic questions about the nature and structure of mind and matter arise. Mind is matter, and yet it is more. Mind is both within physical reality and beyond it. A lesion of the brain changes personality. Neurohormonal[3] events accompany every emotion. Yet our thoughts and feelings also affect our bodies.

A common, simplistic view is that healing results from a triumph of mind over matter. My concept suggests that the inseparable duo of mind and body are part of the same tissue substance, and yet there are undeniable differences. The word mindbody can be used to describe the inherent, inseparable nature of the mind and the body.

Regardless of our theories, medical scientists need to take notice of healing in its various manifestations. The concept of subjects considered legitimate branches of medicine needs to expand to include more than just the physiological and structural aspects of the body as a basis for understanding health and illness.

Holistic health is the approach to health and disease which seeks to include all factors that can possibly affect human life. The word comes originally from "wholistic," meaning "pertaining to the study of wholes." The "whole" is always greater than the sum of its parts. Both modern systems theory and gestalt psychology address this point eloquently. What is more important is that in a system or a gestalt, every part interacts with every other part, so that a change in one part affects every other part. If a family member begins to act strangely and is labelled crazy, that member's behavior affects every other family member. If one part of the body malfunctions, other parts are affected. In the sociocultural system, the popularity of disco music has far-reaching effects upon people who are not even remotely interested in it. Sales of clothing, records, rental fees for studio space — all are affected by changes in popularity. Holistic medicine refers to the branch of medicine that concerns itself with the *general* aspects of health and disease, as opposed to specialties more concerned with specifics such as urology, neurology, endocrinology. Holistic medicine has insights to offer every discipline, but is separated from the other branches of medicine in its concern for the overall, rather than the specific. The branch of medicine which most closely approximates holistic medicine is behavioral medicine, an interdisciplinary child of psychiatry and psychology. Classical psychiatry, unfortunately, sometimes functions to preserve the artificial separation between mind and body by taking care of the "mentally ill," so the "real doctors" can treat the sick. The word "holistic" is used pejoratively in most medical centers. Most professors of medicine have decided that holistic medicine has little to offer their students.

Holistic has also come to mean to some people treatment with vitamins or nutrition or other substances that traditional physicians do not use. Such substances could include homeopathic remedies, Bach flower remedies,[4] herbs, or various potions. Unfortunately, many have come to place holistic medicine in the category of encompassing anything physicians who might qualify to join the *American Medical Association, do not do.* Advocates of nutrition as the *only* cure for everything call themselves holistic. Yet they, too, treat the person from the outside, and address only a small specific part of the individual's behavior. The giving of various external remedies without a consideration of the whole person in the context of his or her family and environment is not holistic.

Such emphasis on external remedies is the same as the belief that we can become healthy by taking what the doctor prescribes. This ignores the possibility for transformation and growth that is inherent in illness. Many are so busy looking for the miracle drug or herb that will cure every ailment, that they ignore the mundane miracle that occurs when disease improves through the efforts of the patient instead of through the doctor. Perhaps doctors as well as herbalists and acupuncturists become so enamored of the "savior" role that it is difficult to relinquish.

In the examples to be developed, the interaction of as many of these factors that impinge upon the person as is possible will be considered. The basis of discussion is a general theory of illness and healing. This is similar to the kind of study anthropologists make of primitive cultures, yet we are studying our own culture. The success of modern drugs and surgery does not preclude concurrent usefulness of procedures such as visualization[5] in helping cancer patients cure themselves. We must be able to explain how primitive magician healers, such as the Ethiopian *debtera*,[6] can, in cooperation with their clients effect changes in disorders that in most American cities would be treated exclusively with drugs or surgery.

Most medical and scientific writers ignore the fact that such events have been reported by anthropologists and continue to be described in every corner of the world; from Brazil to East Africa[7] to the Kalihari Desert,[8] these so-called "primitives," without access to pharmaceuticals or surgery, occasionally "outdo" we modern, sophisticated people. Even in modern-day America, faith healers of the Pentecostal church,[7] as well as other church healers, participate in events that can only be labelled miracles. If these are really miracles, can we discover predictable events or prerequisites that precede such miracles? If yes, can we help our clients to access such information? These are the relevant questions for medicine, especially when the side effects of medical treatment can be so devastating.

Dr. Alex Comfort[9] of the University of California Medical School at Irvine has written about how much easier it was to practice medicine and give relatively inactive placebos in the time before our modern powerful pharmaceutics. He states, "But the fact remains that an estimated 50 to 60 percent both of medication and of laboratory investigation is probably superfluous, if not harmful, which raises the economic as well as the therapeutic significance of the physician's judgment to a very high level indeed. We could try to emphasize this in medical school. Or, we could start importing the concept of barefoot doctors from China — they probably do less harm than the shamans with live pharmacological ammunition, and everyone could afford to be sick again."

Patients successfully treated with drugs for one disease (Hodgkin's disease) have a much higher chance of developing another disease (leukemia). Many physicians treat the patient with severe bowel inflammation (ulcerative colitis or regional enteritis) with relatively ineffective drugs, waiting for the time when the bowel must be removed and a colostomy is placed. The colostomy patient has the end of his or her intestine draining onto the skin with the products of digestion being caught in a plastic bag. The psychological effects of this can be devastating, an issue many physicians rarely consider. If we can learn how to intervene effectively before surgery at levels beyond our current knowledge, perhaps we can prevent some of the misery and suffering modern medicine leaves in its wake.

Holistic means that we must consider every single factor that could conceivably affect the patient. A complete list of these would include everything we could conceptualize as playing even a small role in human affairs. A short list could include diet, heredity, environment, stress, emotions, attitudes, beliefs, family system effects, community system effects, religion, acculturation, and many more. A holistic health practitioner does not necessarily work at each of these levels, but with an understanding that all exist and are important. The holistic practitioner also knows that all are interactive. Changing diet may change the contribution of other factors. Decreasing sugar intake may reduce genetic susceptibility to diabetes. A patient may be more or less stressed from a given diet. Did the diet change because the religion changed? What effects will that change of religion have on the client's health? How will the community and the patient's family react to the new diet and/or the new religion? What beliefs led the client to believe this new diet would be helpful?

Consider a patient who changed her diet every six months. Her family had taught her that she must eat right to be healthy. This she believed, but was confronted with the question of who decided what it meant to "eat right." She had read about one woman who was reported to live only on water, air, and sunshine. Was this the best way? Or was it best to be a vegetarian, or to fast? She would follow a particular dietary practice for six months. Then she would become disenchanted because her various problems remained despite the new diet. One of these problems was being overweight. Despite her dietary changes, she remained on a cyclical path between what she considered her normal weight and what she considered overweight. Therapy consisted of helping her to take a new perspective from which she could examine her beliefs about food and could consider what food had symbolized in her family. Then she was able to lose weight rapidly and easily.

Many medical thinkers dismiss stories of "miracle cures" as the random product of "spontaneous remission." This concept describes a belief that a certain small percentage of diseases spontaneously cure themselves for no reason and in a random distribution. The assumption is that the cure has no relation to anything the patient did, including lifestyle change and change of attitudes. So many stories of healing exist even in a small bookstore that it is hard to know how doctors can continue to ignore such phenomena they do not understand. A famous example is that of Norman Cousins,[10] who was told by his doctor that he had a disease (ankylosing spondylitis) that would freeze his joints stiff. He was offered the choice of being frozen stiff in a position of sitting or lying. Instead, he used high doses of vitamin C with a constant diet of humor. Friends brought him Marx Brothers movies and told him joke after joke. Through this combination, he changed his perspective on the world — his beliefs, attitudes, and entire lifestyle. His disease disappeared. As eloquently as Cousins writes about his experience, most doctors dismiss his recovery to the garbage can of spontaneous remission, a random-chance phenomenon.

Illness and Blame

Because of a fear of blaming the patient for his or her illness, a mindbody approach to understanding health and illness is frequently dismissed. Thus, the issue of blame must be addressed early in our exposition. We will do so by discussing a patient with cancer who had to resolve the issue of blame for himself.

Blame has been a recorded problem at least since the writing of the Old Testament. In earlier ages, blame was usually ascribed to events external to the person. Through healing ceremonies and rituals, evil spirits (objects of blame) could be forced out of the person's life. The Kung of Africa's Kalihari Desert provide a modern-day example of the efficacy of their own brand of a supernatural[11] theory of illness.

Biblical Job sets the most striking example of the problem of blame. Most churches teach that Job became ill and lost his worldly possessions because he fell into God's disfavor. His illness served as a test of faith. For centuries, the Roman Catholic church of the Middle Ages fostered the concept of illness being the product of sin. *The medical model was perhaps a needed rebellion against the religious concept that a sick person was a sinner.* The medical model proposed that disease was caused in the body, a reactionary "scientific approach to balance the pre-existing religious one." Causes could be treated through external agents rather than by prayer and contrition. The medical model provided an alternative to the rigid doctrine of the Church of that time. To most people from the 16th century until now, the medical model *is* supernatural in an animistic and magical sense. Germs and the concepts of molecular biology are as animistic as ghosts or spirits. There is a magical quality to the power with which most patients imbue their physician. Now, however, the medical model needs to give birth to a new holistic approach arising from the need to rediscover a balance. To take back responsibility for health is not to be a sinner if a person finds him or herself sick.

The resistance to believing that the patient plays a role in his or her illness has been the desire not to blame or "lay a guilt trip on" the patient, that she or he in some way "caused" the illness. Newspaper writing about illness betrays the belief that the patient has no responsibility for the illness by always describing the patient as a victim. The problem of disease in children raises some special questions that will be addressed in Volume II. For now, we will limit our considerations to adults.

Xavier, the cancer patient I will describe, was caught between the belief that he had, in some part, contributed to his cancer and the belief that he was a victim of a disease over which he had no control. As we see how this conflict was approached in his case, some general answers can be discovered for the problem of blame.

Xavier was a 32 year old man who came to me with a diagnosis of malignant melanoma (a skin cancer) which had metastasized (spread) to other organs of his body (brain and lung). He was not sure if he believed visualization could help, but he felt he should try anything. He did not want chemotherapy, but had had a course of radiation therapy and was being followed at one of the local medical centers. His main belief was that his best hope was treatment with laetrile and nutrition. He was receiving care at a clinic that offered a special nutritional program advertised to cure cancer. The nutritional therapy included the use of laetrile, which Xavier had to travel to Nevada to obtain and which was very expensive.

Xavier's history revealed that his father had moved to Macon, Georgia, when Xavier was in the first grade. Before that, his family had lived in Chicago. Macon was much less urbanized than Chicago. Xavier's father had traveled ahead of the family by two months to find them a place to live. Xavier and his sister and brother had then come with their mother and had moved into a house at the edge of the city. Xavier vaguely remembered having attended first and second grade in Macon. During second grade, his father was diagnosed as having malignant melanoma. His father traveled to Atlanta for treatment (chemotherapy). Xavier remembered how terrible his father had looked upon returning from Atlanta. This was the contributing factor to Xavier's decision not to have chemotherapy.

Age regression[13] was used to help Xavier discover childhood memories, available to him at a deeper level than waking ego consciousness. He discovered his past experience of his parents' frequent arguments. Xavier's father would sometimes storm out of the house to end those arguments. His parents rarely, if ever, touched one another. The only time Xavier could remember them touching was when his mother had hugged his father at the airport when they were reunited after a two month absence.

Xavier was able to remember the day the children were told their father had cancer. On that day, Xavier's father and mother touched almost constantly. No further arguments occured after that day. Father was treated with great respect and his every need was provided for by mother. The children were encouraged to adopt a similar attitude toward their father.

Xavier also was able to remember the last time he saw his father alive. His father had come into the bedroom to say goodnight to him. Xavier was in the third grade. He remembered that his father looked very tired and sad.

The next day when Xavier rode his bicycle home from school, many cars were parked outside the house. He remembered having had an idea throughout that day that his father was about to die. When he saw the many cars, he was certain his father had died. He remembered taking the news rather matter-of-factly. He did not cry. He remembered being particularly angry at a man he described as very raucous and loud who pestered him incessantly. He said nothing. He remembered someone wondering if he would get cancer in the same way his father had.

Xavier's mother remarried two years after his father died. Xavier identified with his father and hated his stepfather. As soon as possible, he left home for college. He attended Temple University and majored in Journalism and Political Science. His family had become rather wealthy and Xavier's financial needs were provided by a trust fund left to him by his father. Xavier had no religious preference. He leaned weakly toward the belief system of dialectical materialism. His consuming interest was politics, in which he was very active during college. Xavier did not work after college. More than enough money existed in his trust fund to sustain a high standard of living. He devoted himself to various political causes, working mostly not for any pay, but for the joy of having served a cause in which he believed.

When Xavier was 25 he had discovered that not all the people with whom he worked were as honest or held such lofty ideals as he. He discontinued his involvement in politics. He felt "burnt out." He felt that his energy had been drained. He felt less and less capable of advocating a cause effectively. Little progress seemed to have been made since his work began at age 22. He discontinued his political involvement and did not work, as there was no need to support himself financially. He did some gardening and travelled to some rural areas; otherwise, he was relatively sedentary. He felt at that time that his life was relatively meaningless. He had no particular direction that pulled him toward activity. At age 26, he was diagnosed as having malignant melanoma, which had already metastasized[14] to his lung at the time of diagnosis. The doctors thought his prognosis was grave.

At that time, Xavier turned his back on medical treatment. He undertook nutritional therapy and took laetrile. At 27, he resumed a passionate involvement with politics, and began working with several causes and candidates. His cancer regressed (became smaller). By age 28, no evidence of cancer could be found. The cancer growing in his lung had completely disappeared, and the small cancer that had originally been found on his skin had been removed surgically.

Xavier continued his passionate involvement with politics until age 30. Then he felt "burnt out" again, as he had once before. He again stopped working and rested, doing little besides gardening. He again felt relatively worthless.

During Xavier's second period of political involvement, he met Ricki, a woman whom he began seeing intensively and with whom he began to live. Ricki had been active in one of the same causes as Xavier. Along with their political interests, they shared an inability to communicate about their feelings for each other. Both Ricki and Xavier tended to react to stress by throwing themselves into work or by precipitating a crisis either at work or in their relationship. When they had been together for a year, Xavier decided Ricki was working too hard to get through school. He began paying for her schooling. This had the effect of further suppressing any tendency for Ricki to tell Xavier things that bothered her about him or about their relationship.

When Xavier was 32, he and Ricki had been together for 4½ years. Ricki had been seeing my colleague, Gayle, and had referred Xavier to me. She had almost decided to leave Xavier. Then Xavier discovered his malignant melanoma had recurred. A new cancer on his skin was again removed surgically. This time, however, cancer was discovered to have spread also to his brain and lung. Suddenly, Ricki no longer wanted to leave Xavier. She felt a new excitement in their relationship.

She began mothering Xavier, acting very tenderly and compassionately toward him. She told her therapist that she felt she now loved Xavier and wanted to see things through to the end — either recovery or death. Her therapist wondered out loud if they would ever get married. Ricki looked shocked. "What if he *does* recover?" she exclaimed. "Then I'd be stuck." Ricki was caught in a double bind. On the one hand, she did not want to marry Xavier, because of the shock of being stuck if he didn't die. On the other hand, she did not want to marry him, because he might die.

Xavier went for radiation therapy to his lung and brain. His doctors wanted to start him on chemotherapy, but he refused because of his memory of what he believed chemotherapy had done to his father. He began nutritional therapy and laetrile again. Through Ricki, he was referred to me. I began to see Xavier with an initial contract to help him with visualization and applied kinesiology. Immediately I was confronted with the realization that Xavier did not entirely believe our work could help him one iota. So why was he there? My exploration of that question led us to the issue of blame.

Xavier struggled with believing that either he had "caused" his cancer or he had not. If he had caused his cancer, that meant (in his own unique system of beliefs):

1. He would feel pessimistic about recovery, because he should be punished for having given himself a problem like cancer.
2. If he feels pessimistic about recovery because he contributed to his cancer, then he does not deserve to do things that will help him get well.
3. He feels like a "rotten, awful person" — helpless and hopeless — if he contributed in any way toward his cancer.
4. But, if he did contribute to his cancer, he can feel hope, because the possibility also exists that he can help himself to get well.

What if he did not feel that he had contributed to his cancer? Then:

1. He does not have to feel bad about himself, because forces outside his control caused his cancer.[15]
2. He does not feel like such a "terrible, awful person" (Xavier's words) if he did not "cause" his cancer, and therefore feels more optimistic.
3. Being cured is out of his control. He can do nothing to help himself. He must rely completely on the skills and

abilities of others. He finds himself completely limited by others' limitations. This makes him feel helpless and hopeless.

Xavier's position with regard to who or what caused his cancer contains a double bind.[16] The double bind occurs because he can do nothing to help himself. If he did contribute to his cancer, he feels helpless and hopeless in the face of his guilt, and yet there is hope, since anything he could help create, he can also help to reverse. The key belief is that he feels terrible about himself if he did something to contribute toward developing cancer. Underneath the double bind, Xavier probably holds a basic belief in his own low self-worth, which leads him to feel hopeless regardless. He probably feels hopeless and helpless already to do anything with his life (he confirmed this). Cancer gives him another opportunity to demonstrate how hopeless and helpless he feels, but, since he can view the cancer as something "not-of-himself," he can project outwardly that his feelings of helplessness and hopelessness were from the cancer. He felt that way long before he found out he had cancer, but for other reasons that were perhaps too frightening.

Simply stated, we have a linear relationship between three beliefs:

1. If Xavier can cure himself by changing his life (attitudes, activities, relationships, etc.), then it means he "caused" his cancer.
2. If he "caused" his cancer, then he must be an evil or mad person to have done such a thing to himself.
3. If he can help himself by changing elements of his life, then he is at fault for not having done so earlier, or for even allowing a cancer to develop in the first place.

The net effect of his double bind is to block himself from effectively helping himself. *If he believes in his capability to help himself, he feels very low self-esteem*, because he has not already done so. It is difficult to generate the neurohormones of healing in a neural state of depression and low self-esteem.[19]

Most doctors would have tried to convince Xavier that he did not have any responsibility for the cancer having developed within his body. This might have denied his true inner feeling, however. One quickly loses rapport with the patient by doing so.

I explored this issue by asking Xavier to assume he had contributed 0% to the development of his cancer. This led him to five conclusions:

1. Only other people could help him to achieve a cure.

2. He does not have to worry about whether or not he personally is doing the right or the wrong acts to help himself. Others are completely responsible, so Xavier can do whatever he pleases, because what he does, does not matter (regarding the cancer, anyway).
3. Xavier feels better about himself in terms of his sense of self-esteem.

The prices paid for these benefits were:

4. Xavier is helpless to help himself in any way.
5. There is nothing Xavier can do for himself that would make any difference whatsoever, which is very depressing. His only hope is what medicine or the nutritionist could offer him. Medicine could not offer him more than a few months, and the nutrition and laetrile was not helping. His cancer was growing.

He discovered that the implicit reason for his double bind was his belief that, if he participated in the development of his illness, he should feel responsible and feel guilty about himself for doing such a thing, *even unknowingly*. If Xavier did hold some responsibility, then he would have to worry about whether or not he was doing all that he personally could do to create the changes he needed to get better. If he could do so but did not, then he would feel even worse about himself. In a sense, his double bind is a kind of performance anxiety that he will fail himself when faced with the demand to help himself.

Can Xavier truly believe that he has no responsibility for the development of cancer? I asked him what percent responsibility he could claim and not feel as though he were an evil person for having contributed toward his cancer. If his part was only 10%, would that be small enough not to feel bad? Was it necessary that it be less than 5%? Or 1%? Would he still feel evil if he had only contributed 1% to the forces that led to his cancer? He answered that even if he had contributed just 1% of those factors, he would feel as evil as if he had contributed 100%. For him, it was all or nothing, and he could not believe he had contributed nothing.

If he could accept no responsibility for his problem, I could have worked just with his self-esteem. We would not have had to consider the issue of what he could do to help himself. Help would be the province of the "real" doctors at the medical center and of the nutritionists and the dispensers of laetrile. Since he could not agree he had played no role, we had to begin from the position that he was in part responsible. I drew a diagram for him, which is reproduced as Figure 1.

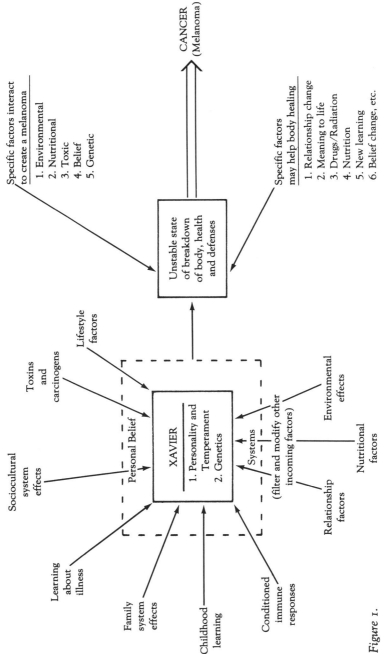

Figure 1.

Figure 1 illustrates some important concepts. The factors or events that contribute to the origination of a disease may be completely different from the factors that can lead to its cure. We may never know the various percentages each of the factors listed on the left side of the diagram contributed to Xavier's cancer. (The list is by no means considered to be complete.) It probably would not help Xavier even if we did know how much each helped. If we assumed for sake of argument that each factor contributed an even 12%, in planning for treatment, we have more probability of affecting some of these than others. We probably cannot change Xavier's genetics or his childhood experience.[21] We *can* change some of the other factors. For example, even if relationship dynamics only contributed 12% to the problem, if Xavier can experience an 80% change in that factor, perhaps its contribution towards cure will be 25%. Assume we need to reach 100% cure. If an 80% change in his relationship dynamics contributes 25%, and a 60% change in his beliefs and attitudes adds another 25% toward cure, then, perhaps, surgery, radiation, and nutrition will each add another 20%. With 110% of what's needed for a cure, Xavier will have passed over what could be called the cure threshold.

For Xavier, a central issue was his belief that life held no meaning. Feelings of depression, helplessness, and hopelessness sprang from that. Xavier believed in materialism. He did not believe in an afterlife. Meaning in life came from the sum total of what he did to help others while on the earth. He did not feel as though he had contributed very much during his life. He was pessimistic that he could contribute very much, since he found himself weary of his political endeavors, successful though they may have been in many aspects. Another issue was that he had learned to solve relationship problems with illness. Couples' therapy could help that. After much delay, Xavier and Ricki were seen as a couple for three sessions. The therapist encouraged Ricki not to respond to Xavier as though he were a sick man with only a few months to live. Such behavior was counterproductive for Xavier in many ways. In the way Xavier's family functioned, Xavier's father's illness had the effect of enabling Xavier's father to be completely taken care of by his wife. Arguments ceased. Expectations decreased. Tranquility reigned in the relationship at the expense of Xavier's father's health. Such effects are not consciously planned, but nevertheless affect behavior through the dynamics of the family.[22]

Xavier also wondered if he could make sufficient changes in any or all of the areas he needed to change to obtain a cure. I told him we had no way to determine that. Theoretically, it seemed very likely that he could increase his survival time. Cure was another issue. I wanted to believe that he could change enough to obtain a cure and wanted to believe that he would, but I could not offer him a guarantee. What if he tried to find a cure with every resource he had, changed everything he could, did everything he could, and discovered all that was still not enough? Given that, would it be worth even trying? Xavier thought about this question and decided the only way he could feel good about himself was to have tried with every resource he could muster to change everything he could change, even if this were not enough. Even if he had to die, having exhausted his ability to help himself and having done something meaningful, he could die with some sense of peace.

I suggested a new way to rephrase his simple statement that "he had caused his cancer."

> People are faced with a variety of complex issues that force decisions. Sometimes people make decisions that are incongruent with the health of their bodies. Under certain circumstances, cancer can result as a side effect of those decisions. People make decisions based upon all data available to them at the time and in the firm belief that they are doing the best things for themselves that they could have done at the time. People can re-make those decisions, so as to be more congruent with the health of the body. Under certain circumstances, alone, or in combination with other modalities of treatment, these re-decisions are sufficient to allow the person to cross over the threshold for cure and to become disease free.

I asked Xavier if a friend had unwittingly, while walking down a street, contributed to the commission of a crime in the thought that he was doing the best he could do in the situation in which he found himself, would he be guilty, given his having acted in good conscience throughout, having only later discovered that he had acted at cross-purpose to what he would have done had he known all the facts? What about a friend who came upon the sight of a man being beaten by another? He defends the underdog who then runs away, only later discovering he has allowed a rapist to get away from a citizen who was apprehending him. Xavier answered that his friend could not, of course, be blamed for such a mistake. I suggested the same was true for Xavier. Moreover, he did not have to view cancer as a crime.

Xavier realized that the deeper issue was that he was afraid to accept the challenge to do everything he could do to cure himself. He was not sure he was ready to do what he felt he must do to cure himself. Also important was his general lack of faith. He had no faith in any of his treatments — no faith in radiation, nutrition, laetrile, or visualization. I discussed the concept of a "faith barrier" that needed to be transcended for his treatments to work even better than they were working now. While radiation was effective, it could be so much more effective if the patient believed very strongly that it was helping him.

Xavier discovered that politics had provided a meaning and direction for his life. He decided that his best bet for finding a cure was to rediscover a meaning for his life. He decided that the most meaningful act he could do was to go to Afghanistan as a photojournalist and to expose the current events there. This would be using his talents. Then, even if he died of cancer, he would feel as though his life had had some value to humanity, because he had acted for the good of the rest of the world and of the Afghanis.

An incredible change in his lifestyle would be needed for him to go to Afghanistan. We talked about other life changes he could make, but he thought he needed a drama such as the proposed trip to Afghanistan through Pakistan. He had never used his journalistic training, even though he wrote well and was very competent with a camera. He did not speak Afghani. At the writing of this chapter, Xavier is trying to decide if he will journey to Afghanistan or embark upon some other equally meaningful venture. If he accepts the challenge, perhaps his cancer will disappear and he will experience a "miracle cure." On the other hand, he may choose against accepting his challenge, in which case, cure might not result.

REFERENCES AND NOTES

[1] San Francisco Chronicle, page 39, Friday, March 20, 1981.

[2] Zukav, G. *The Dancing Wu Li Masters: An overview of the new physics.* New York: Bantam Books, 1980.

[3] Neurohormones are chemicals manufactured by the brain which affect and regulate behavior and physiology.

[4] Bach flower remedies consist of medicinal potions distilled from specific types of flowers.

[5] Visualization as a technique will be considered in depth in a later chapter. Briefly visualization is a psychotherapeutic technique relying on mental imagery to facilitate emotional change.

[6] Young, A. Magic as a "quasi-profession": The organization of magic and magical healing among *amhara. Ethnology,* XVI (3): 245-265, 1979.

[7] Figge, H. *Geisterkult, Besessenheit und magic in der Umbanda Religion Brasiliens.* Freiburg/Muenchen: Verlag Kark Alber, 1973; Bourgiougnon, E. The effectiveness of religious healing movements: A review of recent literature. *Transcultural Psychiatric Research Reviews,* 5:5-21 1979.

[8] Katz, R. The painful ecstasy of healing. *Psychology Today,* pp. 81-86, December, 1976.

[9] Comfort, A. Folk medicine isn't all bunk. Medical Opinion, pp. 47-48, February, 1977.

[10] Cousins, N. *Anatomy of An Illness.* New York: Random House, 1978.

[11] Murdoch and colleagues[12] have defined supernatural theories of illness as being composed of theories of mystical, animistic, and magical causation. Theories of mystical causation include "any theory which accounts for the impairment of health as the automatic consequence of some act or experience of the victim mediated by some putative impersonal causal relationship. . . ." Theories of animistic causation include "any theory which ascribes the impairment of health to the behavior of some personalized agent — a soul, ghost, spirit, or god." A magical theory refers to "any theory which ascribes illness to the covert action of an envious, affronted, or malicious human being who employs magical means to injure his victim." It is very likely that these concepts, however distorted by anthropologists, are the forerunners of some of modern holistic thought. Holistic thought would hold that illness is to some extent (not necessarily automatically) the result of acts and experiences of the individual. Patients often speak of a higher self or soul having contributed to the development of an illness to help them see the consequences of their behavior and thereby learn. The ways in which family members and members of an emotional network of people affect each other almost does seem magical (even though it can be explained in the context of modern systems theory).

[12] Murdoch, G.P., Wilson, S.F. and Frederick, V. World distribution of theories of illness. *Ethnology,* 17:449-470, 1978.

[13] Age regression is a type of hypnosis discussed in detail in a later chapter, which helps a person return in their mental experience to vivid memories of an earlier time.

[14] Metastasis refers to the process of a cancer spreading to other organs.

[15] Xavier uses the word "bad" here, even though "bad" is not a feeling. Actually he felt guilty and described the experience of castigating and reproaching himself as bad. Such language refers back to a highly self-critical belief system.

[16] For a discussion of the nature of double binds the reader is referred to References 17 and 18. Briefly, a double bind occurs when two seemingly opposite choices both lead to the same outcome.

[17] Peterson, G. *Birthing Normally: A personal growth approach to childbirth.* Berkeley: Mindbody Press, 1981.

[18] Watzlewick, P., et al. *The Pragmatics of Human Communication.* New York: W. Norton, 1968.

[19] For a further discussion of the neurohormones of healing, the reader is referred to Reference 20.

[20] Simonton, O.C. and Matthews-Simonton, S. *Getting Well Again*. Los Angeles: J.P. Tarcher, 1978.

[21] Although we may be able to affect these factors indirectly by changing Xavier's habits of responding that are derived from the factors. Chapter 3 will contain more examples of this.

[22] For more information on family dynamics, see Reference 18.

Chapter Two

The Importance of Belief

The science of belief is the study of the effects of beliefs upon human functioning and the world.

A belief is an assumption made about the world that may or may not be conscious, is connected with a great deal of emotion, and determines the interpretation of sensory perceptions. Beliefs determine how we organize our perceptions of the world, how we react to other people, and what situations we will create in our life. Beliefs may not be conscious but are the working assumptions we make about the world.

Most of us gain our initial set of beliefs from our parents. We must. As a newborn infant, as a one year old child, our parents take care of us. Without them we would die. We rely on them to perceive danger for us, as we are too young to be so aware. Because of their success in keeping us alive, we often grow up believing as they do.

Our parents have a variety of reasons for believing as they do. Some may be sociocultural; some religious; some for other reasons. As we grow and change we discover that some of the incorporated beliefs of our parents no longer serve us well. For example, for those planning an alternative birth, if their mother firmly believed that the mother should not be conscious for birth, a change of belief is necessary to decide upon a natural birth. Or, if one's mother or father taught that it was wrong to show love, we might want to change that belief in our own parenting. We might want to be clear about showing love to our children and to our lover.

A sociologist[1] did a study to understand why people buy certain cars. He wondered if it was because of race, income, exposure to advertising, or other factors. He interviewed new car buyers to discover why they had bought their car. He discovered that people's car buying habits could not have been predicted by data given at random to a computer. Blacks did not necessarily buy a Cadillac. Upper class individuals did not necessarily buy a Porsche or a Mercedes Benz. Each person or family had a unique theory that explained their behavior, but which could not have been predicted except by asking them. For example, acquaintances of mine bought a large, gas-guzzling station wagon because they believed a normal, healthy American family should have one. Even though their family wasn't so large they needed such a car, their beliefs were such that the car symbolized a sense of solidarity which their family sorely needed as it was in a period of relationship crisis. In most such studies of the social forces that determine human behavior, unique individual beliefs emerge as the most important factors that predict behavior. Knowing someone's belief system gives us the best opportunity to predict what they will do in specific situations. Carlos Castenada has written somewhat differently about this:

> For the purpose of presenting my argument I must first explain the basic premise of sorcery as don Juan presented it to me. He said that for a sorcerer, the world of everyday life is not real, or out there, as we believe it is. For a sorcerer, reality, or the world we all know, is only a description.
>
> For the sake of validating this premise don Juan concentrated the best of his efforts into leading me to a genuine conviction that what I held in mind as the world at hand was merely a description of the world; a description that had been pounded into me from the moment I was born.
>
> He pointed out that everyone who comes into contact with a child is a teacher who incessantly describes the world to him, until the moment when the child is capable of perceiving the world as it is described. According to don Juan, we have no memory of that portentous moment simply because none of us could possibly have had any point of reference to compare it to anything else. From that moment on, however, the child is a *member*. He knows the description of the world; and his membership becomes full-fledged, I suppose, when he is capable of making all the proper perceptual interpretations which, by conforming to that description, validate it.
>
> For don Juan, then, the reality of our day-to-day life consists of an endless flow of perceptual interpretations which

we, the individuals who share a specific *membership*, have learned to make in common.

The idea that the perceptual interpretations that make up the world have a flow is congruous with the fact that they run uninterruptedly and are rarely, if ever, open to question. In fact, the reality of the world we know is so taken for granted that the basic premise of sorcery, that our reality is merely one of many descriptions could hardly be taken as a serious proposition.[2]

Don Juan views each person's life world as different, as individual, and as equally valid. The shared reality that several different people would all agree to is seen as simply the product of consensual validation, a process which has been defined as one in which a group of people define certain experiences as real, and advance certain explanations to interrelate those experiences.[3] In this definition phenomena that do not fit a particular group's construction of reality are excluded by training group members to utilize selective awareness or to define differing perceptions as specific states, such as "mental illness," or "sickness," or "senility." Doctors engage in such behavior when they ignore the available data about healing discussed in earlier chapters.

Recently I spoke to a medical student about a speech she was to give at a senior citizen center on hearing problems of aging. I suggested she not suggest to the audience that hearing loss was an inevitable consequence of aging. I discussed how some hearing loss might be understood as a desire not to hear others telling the older person what a burden they had become. "What about otosclerosis?" she asked. "That's a real disease that alters the structure of the ear." "Why is it," I asked her, "that alteration of function cannot, in your mind, correlate with change in structure?" Her answer was that she could not imagine how that could occur. I pointed out that aborigines might not imagine how we could fly either, but we think nothing of flying to Los Angeles for the week-end. Her belief was that functional (desire not to perceive) and structural change (thickening of the ear drum) could not be related because she could not imagine how.

A strong belief in the supremacy of technology can have paralyzing effects.[4] A diary of a Maine midwife of the 17th century describes how 700 women delivered with only one stillbirth without the benefit of any technology.[5] Health education for women to believe wholeheartedly in the necessity of technology for childbirth had begun earlier in England as almost a systematic program to change women's beliefs by allopathic physicians. It is well described by G.J. Barker-

Benfield in *The Horrors of the Half-Known Life.*[6] Physicians began to teach women that birth was abnormal. Doctors with instruments were required to help the woman give birth. Reliance on technology was taught, crude and primitive as it was. Barker-Benfield reproduces a quote from an early obstetrical textbook for physicians on how to manage labor. The doctor was told to go to the house and break the waters. Then he should go away after telling the woman that the baby would come soon because he broke the waters. If the baby delivered while he was gone, he could take credit for it because of his intervention. If the baby hadn't delivered when he returned, he delivered it with forceps and still took credit. The book taught medical students and doctors how to make themselves essential to the birthing process.

Despite some evidence to the contrary, most modern obstetricians still believe childbirth is a tremendously hazardous process without benefit of technology. Data to support this is often drawn from inner city London slums or similar environments which did have high maternal and infant death rates. Doctors conclude that it is the process (birth) that is dangerous, rather than associated variables such as the terrible nutrition, the miserable quality of most people's lives, and the many environmental hardships.

Other examples come from early histories of "lying-in" hospitals in which doctors often went from autopsy to delivery without hand washing. Maternal mortality sometimes exceeded 50%.

We will probably never know how dangerous birth really is, because it can't be considered in isolation from the woman's belief system, her ambivalences, incongruencies, anxieties, stresses, etc. Doctors still insist that it can be. They speak of the inevitable "wastage of reproduction" just as internists may speak of disease marching inexorably toward death. These are just belief systems.

What we believe is what can come true for us. If we believe that the hospital is the safest place to birth, then it will be. If a woman believes on the deepest emotional level that the hospital is the only safe place to birth, then if she tries to deliver at home she won't be successful. Many doctors and midwives have experience with women who would not deliver at home and, as soon as they reached the hospital, would quickly birth their child.[7]

The daughters of physicians can illustrate the issue of belief. A local Berkeley midwife told me that only after seven years of practice did she attend a successful home birth of the daughter of a physician. I wondered why this was so. I realized that even at my house, we talked more about complicated births than we did about normal births, even though our stated emphasis was on normal birth. Realizing that, we made a point to be careful to discuss only normal births when children were present. Then we talked about how beautiful and wonderful births were. Children need first to be acculturated to the belief that birth is beautiful instead of complicated. Daughters of physicians, daughters of nurses, and many medical people have trouble giving birth because they have been hypnotically conditioned to believe that birth is abnormal. Throughout either growing up or going through training, these people focus only on the abnormal. The belief among medical personnel that birth is dangerous is then even further reinforced since it is confirmed by personal experience. If we as a culture only hear that birth is abnormal — it will begin to become so.

The importance of belief is illustrated in a well-documented case study related to the drug krebazolin.[8] It had just been released by the FDA as an experimental anti-cancer drug. Initial reports had been very favorable. It was given to a man with stage 4 intractable cancer (lymphoma). He was thought to have little time to live. Large tumor masses were visible protruding beneath the skin in many parts of his body. His physician expressed strong optimism about his chances for recovery with the new drug. Soon after beginning the drug, his cancer began to regress. The lumps disappeared. On X-ray, there was clear evidence of the cancer masses regressing (beginning to shrink). As follow-up progressed, eventually there was no evidence of tumor masses.

Just then a news release about a double-blind, controlled study showing that the drug was worthless came to the patient's attention. After reading the newspaper, he promptly relapsed. The tumor began to grow again. It was visible on X-ray and was palpable through his skin. His doctor told him the study he had read about was inaccurate, because, even though the drug was actually worthwhile, the researchers had tested a bad batch. The doctor began sterile water injections, telling the patient this was a new, improved batch of drug. The tumor disappeared, both on X-ray and to feel. The man did very well until the Food and Drug Administration released its final report showing that the drug was indeed worthless. The man died two days after reading about that final report in the newspaper. Obviously the fact that this patient believed in the drug was more important than whether or not the drug worked in double-blind, controlled studies.

Another example illustrates the interaction of beliefs and drugs. I was referred a pregnant woman, who had severe vaginitis for whom none of the usual preparations her obstetrician had tried had helped her condition. She was infected with three different organisms — yeast (monilia), Trichomonas, and Hemophilus. Her doctor was frustrated with his efforts and with her and hoped I could be of some assistance. Twenty-four hours after our first visualization session, Cathy, the patient, promptly announced she was sure visualization would not help her. She wanted "real" medicine. I prescribed AVC cream, which is a relatively non-specific remedy that had not helped her in the past. A day later she was entirely well. This is virtually unheard of with AVC cream. I had discovered in the visualization that her illnesses functioned as ways of getting back at other people, most particularly her husband with whom she was very angry but to whom she was unable to express that anger. Denying him sex was a passive-aggressive way to show that anger. She could "get back" at her obstetrician by (1) not being helped by his every effort and (2) showing that my visualization couldn't help her either. His referring her to a psychologist led to a flight to health by physical means, since she resented the implication that there was a psychological component to her problem. After successful couples' therapy (which she did agree to) her vaginitis did not return. In couples' therapy, I taught her and her husband how to express anger directly and fairly.

For the client's beliefs to help the healing process the client should be neutral to positive about the chances for success and the person giving treatment needs to believe in his/her ability to be effective. Because of a lack of belief (faith) not all people can be helped by every technique or therapy. If a person believes strongly enough in a negative outcome to treatment this can also occur, although I believe the body heals much faster in response to beliefs congruent with health than it breaks down in response to beliefs incongruent with health.

Carl and Stephanie Simonton[8,9] at the Cancer Counselling Center in Fort Worth, Texas, have done some interesting work on emotions and cancer that have relevance to our study of beliefs. In their work, the best predictive factor for recovery from cancer was the emotional commitment the person had to getting well. The Simontons are helping patients to improve the quality and length of their lives (some even becoming cured) with visualization and belief change techniques. Many of the people helped by the Simontons had been given up by their physicians after having received all the conventional medical cancer therapy.

Carl Simonton[9] stated in one of his publications, "It has become increasingly clear to me that there are very strong psychological factors that predispose a patient to the development of cancer and that as these factors are changed the patient's response is affected. . . . The altering of attitudes is indeed a responsible task and cannot be undertaken lightly. It is also an exceedingly difficult task. In order to accomplish this, the investigator must himself have a very strong belief . . .

"When approaching these areas, the physician or investigator now assumes a role similar to that of the philosopher or preacher, and so he may be seen by those viewing his work. However, it could be said that we are all philosophers and/or preachers to whatever degree we express our belief systems and are strong in our convictions."

In Simonton's[9] first study of 152 patients in which he correlated patient response with attitude, a 98% correlation was found between patient responsiveness to treatment and the attitudes Simonton had thought would be conducive to recovery.

Arigó is another fascinating person to study for our science of belief.[10] Arigó is a Brazilian village healer who has been extensively studied by a team of physicians from the U.S. and Canada. He saw a tremendous volume of patients per day. His only tools were his hands and a rusty knife he carried. A team of American doctors visited Arigó, who agreed to let them diagnose his patients after he saw them. After the patients left Arigó's small shack, the team of doctors would make a diagnosis in a modern, mobile diagnostic van brought along. Ninety-five percent of the time the examining doctors and Arigó agreed about the diagnosis.

Arigó was found to have impressive success with some of the people who came to him for healing. Sometimes Arigó would tell people he couldn't help them yet, because they needed to learn something from their illness that they hadn't learned yet. He would ask them to return when they had learned what they needed to so he could help them. Occasionally Arigó would tell people he could not help them because it was their time to die. The doctors studying Arigó recognized a deep level of philosophy and respect underlying his work and a recognition of the importance of the learning potential of illness.

Illness always has a learning potential.[11] Sometimes our society rewards illness to such an extent that the patient has difficulty improving. An example will illustrate this:

A 32 year old woman (Randi) came to see me for help with severe back pain. She had been on complete disability payments for the past five years, for severe back pain and lower extremity weakness. Recent medical examinations had confirmed weakness and atrophy, but with no apparent identifiable disease. Randi had successfully earned an M.S. degree in design engineering from Purdue University and had worked for one year as an engineer in Houston prior to the onset of her weakness. She had not worked since then.

During therapy, several important issues emerged. Randi felt pressure from external sources (her internal image of "society") to succeed. She experienced this pressure as so overbearing that she became angry at "society." She felt oppressed and victimized and took a political stance that her problems were a natural by-product of life in a capitalist society. She angrily stated that she deserved payment from that society to compensate her for her suffering. (She said this as if expecting me to challenge her that she was doing wrong.)

We learned that when she began to make money from occasional odd jobs Randi experienced a part of her panicking and planning ways to sabotage that success. Sometimes this would consist of a sudden switch to doing bad work, or giving her employer a sense that she had somehow cheated on the price, or taking so long to complete the project that everyone was frustrated. After such frustration Randi would again berate the capitalistic organization of society as having oppressed her.

She discovered feeling that her parents had held unreasonable expectations for her. She had rebelled against her perception of their desires during the process of adolescent differentiation by constellating her identity of herself as a socially unconventional person, often doing outrageous things according to her perception of her parents more conventionally rigid moral standards.

Sexual freedom and the women's movement were new, radical ideas to most people in the small Louisiana town of her childhood. After an abortive love affair with a young, "radical" Washington, D.C., attorney (following college at American University), Randi felt devastated. She immersed herself completely in graduate school, and reported having felt emotionally numb.

When Randi did begin to improve (in the sense of feeling higher self-esteem, less oppressed, and making money from her odd jobs, she began to feel very guilty about accepting the money from disability that came each month. As her self-esteem improved and her feeling of being oppressed decreased, her strength returned and her pain diminished. Randi's rising guilt about accepting disability money served as the trigger for her saboteur part to "upset the apple cart" and undo her success. An added problem was that the disability program made no provision for intermediate steps away from complete dependency to self-sufficiency. She could not honestly begin to earn money and keep the disability until she was sure of being self-sufficient. She was forced to conceal her earnings from disability. This transition difficulty built into the program reinforced her sense of oppression and gave her the kernel of truth to grow a stalk of capitalistic oppression.

As true for Randi, patients on disability may need a phase of being able to give up their symptom and still feel good about themselves for taking the money that comes every month. There are some very negative aspects (from the point of view of healing) to the way our society handles illness that are conducive to maintaining the sick role. It is important to stress there is nothing wrong with being sick or having problems. It is just another type of learning potential for growth.

Feelings of hopelessness contribute toward a person becoming more susceptible to illness and death.[12,13] The onset of a disease may frequently follow an important change in an emotional relationship.[12] A profound feeling of psychological impotence often precedes illness and death.[13] Such patients feel both hopeless and helpless. They have a depreciated image of themselves, they have lost gratification in their lives and their futures seem bleak. Their belief systems center around beliefs in personal impotence, poor self-worth, and the lack of the future to offer any hope of change.

REFERENCES AND NOTES

[1] Personal communication, Barney Glaser, U.C.S.F., Department of Medical Sociology, 1979.

[2] Castaneda, Carlos. *Journey to Ixtlan: The lessons of don Juan*. New York: Simon & Schuster, 1972.

[3] Berger, P.L. and Luckmann, T. *The Social Construction of Reality*. Garden City, N.Y.: Doubleday, 1966.

[4] Ilych, Ivan. *Medical Nemesis*. New York: Simon & Schuster, 1974.

[5] Wertz, D. and Wertz, R. *Lying In*. New York: Ramdom House, 1977.

[6] Barker-Benfield, G.J. *The Horrors of the Half-Known Life*. New York: Harper & Row, 1977.

[7] See Reference 17 of Chapter 1 for more information.

[8] Simonton, O.C. and Matthews-Simonton, S. *Getting Well Again*. Los Angeles: Tarcher, 1978.

[9] Simonton, O.C. Reflections on three years of cancer research. Los Altos: Academy of Parapsychology and Medicine Bulletin, 1972.

[10] Puharich, H.K. The Work of the Brazilian Healer Arigó. *The Varieties of Healing Experience: Exploring psychic phenomena in healing*. Los Altos: The Academy of Parapsychology and Medicine Bulletin, 1972.

[11] Illness does not mean that the patient is bad or evil.

[12] Schmale, A. H., Jr. Relationship of separation and depression to disease: I. A report on a hospitalized medical population. *Psychosomatic Medicine* 20:259-277, 1958.

[13] Engel, G. A life setting conducive to illness. The giving up — given-up complex. *Bull. Menninger Clinic* 32:355-365, 1968.

Chapter Three

Psychotherapy and Diabetes
An Existential Approach to the Therapy of Physical Illness

Understanding of health and disease comes from a study of the process of clients who have experienced significant improvement of a physical disease. In this chapter, the history of a client is described. This client had diabetes and decreased her insulin requirements eightfold. Many health professionals do not think patients can improve to such a degree the status of their diabetes without drugs or dietary changes. The case example I will describe shows this is not so. Wanda *does* improve her diabetes — not with drugs, but by organizing and reorganizing her inner resources and perceptions. This reorganization results in a change of basic beliefs and attitudes. After describing how Wanda did this, I will discuss a theoretical framework within which such change is possible. Any theory of health and disease must be able to explain Wanda's success.

Wanda's Experience

Wanda had been trying to improve her diabetes with a variety of techniques for the year previous to seeing me. Her friends told her that I was involved with "holistic health" and might be able to help her. In the year before seeing me, she had been using applied kinesiology,[1] fasting, and other techniques. She had been using a large, local prepaid medical group as her medical care provider. Her doctors were opposed to the methods of treatment that she had experimented with. Medical

records from that institution described Wanda as having had "a complicated medical history of psychoneuroses with psychosomatic-type
pain," and "problem with drug abuse." She had been seen in their
clinic for the past ten years, and her diabetes was described as being in
"rather poor control." She had been treated with diazepam[3] (10 milligrams every four hours for chronic abdominal pain), and had also been
diagnosed as having chronic monilial vaginitis.[4] She had a history of
intermittent episodes of high blood pressure (hypertension). She had
hemorrhoids that came and went and occasionally bled. She sometimes
had urticarial attacks,[5] and problems with chronic diarrhea. Two years
before seeing me, her insulin intake was 100 units a day of both NPH[6]
and regular insulin. She was still in poor control. When she began
seeing me her intake was about 80 units per day, a fairly large dosage, of
both NPH and regular insulin. She had had necrobiosis[7] on her right leg
nine years previously, after an incident in which her brother kicked her
repeatedly on the shin. This had been treated successfully by a vascular
surgeon. The psychological assessment by her internal medicine specialist read as follows: "The type of problem she has is not quite clear to
me, but she is very introspective, and very interested in her own mental
mechanism, and at times attends groups to get help."

At first I knew very little about Wanda. She usually wore loose-
fitting, non-traditional clothes. She was overweight. Her initial way of
greeting me was always with a hug. This hug became a ritual of each of
her visits.

Wanda could be loud and raucous, or talk softly and cry. Her
woman lover, Terri, frequently accompanied her to our sessions.
Before Terri, Wanda had involvements with men, including a three-
year marriage. Wanda and Terri lived in a house with another woman,
Darlene who had just had a baby.

Wanda developed diabetes at age 15. The summer prior to her
sophomore year in high school, she had been away from home at a
camp in Minnesota. She ate *only* candy for those three summer months.
On the first day of school she developed diabetic acidosis (coma) and
was begun on insulin. Her father was also diabetic. He developed
acidosis[8] and coma during World War II on the day he was to be
shipped to the front lines to fight as an infantryman.

In initiating the process of discovering Wanda as a unique person, I
began with the technique of exploratory visualization. This technique
involves a combination of indirect hypnosis,[9] visualization and mental
imagery techniques,[13] the telling of stories, progressive relaxation training, and psychotherapy.

Exploratory visualization is a very descriptive technique. Description helps to create a map of the patient's inner world. At first these maps might be as accurate as Columbus' first map of the world. Then we discover and approximate the shape of the American continents. Next we discover a general sense of the interior landscape — the presence or absence of deserts and mountains, rivers and lakes, cities, prairies, farmland, and forests. Where are they, how big are they, and what novel characteristics do they possess? Theory *cannot* guide us. To rely on theory is to make *undue assumptions and mistakes* about this new individual. The individual has a series of such inner landscapes, a collection of worlds as potentially variable as new planets. What is the atmosphere? What are the life forms? Are they carbon based or are they based upon other elements?

Wanda's previous history showed many problems, including very poor control[16] of her diabetes. The process of therapy consists, in part, of the use of techniques (visualization, indirect hypnosis, applied kinesiology) to help Wanda discover her own inner landscape, especially her belief systems. The concept of belief systems should become increasingly clear as Wanda's experience unfolds.

Wanda believed in reincarnation, and when she was deeply relaxed and helped through an age regression procedure, she would frequently find herself in other times and places other than what she defined as this lifetime. Two months into our work together, through "past life" experiences, we discovered beliefs that Wanda held about herself on both conscious and unconscious levels. The following beliefs were identified:

1. *Belief in Karma*
   Wanda believed that she had been a victim or had been victimized in many past lifetimes because of karma she had to work out (i.e., her diabetes was a punishment from karma accumulated in past lives).

This can be further broken down to:

   A. I am a victim, and
   B. This is because of my karma from past existences.

A past life regression would occur whenever Wanda experienced herself as being in another time period. It was not necessary for me to believe in past lives or even contemplate them in Wanda's way in order for me to help her. I could treat her "past life experiences" similar to any other experience she might describe. I believe "the client is always right," until he or she changes his/her mind. It does not help, nor is it correct experientially, to tell them they are "wrong." Therapy should consist of the therapist helping the client to set up a series of experiences through which he or she can re-evaluate his/her beliefs. Then the client may *decide* to change particular beliefs. Arguing with Wanda would have been counter-productive. However, my entering into her belief system could benefit her.

Most of Wanda's past life experiences involved her refusal to comply with the requests and demands placed on her by those in power over her. This refusal would lead to her being killed by them. This belief can be stated as:

2. *Belief in the Consequences of Refusal*
   A. I frequently find myself in situations in which others hold power over me.
   B. These others try to force me to do things I don't want to do.
   C. If I resist their demands, I will be killed, or
   D. If I don't do what others want, harm will come to me.

   We *could begin* to hypothesize that her diabetes *may be* intimately connected to:

   A. A belief in herself as a powerless victim, and/or
   B. A belief that resistance to the will or demands of others leads to physical tissue damage. Perhaps the demands of adolescent differentiation from her family helped to activate her diabetes. Sickness could also be a form of acceptable teenage rebellion.

Why Diabetes?

Why not asthma or cancer? There are many possibilities, among which we could consider:

   I. The influences of heredity play a role; i.e., a familial predisposition to diabetes as an illness.
   II. There is some symbolic/expressive meaning to the choice of diabetes.
   III. Her family conditioned her to believe that diabetes was the illness she could easily get were she to become sick.
   IV. Social beliefs about heredity influenced her.

In one particularly illuminating session, Wanda experienced a past-life regression in which she found herself to be a Samurai in Japan during the Middle Ages.[17] She visualized herself having been trained to fight for the Emperor's entertainment. Her father in her current life was her trainer in this past life drama. When she realized what she was being trained for (she saw herself as male) she rebelled and refused to enter the arena and fight. Her trainer told her she would disgrace her family and him. If she refused to fight, he would kill her. She did enter the arena, and fought an 18 year old (she was 29). She saw herself deliberately taking a wrong step so that he could kill her. He chopped off her head with a sword. She experienced strong feelings of grief and sadness for having died in such a useless way.

In a later session she experienced a past life in which she and her current lover, Terri, were shepherds. Because of a stance they had taken relative to their beliefs, someone was coming to kill them. There was nothing they could do. She described calmly meditating while waiting to be killed; in her visualization she saw herself and her friend die.

From these experiences we can hypothesize that she believes:

3. If I take a stance or have my own beliefs, I will be killed or will die.

The above premise relates to a previous hypothesis. During her teenage years, Wanda had to rebel. She had to develop her own beliefs independent of her parents' beliefs. Yet she believed that doing this would cause her to die. Hence (in her mind), *what she must do to live causes her to die.* A complementary aspect of this hypothesis is a strong belief in powerlessness.

In further sessions Wanda experienced several lives in which she was killed in various ways. In many of those lifetimes, she saw herself being killed because of her beliefs. Once a fish hook spear had to be pulled all the way through her to come out. In another past life Wanda reported having had a clitoridectomy and closure of the vagina while on the rack as a woman whose beliefs symbolized unruliness and retaliation to the culture and time period being visualized. She reported an experience of being killed with torture stars in China and of being hung. In her visualization of a hari-kari experience in Japan, she reported having *decided* from then on that she would become sick through physical disease rather than being killed *per se.* The recurrent situation was that someone in power wanted her to do or believe in something against her will. The only way to resist was to be killed or to get sick with a disease and die. Thus, we have another possible belief:

4. If you have to die, it is better to die from a physical disease than to be killed (perhaps an identification with being ''in control'' of her death).

Another aspect of this is the tremendous amount of violence and rage stored amidst her inner landscape. Perhaps this suppressed rage had been turned inward and was eating away at her pancreas. Perhaps she was afraid she would murder someone if she expressed these feelings. Her brother had once beaten her unconscious when she criticized him in the way that their father criticized her. The family dynamics now began to emerge as an important issue.

Wanda's parents placed tremendous emphasis upon academic success. To their dismay, Wanda did not do well in elementary school. She required special tutors to help her learn to write and spell. She had what would probably now be classified as learning disabilities (perhaps related to the tremendous pressure to succeed — a "freezing" response in the face of unmanageable anxiety). Her parents were always demanding that she do better. Their love was conditional upon her report card. She struggled against her learning problems to please them. Finally, during her freshman year in high school, she succeeded. She was at the top of her class with all A's. Hence, her parents let her go away for the summer, during which time she ate only candy (in her perception, to compensate and reward herself for the severe stress involved in succeeding).[18] Thereafter, during her sophomore year and the remainder of high school, she could do less well, and "save face" by blaming her lack of success on her diabetes. The diabetes could serve as a savior of sorts, from the agonizing pressure to perform. This was consonant with her parents' beliefs. Her mother was from a wealthy family; her father was not. He had struggled to prove himself to his wife's family until his diabetes began. Then he was no longer expected to, because he was sick. This gave him a permanent "one-down" position in the family, but *a position in which there was no expectation on anyone's part that he would move up from.* Wanda now occupied a similar position vis-a-vis her parents, as her father had occupied vis-a-vis his wife's parents. While having certain drawbacks (diabetes), the position was fairly comfortable (no expectations of success).

Wanda's brother handled the family pressure differently. He chose to go to Vietnam in the U.S. Army. Wanda remembered him as very much enjoying killing the Vietnamese. He reinlisted three times and spent eight years in Vietnam in combat duties. The family seemed to have more murderous rage than it could contain. For Wanda, it was directed inwardly; for her brother, outwardly.

Wanda identified in some significant ways with her father. She saw him as powerless to her mother. Men appearing powerless to dominant women who "married beneath themselves" was a symbol in Wanda's father's side of the family, which is diagrammed in Figure 1.

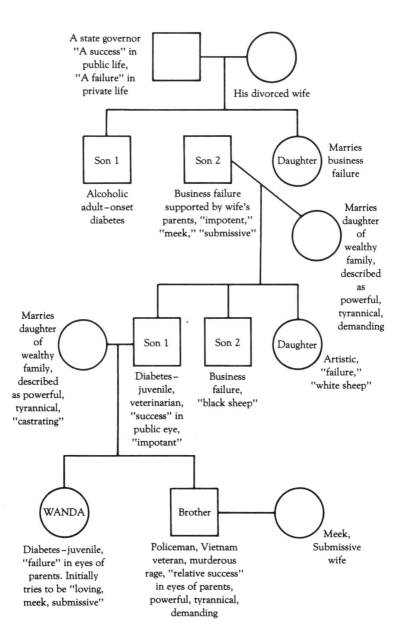

Figure 1.

Prior to our work, Wanda had no memories of her life before age 15. Her development of pre-teen memory was a success in itself. It was through association with the visualizations of her past-life experiences that she became capable of early childhood memory. Prior to this time, Wanda had amnesia for her early childhood experience. Suppression of memory is not an uncommon phenomenon in the development of disease. Wanda remembered the feelings she had had as a young child when she failed her parents. This association was a key to her early memories of elementary school. Most of those memories were connected with experiences of having displeased her parents and of not being the brilliant, intelligent child she felt they wanted her to be. Some additional childhood beliefs emerged, which seemed to still hold strength in the present:

5. I'm not good enough to please my parents.
6. When I try to do what they want, I only experience failure and feel worse than ever.

The experience of making things worse by trying to make them better probably fostered her need for rebellion. Wanda expressed feeling that diabetes was a successful way to rebel against her family's desires. In describing her summer sugar diet, her large weight gain, and being rushed to the hospital on the first day of school, Wanda related that her father had had much the same experience. This reflected two beliefs:

7. In many ways (especially in my physical body processes and disorders), I'm very much like my father. Also,
8. I can get back at my parents by developing diabetes.

Two other childhood beliefs arose to take the form of corrolaries to the above:

9. If I find myself pleasing my parents (pleasing authority; doing what other people in power want me to do; pleasing myself; or succeeding) the stress is overwhelming, and I have to capitulate in a way that will allow me to save face and still get back at the authority (by getting sick). Thus,
10. Getting sick (diabetes) is a way to avoid having to succeed without losing face.

Wanda was next able to identify a part of herself that worked against her. This part of her would help her to forget her insulin when she went on vacation or on trips, or would cause her not to eat properly — to binge, or to wait too long without eating (which would make her susceptible to an insulin reaction).[19]

In one session, representative of the visualization technique I use to map belief systems, deep breathing helped Wanda relax. I asked her to take some slow, deep breaths, suggesting she direct her breathing and relaxation energy into various parts of her body during inspiration. We began with the top of her head and moved on to the back of the head, the forehead, the area behind the eyes, the jaws and face, the neck, and the back. Before beginning, I instructed her to breathe deeply and had given her an indirect hypnotic suggestion to imagine herself in a place very conducive to her receiving the help she needed. When she began directing energy to her back, I gave instructions for her to see herself lying in a warm, grassy meadow, feeling the sun upon her skin, while hearing water flowing through the meadow. Then I linked the idea of water flowing in the river, down the hill, to the notion of the relaxation process spreading down her back, vertebra by vertebra, indirectly relating each vertebra to a waterfall in the river. To this I included indirect suggestions that she could go deeper down inside herself. Then a linkage was made between the pelvis and a pool in the river. In the river pool, the water collects and then flows out in two separate tributaries which I then compared indirectly, in the form of a metaphor, to the relaxation energy flowing down through her legs. There were more indirect hypnotic suggestions to go deeper down as the relaxing energy flowed through her knees, her ankles, her feet, and into her toes.

I gave her suggestions to imagine herself going to a place where she could meet the part of herself that was trying to sabotage her process of getting well. I told her to cover her body with white light[20] as a kind of protective armor to keep her safe in any situation she encountered. I made sure she knew she could instantly return to the room in which we had begun if things became too frightening. She raised a finger to indicate she was experiencing herself in a place where she could meet her troublesome part. I asked her to go get that part of herself. She was quiet while she did so and then began to describe her experience. It became difficult for her to see what was happening. I used a focusing technique of asking her to describe in minute detail her imagined environment. She was in a desert. There was no food or water anywhere. She felt as though she were giving herself a test and was failing. She felt as though she had placed herself in a survival contest that she was failing.

This suggested another belief:

11. Improving diabetes is a test with many of the same emotional qualities as the tests of success her parents created for her while she was in school.

I asked her to find a guide to help her, but she could not. She was crying and feeling very much like a victim. It seemed worthwhile to transform this victim experience into its opposite. I had a spontaneous vision of her as a ruler, a minor governor or a city ruler, of a desert city with many minarets and mosques. I described my vision to her and she quickly began to embellish my description, claiming the place as one who knew and ruled it. She described feeling very indifferent to people and love. This led her to describing an experience of being just an "energy body." As this "energy body" she felt many malevolent impulses and let her "child" go out of control (in the sense of transactional analysis ego states of child, adult, and parent). She tried to destroy the earth with her energy. She reported being restrained by other energy beings who would not allow her to destroy the earth. She felt a weight of many thousand pounds crushing her, a weight many thousand times greater than the earth. She described being restrained by purple fields of energy. The energy of this restraint became very intense and she began to shake and to become terrified. I quickly gave her a hypnotic suggestion to allow herself to return to waking consciousness if necessary, and recognize that all that she had discovered would be accessible to her consciousness at the right time, but not when or in an amount she would be unable to cope with. I had the feeling that she was moving toward an insulin reaction, which I did not want to have occur in my office.

Once she had digested some of the less anxiety-provoking material from that existence, she returned to a waking level. It was difficult for her to return to a waking level, and I used some simple focusing and body movement exercises to help her reorient herself to the present.

This experience led to a recognition of more beliefs:

12. If I really let myself have power, I might kill or destroy someone or something.
13. I have to keep my power under someone else's control so I won't kill or destroy.

Whether or not Wanda really was an energy body trying to destroy the earth is immaterial. The experience can be seen as being *also* symbolic and expressive of her childhood. As a child, she would have liked to destroy her world of home and family, but the yoke of family rules and conscience suppressed her destroyer part (Shiva)[21] so completely that it went to work on her. Scientists have found that many diabetics make antibodies which attack parts of themselves as though attacking foreign invaders.[22] A transcript of a dream Wanda had during the fourth month of therapy further illustrates the issues with which she struggled:

Wanda: She's (Darlene) getting so good that all we other people in the house have to do is walk in the door, man, and she sees us, sees everything.[A] She'll say, "Oh, you've got a dark hole in your aura right there."[B] Everything, and shit has been breaking loose, everything. What happened yesterday — I've been scared to death to let anything past my power. Okay. So this has always been closed off. Yesterday, Corey and I had our regular little argument, and I just, it's just so hard for me to separate myself from everybody else, so that I know what's going on over there with them and I know what's going on with me.[C]

That's when you lose control. And *I lose control when it hits my power,* and then there's that block. *I've been told my whole life "you're too fearful, so shut down, because if you don't shut down it'll wipe you out."*[D] Okay.

So I felt this starting to seep through my power, with me unable to keep it down; I just started breathing like crazy to try to keep myself separated.

And her stuff just came shooting on through and I just went crazy. And I acted out her

[A] Wanda begins the session by describing one of her close friends who lives in her house. "Seeing" here refers to awareness as described by Casteñada's don Juan.

[B] A positive, beneficial aspect of Wanda's belief in Darlene's ability to read her aura was that she stopped trying to conceal her feelings, because anyone could see from her aura what she was feeling. Possibly this development of the ability and feeling of the desirability to express feelings had much to do with the improvement in her diabetes.

[C] Now Wanda is describing an argument with her mother, Corey. "Past my power" and "hits my power" translate into "interfere with my sense of self" or "threaten my self-integrity" or "cause me to be disoriented in my groundedness in the world."

yang side, her violent yang side. And *I've always been in fear that I would lose control of it, that somebody would get killed* out of it; but I just let it happen, whatever came down, I just trusted that the good Lord was going to be hanging onto my hand, you know?E So, it got to the point where I just wanted to choke her to death, and then I just quit. It was like somebody had just turned off the button.F And I came back to my body and it was the revelation that I cut off my children because they see too much, they're too fearful, and I lost control of them.G So here's the parent out here, being in total fear of them, cutting off at the power, so that they couldn't get through with all that stuff that I didn't want to feel. Which has been my entire parents' trip; not to feel. So it was like I came back into myself and realized what I had just acted out, and that my whole life I've been growing up like that, acting out other people's stuff, never being able to separate it from my own, saying "well, that must be me, that must be my stuff that I'm acting out." When I couldn't even separate it. Even though I've got that stuff, though maybe not to that intensity. So the intensity comes when I'm getting their stuff on top of my own. I'm so fearful of it. It's bad enough with your own, but when you add on

D   The parental injunction here is not to feel, because "allowing the feelings full range of expression will make you crazy."

E   This passage neatly illustrates Wanda's fear of losing emotional control and becoming violent.

FWanda is learning that she can feel her emotions and even express them, and that she won't murder anyone.

G   "Cutting off her children because they see too much" means divorcing the emotional parts of her (which she calls children because they're connected with the repressed playful, fun-loving parts) from the remainder of her ego. When her "kids" are included, her entire self is aware of how she feels, and aware that her parental injunction was not to feel.

everybody else's, it just becomes terrifying. So I got in touch with that kind of castration of my kids, and it's my kids who have all that power; it's my kids who read through their second [chakra] and get all that information. And when I started getting into the psychic field they kept telling me that to heal from your second [chakra] is the most powerful thing you can do, but to maintain control over it is like a horrendous job that you've got before you. And that nobody really knows how to do it.[H] And, what I'm finding out is that you've got to operate from all of them [chakras] to do it.[I] And if you've got this shut down because of the fear, then you're gonna constantly lose control of it. Twenty-four hours a day you're gonna be in fear. So, I went into the shower and I turned the sucker onto cold, and I jumped in so it would ground me, and I just let my kids come out; I let my parents come out and I just really got down.

And for the first time in my life I loved me. I mean, I could touch me and say, "oh you're so perfect." (laughs) It was like I never saw that positive side before.[J] Because I could separate it for the first time.

Lewis: And what else happened?

Wanda: My energy was trucking. And it lasted three

[H]   Wanda needs her emotional parts integrated into her personality to know her boundaries, in order to separate her own feelings from those of other people around her. With separation of her emotional parts, Wanda can recognize parts of herself in many of the actions of others. Because of her lack of clear understanding of how she and others are related in feeling similar feelings, she jumps to the assumption that she must feel identically with the other person.

[I]   Operating from all the chakras means integrating all the elements of the personality. She's saying that if she's afraid of any of her parts and is refusing to integrate them into her personality, then her ability to heal herself or another person will be compromised.

hours; then I proceeded to go downhill, and become violently ill. And I threw up blood, old blood from my stomach. My whole father's side[K] was shut off like my head had been cut in half. So I was getting tremendous father pictures. I couldn't get hold of any of the pictures; I didn't know what the fear was. And it became more intense as the sun went down. And that was the infection, that was the resistance, was not wanting to see that shit. So I'm turning it off, I'm getting this tremendous headache. All the muscles, everything, were off.[L] And last night I had this dream. And this dream — I never had a dream like this — and I was with the family and we had an apartment, or a place where people could stay when they visited, like it was empty. And one of my foster kids came to see me, to visit, and we put him in this room, in this apartment. Free apartment. And it was nice and clean when I put him in it. And he got up out of bed, and he came in and he said "there's something wrong with the bed." And when we went back in, it was like things started to crawl out of the walls; it was like everything just started to fall apart, like decay.[M] And his mattress was full of dead mice; I mean it was like the mattress broke in half and it had all these dead mice in it. I had no fear of

[J]   As she accepts all her parts, including her critical introjected parents, she can really begin to love herself. If we can accept even our less savory parts, then we can really begin to appreciate our positive aspects.

[K]Father's side refers to her logical, intellectual side, left brain functions in the split-brain studies. Getting hold of the pictures means creating a clear visual image of the fear. Wanda uses her visual mode frequently and effectively.

[L]   Refusing to examine the images from her critical father part leads her to a tremendous headache. "All the muscles" refers to applied kinesiology; all of her energy meridians were out of balance.

[M]   Symbolically (and any symbol must be grounded in validation from Wanda) as Wanda opens her awareness to the less savory parts of herself, it, except that I thought this was the weirdest thing I'd ever seen. And there was this attic-like thing where you take the thing over and you crawl up there, and there had been this smell. We went up there and somebody had taken a guinea pig cage, with the guinea pigs, and left it. And the guinea pigs had gone crazy, multiplied, and died. Carried out their life, you know. And it was like there were dead bodies all over. And the guinea pigs are giant! I mean they're not just little guinea pigs, they're like that.[N] And they're running all over. And then mice started jumping out of the walls. And Will is just looking around going "Mother, what the hell is going on?" And I'm looking at Will saying, "I don't know what's going on." And then these birds come flying in the door, these beautiful birds, and they were blue, this intense turquoise blue, and they were mated.[O] And they were fucking each other on these two chairs. And I thought "These birds are beautiful," and then I saw what they were doing, and I'm going "What are they doing?!" "What is this that's happening?" And so I kind of shoo them out the door and they fly away, and then balloons start coming out of the walls, and then they blow up and then they pop, and then I'm going, "Well, somebody's carrying on a real heavy-duty

first she feels overwhelmed by decay and death and bugs crawling out of the walls. It's a frightening possibility (the foster kid is scared), but Wanda is learning to view her "negative" aspects without the fear.

[N]   (indicates size with her hands)!

[O]   As Wanda learns to appreciate the previously hidden aspects of herself she can begin to experience the beauty of some of these parts. Yet sexuality is connected with these parts. Sexuality has been repressed. Wanda's first response to the recognition of her previously repressed sexuality is to try to shove those parts out the door, but they just keep coming back as balloons out of the walls, blowing up and popping like the practical joke." And this place is falling down. Dead bodies everywhere. But they're animals. And so the landlord comes in, and the landlord is some landlord I had somewhere in my past, and he looked at me like "I'm going to get this apartment away from you." And he had that little twinkle in his eye, you know, like, "This is what I'm doing to make this happen." And what I'm getting are these two sides of me, this side the repulsion at seeing this happening, all the dead bodies and the mattress all decayed and the walls falling down — and not figuring out any of it. Not being able to make any sense out of what's happening. And then the landlord leaves, and he goes out and he works in his garden. Like this is perfectly normal! What is this guy doing, you know? He's trying to figure out what this is. And he's out there with some new contraption that he's laying down there to plant his new plants in. And that's when I wake up. And it's like the weirdest dream I've ever had. And it's like for the last two weeks all I've been dreaming were father pictures, all the men in my life that have been violent have been in every single one of them — covert violence. That silent violence. The night before that I dreamed that I was married to a hit man, and that I didn't know that's what he was

physiological experience of orgasm. Maybe it's a practical joke her higher self is playing on her.

doing, but I was just having a gay time with all the fun. And then I realized that that's what he was doing and I helped him participate, but I never wiped anybody out, I just let him do that. But I would always participate. And then at the end of the dream we came to this place and here we're having an orgy.[P] And there must have been 20 of us. Just carrying on this orgy like gangbusters.[Q] And that's the kind of dreams I've been having. I mean just totally from my second [chakra] (laughs). Just incredible. And it's like all father stuff — all of it.

Lewis: You want to try? We could try to figure out some of the stuff . . . .

Wanda: Oh, I would, I mean, it was wild.

Lewis:[R] How about getting into a really relaxed space where you can just tune into the dream? And just start it up again, only this time . . . roll back the screen, rewind the camera. Okay. Let's start it from Will's perspective. Okay. You might start with Will's coming into town, what he's thinking and what he's doing. He's going to come into town, he's gonna visit you, what he might be thinking. Just be Will.

[P] Sexuality in her family, her family's past, and Wanda's experiential past with men has always been linked with violence.

[Q] Perhaps the power and force of orgasm tends to release by association (neuro-physiological?) the power and force of her repressed emotions.

[R] I'm beginning a gestalt technique for first person experiential dream interpretation. I've already helped her by anchoring techniques to be able to enter a deeply relaxed, hypnotic trance level with just the verbal instructions to get into a very relaxed space.

Wanda: Okay. I'm scared to death to come see Wanda. I don't want to come see her.

Lewis: How come you don't want to come see her?

Wanda: Well, she's always telling me stuff I don't want to hear, and when she does talk to me I never understand her. And, she just, I'm always afraid I'm not gonna understand and I'm not gonna meet up to what she thinks everything should be. So when I'm with her I'm in total silence. So I really don't want to come because I can't participate with her.[S] But I have to come because I have to see if she's still alive. And I really do love her, but . . . I don't even know how. I just have a need to just check her out. So I go to see her, and she says that they have an apartment that I can stay in. I'm in this apartment and I'm laying down. She gives me this bed to sleep in, and everything's real nice and clean, and I get in the bed and I'm laying in the bed and it just stinks. And I just can't take that smell any more and I just don't know where it's coming from. And I've looked everywhere. I'm really afraid so I better go get her. And she comes back in this apartment with me and we start to look around to try to figure out what this smell is, and as we look around it's like everything kind of starts to fall apart, it's so old. It's an

[S] The part of Wanda represented by Will (a foster kid) is afraid to step into the "active space"[25] of Wanda's consciousness.

illusion. It's like somebody put
sheets on a rotten mattress or
something. The mattress falls
apart. There's mice around.
There's dead mice. I've never
seen anything like this before,
and I keep looking at Wanda to
see what her reactions are, and
she looks like she's scared and
she doesn't know what it is. And
that just makes me more
terrified. And I'm not saying
anything, I just go around
looking at everything. The more
she looks at everything, the
more bodies fall out. And wild
animals jump out. And this one
guinea pig jumped in her lap,
this huge . . . and I'm so scared,
and the only thing I can do is
keep my eyes on her because I
don't know what's going to
happen next. It's like she's the
only thing I can ground myself
with. I'm so afraid she's gonna
leave because she's too scared to
stay. She's not so, she's not
really scared, but she acts really
confused. And I know she's
kind of scared underneath. And
she opens the door and these
birds fly in. And she gets all
excited. And she sees them
fucking. So I walk over to where
she is because I can't see too
good because she's standing in
front. And they're like
iridescent. And they're like
mated, they're two pairs. And all
of the sudden like she gets
scared so she shoos them out of
the house. And then she shuts

the door like it's going to keep
everything out.[T] But everything's
inside. And then the walls start
to do funny things, like the
wallpaper peels away. And mice
jump out of the walls. Then she
turns around and tells me that
there's balloons on the walls,
floating up. And they pop. And
I'm so scared that she's just
gonna get scareder than I am.

Lewis: So what do you do
next?

Wanda: I'm just standing
there in total silence like I'm a
rock, because I'm afraid to
move. She's running around
trying to figure it all out. And
she's telling me she doesn't
know what's going on. The mice
are everywhere; there's mice
everywhere. Just on everything.
There's big ones and little ones.
Guinea pigs. There's rats and . . .
she's not afraid of them. It's just
when she sees them dead that
she gets afraid. Then the
landlord walks by the window,
so she goes to the door and calls
him in to show him what's
happening. I'm just standing
there hoping no one will see me.
She's talking to the landlord; he
acts like it's no big thing. Like
he doesn't even see it, and he
doesn't even know what she's
talking about. She's so
frustrated, she's practically
jumping up and down. Then he
just tells her he'll take care of it.
And then he leaves her just

[T]   This again refers to her fear
of sexual expressiveness.
Shutting the door of her
consciousness to keep
everything out is unsuccessful
because the idea that the conflict
is external is just projection. The
animals and the fears and the
smells all represent inner parts
of Wanda.

standing there and walks out the door. And he walks over to his garden and there's somebody in his garden helping him plant some things. And it's like he's totally oblivious to what's happening. The place is actually falling down!

Lewis: Then what do you do?

Wanda: I don't know what to do about it. I just stand there. And she's crying. Until Wanda tells me what to do.

Lewis: What if Wanda never tells you what to do?

Wanda: Then I'd never know.

Lewis: And what would happen to you if you never know?

Wanda: I'd just stay in the house forever.

Lewis: How long can you stay there with the house falling down around you? Are you able to do something?

Wanda: I can't do anything. I'll just have to wait and see what everybody else is going to do. I don't even know what to ask her.

Lewis: Let yourself see Wanda turning into one of those birds that just spins around. And they're all gone now, the rats and the guinea pigs. The mice. There's nothing to keep her here, she just turned into a bird and flew out. You're all alone.

Wanda: We're always all alone, I guess. We never know what to do when that happens and we really understand that we're all alone. She really wants to just go away. She wants to get stoned, pop some pills or something. I just let her go away, and there's no one to help me.

Lewis: Can't you ask one of the guinea pigs for help?

Wanda: (long silence) Ok., I do. I ask the large one for help and he says, "Why do you put yourself here?" He says, "Why do you put yourself here in the first place if you don't want to be here?" Then he tells me I'm supposed to be. And then I tell him, "Well what am I? What is it that I actually am?" I try to get him to answer but he just keeps running away and not giving me what I need. So that's what he says, "just sit down and enjoy it, whatever is there." And I tell him I'm afraid. He says, "Just be afraid." And I tell him it hurts to be afraid. Then he tells me, "Who says?" And then I say that it hurts to be afraid and not know what to do. And I'm helpless. And he says, "so you're helpless, so what." And he says he doesn't think that I am. He says, "can't you see the harm you're doing? You need to learn to enjoy any space you're in. And make it fine. Just enjoy learning to reach out, touch, try and hold on to it."

The session continues, but is not necessary to reproduce for our purposes. The section provided here gives a more concrete introduction to what Wanda is like, her own language patterns, and how her beliefs can be deduced from her language.

In the fifth month of therapy, important new information arose about the doubting part of Wanda. This part doubted her own ability to ever be whole and take care of herself. She had a spontaneous regression to an existence during the time of Jesus. She used that experience to discover, in comparison to Jesus, her own self-doubt. She felt she could never live up to Jesus' example. This we could express as another series of beliefs:

14. I don't believe I can ever really take care of myself by myself.
15. Other entities (Jesus, parents) are so self-assured that I can never live up to their example of faith.
16. If I try to live up to others' faith, I'll only fail and feel worse than ever.

By this point Wanda had accomplished a significant part of her goal. She had reduced herself to only requiring 40 units of NPH insulin in the mornings and occasionally 10 units of regular insulin in the evening when her urines had 2+ sugar[26] or more.

Such reduction was significant and important. Wanda's beliefs were emerging for her own recognition and review. On another level she was beginning to develop an awareness of her own behavioral patterns. Especially important was her recognition of emotional response sets arising from her childhood experience of never succeeding in pleasing or being good enough for her parents. Related was the feeling that it was better to be sick than to try to change an impossible situation. Improving her life was viewed as an impossible situation, so it would be better to be sick and not have to try. Anger was clearly important in her psychic economy. Anger was viewed as destruction — various parts of her had to guard against her anger which might reach murderous proportions (as with her brother) and hurt someone. It was better to hurt herself than to hurt someone else. As she began to understand her family, she began to maintain her own sense of integrity when with her family. She disagreed and expressed her own opinions. When she felt angry, she told her parents. Her mother and father began to tell her she was going crazy.

Next we arrived at the following formulation of one of Wanda's beliefs, with respect to the role diabetes had played in resolving a conflict between herself and her parents:

Parents: "Be perfect for us, Wanda."

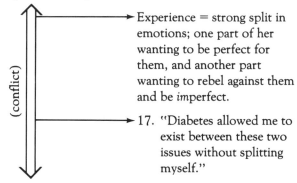

(conflict)

Experience = strong split in emotions; one part of her wanting to be perfect for them, and another part wanting to rebel against them and be *imperfect.*

17. "Diabetes allowed me to exist between these two issues without splitting myself."

Wanda: "I should not believe or do what my parents tell me to do."

Now we begin to appreciate how diabetes could be useful to Wanda:

17A. Diabetes helps me to resolve the emotional split between my parents' demands that I be perfect, and my need to rebel against them and their instructions and be imperfect.

17B. Diabetes can also help resolve the emotional split between my belief that I should be perfect and my natural rebellion against such a limiting belief.

More and more parts of Wanda were beginning to cooperate together and to direct themselves toward health and integration, one result of which was the improvement of her diabetes. The "part of her" concept refers to my view that a person is composed of many separate parts (analysts would speak of introjects and drives). The person can be viewed like the U.S. House of Representatives, in that behavioral decision-making is a result of more than half of the parts of a person agreeing together. Ambivalence results when a significant contingency of parts remain who lobby against the behavioral decision and continually try to muster enough votes to pass an opposing bill. The self or ego is more than the sum of his or her parts, just as the House of Representatives has a "wholeness" that cannot be understood solely from a knowledge of each individual Representative.

Wanda described many separate parts. Her "little boy" part was angry at not having time for rough and tumble play and for kidding around. Her "little girl" part wanted love, nurturing, and acceptance. Her "critical father" part was continually seen orating from his soap box that Wanda would never amount to anything. Therapy consisted of helping the various parts to achieve a sense of harmony together.

By the sixth month of therapy, Wanda had described more beliefs that several parts of her held, in the form of injunctions:

18. You're helpless to change your physical reality.
19. Don't believe in what you can't see.
20. Don't feel and don't show emotions.
21. Don't try.
22. Don't believe that you'll ever succeed.
23. Be perfect.
24. Good is defined by what other people around you (neighbors, etc.) think is good.

The reader can quickly perceive how much conflict these opposing beliefs could generate. Equally strong beliefs with opposite demands upon behavior and emotion seem to be the most likely to have negative physiological consequences. Wanda believed that she should always try *and* that she could never succeed as a result of her attempts. Feelings of hopelessness could easily result from the marriage of such opposites. The Simontons[27] have argued that hopelessness depresses the ability of the immune system to kill foreign cells (cancer cells or bacteria) and makes the person more susceptible to cancer. There is some evidence that this could also be an important factor in diabetes susceptibility.

The nature of hormones and disease is as yet poorly understood. Many hormones have immediate effects on tissue. These include insulin, catecholamines (stress hormones), glycagon, ACTH, parathyroid hormone, and secretin, all of which have very different actions in the body. These hormones, in turn, affect other hormones. Insulin is an anabolic hormone which encourages tissue building (catabolic hormones break down protein and tissue). Insulin (and other anabolic hormones) act to antagonize the intracellular increase of cyclic AMP by accelerating its breakdown.[28] Cyclic AMP is cyclic adenosine monophosphate, which is an intermediate "messenger" released by catabolic hormones and by stress (which releases catabolic hormones). It continues the work of the immediate acting catabolic hormones inside the cell. Insulin also prevents the intra-cellular activation of enzyme systems by cyclic AMP.[29] It makes sense that factors which might change the balance of the body between breakdown and rebuilding (catabolism and anabolism) could affect the body's need for insulin. Simply eradicating stress will move toward a more anabolic state.

W.I. Smith and colleagues[30] have found an increased prevalence of IgA deficiency ($p < 0.001$) in children with juvenile-onset insulin dependent diabetes. IgA is one of several antibodies the body manufactures to protect itself from infection. These children had other immune system associated diseases, such as thyroiditis, chronic active hepatitis, and histories of frequent infection. Four of these nine children had auto-antibodies to endocrine organs. That is, they manufactured antibodies against themselves — in particular, their own endocrine organs. The existential considerations of such a process implies self-destruction, e.g. self-hate, blame, self-attack.

An important event took place in the 7th month of therapy. Wanda decided that she wasn't making progress quickly enough and began a wheat grass fast (against my advice). This may have related to her fear of succeeding in which she identified me as a parent, sabotaging or rebelling against her previous success and my desire for her to succeed further (or it could be unrelated to me). She continued her fast until she developed diabetic ketoacidosis requiring hospitalization. This seemed to be a manifestation of her dialectic of success-failure. When she tries, she fails (a direct result of deliberate action taken by her). Her medication requirements had dropped to 10-15 units of regular insulin per day before her wheat grass fast. After this, they rose to 60 units per day. She had switched from NPH to regular insulin because, as our work continued, her insulin requirements fluctuated more frequently. As she discovered her beliefs and her past, she could react emotionally to it. When she did, her insulin needs would drop. When a part of her was feeling panicked, angry or fearful, but most of her was ignoring that feeling, her insulin needs would rise. Regular insulin made it much easier for her to regulate her insulin intake to match more accurately her psychophysiological condition at the four different times that she checked her urine and medicated herself according to her findings.

In the 8th month of therapy it was necessary to reframe her goals. We talked about Wanda permitting herself to give up improving her diabetes as such a charged issue in success or failure. We also talked to the part of her that believed healing was impossible. I suggested a new plan of her spending only 10 minutes in the morning and 10 minutes in the evening thinking about diabetes (except when she had to check her urine). The rest of the time she was to live her life (emotionally) as though she did not have diabetes, except for taking care to give herself proper insulin (she would never eat a diabetic diet.) The time she used for intensive visualization and past life exploration about diabetes would be redirected into general personal growth activities. This plan she did not carry out, although I thought it was a good one for alleviating performance anxiety. Perhaps she needed a way to rebel against authority; she could help herself in a creative way different than that I had suggested.

During the nine months of weekly therapy, we had discovered that Wanda's insulin requirements were strongly connected with her emotional state. When she was afraid, agitated, or trying not to feel, her urine would show 4+ sugar. When she felt integrated and grounded, her urine would read negative, regardless of how little insulin or how much sugar she had ingested. At this time, she was back to a maximum of 40 units of regular insulin per day.

Progress continued through analysis of a dream that Wanda had which revealed further beliefs:

> She was getting dressed up to go to a class reunion. She was overweight. Her father was sitting outside waiting for her. She had long, thick hair which came to her knees. He saw that she had made an effort to dress up, and, for some reason, this affected him very much and he cried. He cried because he said, "I can't let myself feel." They hugged each other and he cried for some time. Wanda cried too. He said three time, "I can't let myself feel," and cried about that.

During the next session, I utilized biofeedback with a GSR device.[31] I ran the central meridian for a kind of kinesthetic hypnotic induction, until Wanda was deeply relaxed. She and I were able to hear when she became tense and relaxed. I then did a quick relaxation induction using the tunnel technique, involving helping her to imagine herself going down through an elevator and counting down each floor from 10 to 1. I included indirect hypnotic suggestions for her to *go deeply down* and to *become relaxed.* This included suggestions to go down below the level of thinking, all the way down to the level of pictures and symbols and images. At that level she was able to experience a very powerful, emotional feeling connected with her neck which she saw as deep blue and as a kind of barrier. Beyond that there was a rosy shade of pink. She was afraid to go beyond the barrier because she might lose control. As we had switched to utilizing the sex/circulation meridian, I hypothesized a relationship between her sexuality and her fears of losing control. She felt blocked energy at the level of the neck, thereby cutting off her head from the rest of her body. She also felt blocked at the level of the heart (also the level of the breasts), and finally at the level of the symphysis pubis (pubic bone) which cuts off the lower half of the body. Wanda related this to sexual fears. She spoke about her fear of intimacy and sexuality. She feared intimacy, because the other person could then try to enforce their will on her, and she would not be able to say "no."

This suggests another belief:

24. Intimacy is fearful because it makes me vulnerable. to another's power and control.

This became easier to understand in the contect of Wanda's family. Power within the family was gained or lost through sexual relationships over several generations. The men capitulated through becoming impotent. Thus, the belief that:

25. Others gain power over me through sex.

By the end of 10 months of work (one hour session weekly), Wanda's needs for regular insulin varied between 5 and 30 units daily. She continued to use a sliding scale[32] to determine the amount of insulin to give herself at each six-hour period. Her diabetes would be, at that time, described by any internist as well-controlled. She had not lost weight or changed her diet or exercise pattern. In our 11th month of working together, her interest and willingness to continue exploring the issues with me decreased. She stopped individual therapy and began serving as an apprentice to a local holistic health practitioner. She has remained at a level of 0-20 units of regular insulin per day for the past two years.

To summarize, the major problematic beliefs that we uncovered were:

1. A belief that she was a victim of karma.
2. A belief in the power of external evil and the harmful effect of refusing to do others' biddings.
3. A belief that she was not good enough to succeed and that the result of trying was failure.
4. A belief that she was similar to her father physiologically and emotionally.
5. A belief that diabetes would help her get back at others and keep her from being split between conflicting demands.
6. A belief that the stress of success is overwhelming and requires capitulation (getting sick is a way to capitulate without losing face).
7. A belief that getting healthy is a familiar failure/success/please others paradigm.
8. A belief that, were she to take possession of her own power, something terrible might happen.
9. A belief that sexuality and intimacy were ways in which others took power over her and thus were to be feared.

Related to these core beliefs, she experienced a general difficulty in being aware of "negative" feelings, meaning anger, hurt, rage, etc. The more she was unaware of such feelings, the more her insulin needs increased. The more expressive she became of these feelings, the less insulin she needed. The physiological effects of stress for her were centered in her pancreas.[33]

Implications for Theory Building

What does this case tell us about the nature of diabetes in particular and health and illness in general.[34] We know diabetes is a physiological ailment so we have to conclude that a relationship exists between emotions and physiology. There is a variety of evidence demonstrating that stress hormones adversely affect diabetes.[35] Many emotional experiences can promote the release of stress hormones such as adrenaline, all of which will tend to worsen diabetes and increase insulin needs.

For Wanda, the stress of adolescence and her response to the normal separation process teenagers act out with parents provided sufficient stress, coupled with a pure sugar diet for three months, to "burn out" her pancreas. We may never know the relative contributions of genetics, stress, family dynamics, diet, and other factors to her condition. All are important. Significant is the fact that Wanda was able to gain control of, and to improve her diabetes through discovery and expression of her emotions.

Environmental Factors

Genetic studies of twins concordant and discordant for diabetes have suggested that an environmental component exists in the development of diabetes.[24] This could represent conditioning of the patient by the environment that she will get diabetes. The environmental component could be reflective of the stress and emotional factors we have discussed with Wanda, or of other variables not yet considered. A holistic theory must take every piece of data into account.

A relationship between the onset of diabetes and seasonal patterns has also been found.[38] Wanda experienced a seasonal effect with her diabetes. It became worse at traditionally stressful times: summer vacation (Wanda believed due to the increased contact with her parents), exam times, and just before major holidays, including Thanksgiving, Christmas, and Easter. The stress of these holidays was important to Wanda's diabetes for her own unique reasons. Other diabetic patients might experience stress from holidays for very different reasons. Such ritualized, scheduled periods of stress in our society may also help people to become more susceptible to viral infections, dietary and exercise changes, and the use of drugs at specific times during the year.

Nutritional factors are obviously important. Before the appearance of her diabetes, Wanda ate candy only for three months. Beliefs about food could sometimes be as important as specific foods. Wanda believed candy was very bad for her. This would be especially true in a family in which the father was diabetic. Sugar would produce high anxiety, much as the forbidden fruit given Eve by the snake who invited Eve to partake of the fruit against God's (or doctor's) orders. Perhaps, particular vitamin and mineral deficiencies are also important.[39] Some patients may be able to compensate for high levels of stress, conflicting beliefs, and genetic susceptibility by super-nutrition and/or mega-vitamin therapy. In my view, helping these people decrease stress and resolve conflicting beliefs is preferable to vitamin and mineral therapy, but, as a supportive measure in the early phases of therapy, nutritional supplementation could be quite beneficial (depending, of course, on the patient).

Stress and the Onset of Diabetes

"Since times of antiquity, observations have been recorded associating the onset of diabetes with emotional shocks or upsets."[44] Wanda certainly fits this observation. Her diabetes occured after a very successful (from her parents' perspective) school year which she experienced as extremely stressful (almost to the point of ego disintegration). There have been other reports of sudden, stressful events occurring before the onset of diabetes.[42]

In all these cases, it is possible that the patients' stresses were so severe as to be driving them toward breakdown of the ego (insanity, psychosis). This seemed true for Wanda. The emergence of a severe physical illness provides a stability within the person, family, and/or community that metaphysically serves to put the break on a cable car plummeting downhill toward ego disintegration (seemingly also true for Wanda). In this sense, the diabetes is very adaptive toward preserving the life of the ego, even though it is threatening to the life of the body. Diabetes provided a way for Wanda to sidestep the pressure and expectations of family and teachers to succeed, without losing face.[46] Physical illness is one way to handle this problem. Delinquency and schizophrenia are two other approaches. Perhaps some of the families of diabetic patients have such severe sanctions not to be "crazy" or "bad," that these two options are closed. As Wanda improved clinically, her outbursts of angry expressiveness were viewed with horror by her family as a sign of mental illness. Early and more recent research has shown that anger is more closely related to norepinephrine, and fear, to epinephrine. When the fight reponse is aroused in type A personalities, their behavior suggests anger more than fear. With this there is an increase in norepinephrine. Epinephrine has been more closely associated with arousal situations and with the threat of loss of desiderata (social status; access to territory, including water; and access to objects of attachment. The brain is thought to play an important role in this. The amygdala (a part of the limbic system) is thought to mediate the fight-or-flight response through its activation of sympathetic nervous fibers to the adrenal gland, the organ which mobilizes the body (including the pancreas) during stress. The production capacity of the adrenal gland for adenosine 3′,5′-monophosphate (cyclic AMP) is reduced following splanchnic denervation. The autonomic nervous system seems to regulate adrenal response to stress through regulation of the important enzymes, phenylethanolamine N-methyltransferase (PMNT) and dopamine-betahydroxylase. Steroidogenesis and the delivery of glucocorticoids (stress hormones) to the adrenal medulla may depend on the action of a permissive receptor at the synapse of autonomic fibers coming into the adrenal, which allows ACTH to regulate corticoid synthesis. Constant maintenance of the fear response in susceptible individuals (Wanda) may alter physiology so as to deplete the adrenal gland and, through that, the pancreas.

Stress and the Course of Diabetes

The course and control of diabetes and the levels of blood glucose have been shown to be altered by emotional stress. Events generating anxiety, specific intrapsychic conflicts, emotional deprivations, conscious and unconscious threats to security, and actual unpleasant psychologic experience can upset diabetic control.[47] Stressful life situations, either consciously or unconsciously interpreted by the diabetic patient as having relevance to his security, can produce fluctuations in the level of ketone bodies[48] and glucose in the venous blood as well as in the amount of urine excreted.[49]

Relationships have also been found between undesirable life events and worsening of diabetes.[51] Some patients actually learn that when their sugar gets too high, they can create a delirium. In spite of painful physical symptoms and apparent suffering, there is an underlying feeling of well-being. This has been called "paradoxical euphoria."[52] The patients eats too many sweets to produce this condition. Inadequate utilization of sugar despite there being too much sugar in the blood (hyperglycemia) leads the liver to tell the body to use up stores of fat. Fatty acids are produced in increasing numbers, leading to the formation of ketone bodies, resulting in acidosis. This acidosis (excess acidity of the blood) causes a sense of disorientation and alteration of consciousness. This altered psychometabolic state, despite producing painful physical symptoms, will blot out painful feelings and will release euphoric emotions. Patients (including Wanda) accidentally discover this effect and intentionally (albeit perhaps unconsciously) allow themselves to become disoriented to achieve that feeling of well-being and temporary "melting away" of cares and worries. This is a reason for poor control of diabetes that most medical doctors never appreciate. Other studies have also shown behavioral differences between groups of diabetics and other patients and controls.[53] Children who become diabetic have been distinguished from control children who do not become diabetic by having more problems with sleeping and with stealing.[58] C.R. Swift and colleagues[59] studied 50 juvenile diabetic patients and 50 individually matched non-diabetic controls together with their families. Results showed that the diabetic child exhibited more psychopathology than the non-diabetic controls. These children were described as more dependent, having less adequate self-images, greater levels of anxiety (manifest and latent), more pathological sexual identification, greater constriction, more pathological hostility, and greater oral preoccupation. Duration of diabetes was most strongly associated with control: the longer the duration, the worse the control. The classification and self-perception were also associated with control. Control was more disturbed in the more abnormal patients. Perhaps these are the children who would have become more or less psychotic or delinquent had their diabetes not intervened.

Psychological Adjustment of the Diabetic

Some psychoanalysts have observed that diabetic patients may develop a habit of dealing with every external and internal situation in terms of food and his or her diabetes.[60] Does this come before the diabetes, afterwards, or does it develop concomitantly? In families such as Wanda's there may already be a family fixation on food and diabetes. There will be shared beliefs among family members about food (when, what, and how much to eat, how to cook, etc.) and diabetes (who will get it, when, and can they prevent it?). Children in diabetic families may learn to use eating as a way to relax and cope with stress, especially through nurturing themselves with a forbidden sugar-filled treat (chocolate sundae, banana milkshake).

Adolescent diabetic girls have been found to have high levels of depression and low levels of self-esteem.[61] Does the production of antibodies that attack the self (autoantibodies) represent a "bodying forth" of certain kinds of low self-esteem? All therapists and approaches that improve diabetic control also increase self-esteem. The longer the duration of diabetes, the lower self-esteem becomes. Self-esteem is an important issue about which clinicians should be aware with diabetic clients. We need to know which beliefs keep the self-esteem down.[62] Wanda had no way to be successful without entering conflict and feeling like a failure. Her self-esteem could not help but suffer in such a double bind of belief.

Belief Systems and Diabetes

Individual belief systems must be considered for accurate theorizing about health. Belief systems represent the formulae that individuals use to put together (construct) their conceptions of how things work and fit in the world around them. Therapy is a deconstitution-reconstitution process that involves helping clients step outside their beliefs to experience the effects of those beliefs and possibly use the inner resources they discover to re-formulate beliefs and attitudes. Wanda believed that eating sweets was equivalent to feeling good and being loved. She believed this would compensate for a painful inner void of frustration, anger, and disappointment.

Family System and Diabetes

Family researchers and therapists have some important things to tell us about diabetes. Wanda's family illustrated some of the dynamics of the communication process that occur in the families of diabetics. A typical communication sequence would involve Wanda having an argument with her father. Shortly after Wanda left her parents' house after a visit, Wanda's mother would call to tell her that, due to the argument, her father's diabetes was now out of control. When Wanda first began seeing me, her mother's attempt to make her feel guilty through blaming her for causing her father's illness, was successful. To compensate for her guilt, she would have a binge meal of sweets. At the conclusion of our acquaintanceship, she was no longer as likely to respond to such manipulation. She resolved her feelings of guilt about her father's illness by concluding their separation as daughter and father. The separation process of father and daughter had been delayed for years. Wanda's diabetes, in part, seemed to have emerged from the tension of Wanda's struggle for separation-individuation from her parents. That separation-individuation, long delayed, was now moving again toward completion. As Wanda became separated from her parents, the emotional stress from the tension of that unresolved process began to decrease. As that stress decreased, Wanda's diabetes improved.

Parents of newly diagnosed diabetic children often experience an initial reaction, characterized by bewilderment, anxiety, fear, and depressive feelings.[63] Parents of children whose diabetes was in poor control have shown "non-constructive external coping processes," (mainly hopelessness and poor cooperation) in the daily care of the diabetic child.[63] These parents handled their feelings of anxiety and depression through chronic underlying pathological forms, such as omnipotent thinking, denial, and phobias. Parents of children whose diabetes is in good control have been found to be more adequately coping with feelings of anxiety, loss, and depression.

Five years later, children who were in good control belonged to "healthy, well-functioning" family types.[63] Families of children in poor control have been categorized as chaotic with internal cliques and severe conflicts.[64]

Salvador Minuchen, a family therapist in Philadelphia, studied interactions of families of juvenile diabetic patients who were in poor control (multi-recurrent bouts of near-coma, coma, and acidosis) with two other groups of families (children with behavior disorders and "normal kids").[65]

For the brittle diabetics (those in very poor control) he found that:

1. The children were intensely enmeshed in their families' current conflicts.
2. Family members demonstrated a high degree of over-protectiveness and concern for each other's welfare.
3. These families were marked by rigidity and seemed committed to maintaining the family status quo.
4. There seemed to be an inability or unwillingness to resolve conflicts.

These attributes were certainly true for Wanda's family.

Success with Psychotherapy and Diabetics

Few reports exist in which diabetic patients improve during psychotherapy. Perhaps therapists have not attempted to help such patients because they haven't felt improvement could occur without drugs. S.H. Block, an analyst, has written about the successful psychoanalytic treatment of a diabetic patient (adult-onset), such that her internist was able to discontinue all medication.[52] The beliefs of most physicians and medical researchers are such that the insights of Wanda's case history are denied to them. The modern belief that truth is determined by double-blind, controlled studies prevents the exploration of new dimensions of investigation. The implicit assumptions behind double-blind controlled studies are that 1) it is possible to manipulate and study a single variable without that isolation/investigation affecting other variables, some more dramatically than others, 2) we know enough about diabetes and health to know what variables to control for and randomize, and 3) it's possible to randomize people. None of these assumptions are provable, yet they are treated as dogma. From case descriptions such as Wanda's we can begin to arrive at a better understanding of the important factors in the initiation, maintenance, treatment, and prevention of diabetes.

Biofeedback and Diabetes

Clinical biofeedback has been used to help diabetic patients achieve better control and decrease insulin requirements.[66] A 20-year-old woman had had diabetes since age 9. Control had been excellent until age 15 when she developed thyroiditis.[67] At age 16 her diabetic control became very poor and she was hospitalized for 14 consecutive months. Insulin doses of several hundred units per day were common, as were massive swings in blood sugar.

At age 17, she was begun on MJ1999 (Sotalol), a β-adreneigic blocker[68] and family therapy was begun. There was improvement in diabetic control at this time, and she was able to live at home and attend school. Ketoacidosis was still rather frequent and often associated with infections, although less severe. The MJ1999 was discontinued after 15 months.

During her first quarter at college the patient was hospitalized four times for ketoacidosis. She was hospitalized four more times during her freshman year and three times during the fall quarter of her sophomore year.

After a baseline period (winter quarter, 3 months), biofeedback training was begun. The average insulin intake in the baseline period was 85 units daily. The average during the training period was 44 units daily. The average daily dose during the follow-up year was 52 units daily. The variation measure (standard error of the mean) decreased as training progressed, and remained small during the follow-up period.

Conclusion

Diabetic patients can reduce their insulin requirements, especially in conjunction with certain kinds of psychotherapeutic intervention. Theories of health and disease must take this into account. Incorporating the approaches just described into existing medical practices could have many positive benefits for patients, including saving money spent on hospitalization and intensive medical care. It is also important to speculate about the possibility for total remission, or cure of diabetes, were a holistic approach begun early in the course of the disease, perhaps at the time of diagnosis. Such therapy could itself be an intervention preventing the disease from solidifying into a stable, difficult to change, condition.

REFERENCES AND NOTES

[1] Applied kinesiology is a method by which to test and balance the energy meridians of the body through testing for muscle tone and massaging neurolymphatic points on the body surface. It will be discussed in more detail in a later chapter. More detailed information is available through Reference 2 or from the Touch for Health Foundation in Pasadena, California.

[2] Thie, J. *Touch for Health, 2nd edition.* Pasadena: The Enterprises, 1980.

[3] Diazepam is known to most people by the specific brand name of Valium. It is thought to act in the brain to decrease anxiety. Ten milligrams every four hours is a rather large dose.

[4] This is an almost constant irritation of the vagina. Monilial means that the population of a specific kind of yeast cell is high in association with the irritation. Chronic means it just keeps coming back; the usual drugs that kill yeast do not stop it. Diabetics are thought to be more susceptible to this because of the presence of more sugar in their vaginal cells and secretions.

[5] Urticaria is a blotchy, raised rash that can itch severely. Traditional medical theorists believe it is related to allergies or dysfunctions in the autonomic nervous system.

[6] NPH insulin is a long-acting kind. It can usually be given once or twice daily, whereas regular insulin is usually given four times daily.

[7] Necrobiosis refers to dead tissue and relates to blood vessel damage. Diabetics are more susceptible.

[8] Acidosis accompanies coma. When there is too much sugar, the blood becomes too acidic. This can be very dangerous.

[9] Indirect hypnosis is described in a later chapter. In essence, it is the planned use of language and communication to give suggestions to a client to do what is good for him without directly telling him what to do. This is very helpful, because most of us are perverse enough to do the opposite of what another person, especially one in authority, tells us to do. More information on indirect hypnosis can be found in References 10, 11, and 12.

[10] Haley, J. *The Collected Works of Milton H. Erickson, M.D.* New York: Grune & Stratton, 1973.

[11] Bandler, R. and Grinder, J. *Patterns of the Hypnotic Techniques of Milton H. Erickson, M.D.*, Volumes I and II. Cupertino, CA: Meta Publications, 1975.

[12] Erickson, M.H., Rossi, E., and Rossi, I. *Hypnotic Realities.* New York: Irvington, 1977.

[13] Visualization is also described in more detail in a later chapter. It is a technique in which visual images are used in communicating and describing, rather than just talking. It is a much *more experiential* way of communicating than everyday talking because it involves all sensory modes and tends to evoke at least a mild trance. More information on visualization can be found in References 14 and 15.

[14] Bandler, R. and Grinder, J. *The Structure of Magic*, Volumes I and II. Cupertino, CA: Meta Publication, 1976.

[15] Samuels, M. and Samuels, N. *Seeing with the Mind's Eye.* Berkeley: Bookworks, 1977.

[16] Control of diabetes refers to how much of the time the amount of sugar in the blood and urine is high. Ideally, in excellent control, the level of sugar in the blood should not be too much higher than the normal range for people wihout diabetes, and there should be no sugar in the urine.

[17] This was before the popularity of *Sho-gun.*

[18] Perhaps the dynamics of her family that led to sugar being considered a highly reinforcing reward need to be considered along with thoughts of heredity. Food certainly occupied a central place in her family.

[19] An insulin reaction is an acute physiological crisis relating to having too little sugar relative to the amount of available insulin. Diabetics who take their insulin and then

don't eat, may have such a reaction because their dose was based upon the assumption that they would eat.

[20] White light as a protective force was an aspect of Wanda's belief system. As such it was useful and effective at bypassing resistance.

[21] Shiva is the Hindu god of regeneration through destruction, which Wanda identified with.

[22] S. Huang and N.K. Maclaren[23] found that diabetic patients had increased titers of antibodies to SS-DNA (61.3%), synthetic polyadenylicpolyuridylic acid (Poly A-U) (78.8%), synthetic polyinosinicpolycytidylic acid (Poly I-C) (62.5%), and DS-RNA of statolon virus (51.3%) and reovirus (27.3%), respectively, in contrast to asthmatics (15.5, 34.9, 3.9, 20.2, 2.3) or to healthy controls ($p < 0.001$). These substances are representative of DNA and RNA, important components of cells. Again, we find evidence of diabetic patients making antibodies which attack the components of their own cells. These may be the physiological mediators of the way self-destructive (in a purely physical sense) beliefs affect the body. Huang and Maclaren have argued that viral infection and response to it can begin the auto-immune response. E.J. Rayfield and Y. Seto[24] argue from animal models (most notably EMC-induced murine diabetes) that viral infection can create a diabetic state in genetically susceptible hosts.

[23] Huang, S. and Maclaren, N.K. Antibodies to nucleic acids in juvenile-onset diabetes. *Diabetes* 27:1105-1111, 1978.

[24] Rayfield, E.J. and Seto, Y. Viruses and the pathogenesis of diabetes mellitus. *Diabetes* 27:1126-1142, 1978.

[25] "Active space" refers to the part of a computer that is being used in the present to actually do work, accessing stored memory from time to time.

[26] The amount of sugar in the urine is measured simply with test-tape and expressed on a 5-point scale of 0 (normal) to 1+ through 4+.

[27] Simonton, O.C. and Matthews-Simonton, S. *Getting Well Again.* Los Angeles: Tarcher, 1975.

[28] Loten, E.G. and Sneyd, J.G.T. On the effect of insulin on adipose tissue adenosine 3',5' cyclic monophosphate phosphodiesterase. *Biochem. J.* 120:187-193, 1970.

[29] Larna, J. Mechanism of insulin action. *Metabolism* 24:249-257, 1975.

[30] Smith, W.I., Jr., Rabin, B.S., Huellmantel, A., Van Thiel, D.H. and Drash, A. Immunopathology and juvenile-onset diabetes mellitus. IgA deficiency and juvenile diabetes. *Diabetes* 27:1092-1097, 1978.

[31] The central meridian is one of the Chinese acupuncture meridians. GSR refers to a machine that measures the galvanic skin response, a parameter that changes under stress. In this particular machine, a tone became higher in frequence as stress and anxiety increase. "Running the meridian" means starting at the beginning of the meridian with the fingers and tracing the meridian with a rubbing motion. Any sensitive spots located are rubbed until no longer sensitive. This is a way of inducing trance by touch and talk (kinesthetic/auditory).

[32] A sliding scale is a formula the patient uses to determine their insulin dose based upon the results of testing their urine.

[33] The pancreas is the organ in the abdomen that manufactures insulin through beta-cells.

[34] I should add that Wanda is not unique. I have worked with two other diabetic clients who have also significantly decreased their insulin requirements.

[35] One of the sources of this research is the study of the effects of surgical stress on glucose and insulin. Stig Nirstrup-Madsen and co-workers in Denmark found that the brain was responsible for the increase in glucose levels that occur during surgery.[36] They found that epidural anesthesia would prevent a rise of glucose during surgery presumably by blocking the transmission of nerve impulses from the area being operated on through the spinal cord to the brain. The same was true for the stress hormone, cortisol, and for the intermediate stress hormone, cyclic AMP. Cyclic AMP has the opposite effect from insulin. This same group of researchers found that, when the central nervous system-

induced rise in glucose was not blocked by epidural anesthesia, it seemed to be highly correlated with a rise in one of the stress hormones — epinephrine, a catecholamine (also known as adrenaline).[37]

[36] Nistrup-Madsen, S., Brandt, M.R., Engquist, A., Badawi, I., and Kehlet, H. Inhibition of plasma cyclic AMP, glucose, and cortisol response to surgery by epidural analgesia. *B.J. Surg.* 64:669-671, 1977.

[37] Nistrup-Madsen, S., Fag-Moller, F., Christiansen, C., Vester-Anderson, T., and Engquist, A. Cyclic AMP, adrenaline, and noradrenaline in plasma during surgery. *B.J. Surg.* 64:191-193, 1978.

[38] An association with increased incidence of infection with Coxsakie-B viruses; seasonal variations in diet, exercise and other agents, including drugs, toxins, or foods have also been considered.[40]

[39] For example, P. McNair and colleagues[41] found that in 71 insulin-treated diabetic outpatients, those with the most severe hypomagnesemia had the most severe retinopahy ($p<0.005$), other risk factors being comparable. Severe retinopathy represents changes in blood vessels inside the eye, reflecting narrowing ("hardening of the arteries") and closing of arteries.

[40] Kimball, C.P. Emotional and psychosocial aspects of diabetes mellitus. *Med. Clinic. N. Am.* 55:1007-1018, 1971.

[41] MacNair, P., Christiansen, C., Madsbad, S., Laurilzen, E., Faber, O., Binder, C., and Transbol, I. Hypomagnesemia, a risk factor in diabetic retinopathy. *Diabetes* 27:1075-1077, 1978.

[42] G.F. Daniels[43] reported case studies in which sudden stressful environmental occurrences proceded the onset of diabetes. W.C. Menninger[44] reported on 22 cases of psychiatric illness associated with diabetes and found four for whom a psychosis either preceded or developed simultaneously with the onset of diabetes. F.P. Slawson and colleagues[45] evaluated 25 newly diagnosed adult diabetic patients and found that 14 gave a history of what Slawson, et al. termed recent object loss. Many presented patterns of unresolved grief and emotional deprivation. S.P. Stein and E.S. Charles[46] found that a group of 38 diabetic patients had a significantly higher incidence of parental loss and severe family disturbance than a group of 38 matched, non-diabetic subjects who had sickle cell anemia and other chronic blood diseases. Kimball[40] found no correlation between onset and emotional stress in a large scale epidemiological study. This is not unexpected from reviewing his methodology. Wanda, in his report, would not have been considered to be under emotional stress by Kimball's methodology. The stress in her life was largely internal and largely being concealed from herself in the degree of its magnitude. An interesting methodological distinction emerges here. In our phenomenological method, the more the research is distanced from the individual, the less reliable it becomes. In the natural scientific approach it should become more reliable. Beliefs and emotions to not follow the statistical models of the normal distribution. If anything, they are extremely non-parametric. Epidemiological methodology would not be expected to be very helpful. The philosophical underpinnings of modern epidemiology are inconsistent with the experienced nature of beliefs.

[43] Daniels, G.F. Present trends in the evaluation of psychic factors in diabetes mellitus. *Psychosom. Med.* 1:527-532, 1939.

[44] Menninger, W.C. Psychological factors in the etiology of diabetes. *J. Nervous Mental Disease* 81:1-13, 1935.

[45] Slawson, F.P., Flynn, W.R., and Koller, E.J. Psychological factors associated with the onset of diabetes mellitus. *J.A.M.A.* 185:166-170, 1963.

[46] Stein, S.P. and Charles, E.S. Emotional factors in juvenile diabetes mellitus: A study of early life experiences of adolescent diabetes. *Am. J. Psychol.* 128:700-704, 1971.

[47] Grant, l., Kyle, G.C., Techman, A., and Mendels, J. Recent life events and diabetes in adults. *Psychosom. Med.* 36:121-128, 1974.

[48] Ketone bodies are acidic chemicals that increase in the blood as diabetes becomes more out of control. Too many of them lead to acidosis.

[49] Of 50 diabetic patients studied by Hinkle and Wolf, in nearly all cases the onset of the biochemical changes occurred after a period of environmental and interpersonal stress characterized by a loss of significant persons, objects, relationships or cultural values regarded by the patient as indispensable to his security.[50]

[50] Hinkle, L.E., Jr. and Wolf, S. Importance of life stress in course and management of diabetes mellitus. J.A.M.A. 148:513-520, 1952.

[51] I have recently begun working with a new patient who has been labelled diabetic and schizophrenic. This patient experienced similar forces prior to the onset of her diabetes. Eunice was a twin in a military family living in Taiwan. Her father was Mexican-American and her mother Taiwanese. Eunice's father demanded she be first in everything once she started school. From age 6 to 11, she was first in everything — schoolwork, gymnastics, swimming. At age 11, she became diabetic, but, unlike Wanda, she was now expected to succeed and be first despite her diabetes. In "true Army fashion," Eunice's father expected her to transcend her "physical handicap" and continue "first." Now more pressure was brought to bear because she had to "eat right" and "behave" and "sleep well" and "not stay out" because of her diabetes. Finally, when she attempted suicide at age 14, the pressure was off, but her parents completely rejected her and kept her institutionalized until age 21.

[52] Block, S.H. Paradoxical euphoria in diabetes mellitus. Psychosomatics 20(1):61-64, 1979.

[53] For example, B.J. Murawski and colleagues[54] studied adult patients who had had diabetes for 25-48 years using the MMPI. The entire sample had a high depression score with pervasive feelings of pessimism, hopelessness, and depression. The men who developed vascular complications had higher pathological scores on all but one scale when compared with the male complication-free group. I.A. Mirsky[55] noted their hurt pride and intensified fears and feelings of inadequacy. S.A. Karp and colleagues[56] found significantly more field dependence in 80 adults versus a matched control group. H.A. Witkin and colleagues[57] found that individuals high in field dependence also tend to be more socially dependent and have less distinct body boundaries. Karp found that women had greater field dependence scores than private patients and that clinic patients had greater scores than private patients. No social class differences were found.

[54] Murawski, B.J., Chazan, B.I., Balodimos, M.C., and Ryan, J.R. Personality patterns in patients with diabetes mellitus of long duration. Diabetes 19:259-263, 1970.

[55] Mirsky, I.A. Emotional factors in the patient with diabetes mellitus. Bull. Menninger Clin. 12:187-194, 1948.

[56] Karp, S.A., Winters, S., and Pollack, I.W. Field dependence among diabetics. Arch. Gen. Psychiat. 21:72-76, 1969.

[57] Witkin, H.A., Dyk, R.B., Falerson, H.F., Goodenough, D.R., and Karp, S.A. Psychological Differentiation. New York: John Wiley and Sons, 1962.

[58] Oltaware, M.O. The psychiatric complications of diabetes mellitus in children. So. Afr. J. of Med. 3:231-240, 1972.

[59] Swift, C.R., Seidman, F.L., and Stein, H. Adjustment problems in juvenile diabetes. Psychosom. Med. 29:555-571, 1967.

[60] Benedek, T. An approach to the study of the diabetic. Psychosom. Med. 10:284-287, 1948.

[61] Sullivan, B. Self-esteem and depression in adolescent diabetic girls. Diabetes Care 1:18-22, 1978.

[62] In existential terms, we need to know how the person has constituted his or her concept of self.

[63] Koski, M.L. The coping processes in childhood diabetes. Acta Paediatr. Scand. Suppl. 19:1-56, 1969.

[64] Koski, M.L., Ahlas, A., and Kumento, A. A psychosomatic follow-up of childhood diabetes. Acta Paedopsychiatr. 42:12-26, 1976.

[65] Minuchin, S., Baker, L., Rosman, B., Liebman, R., Milman, L., and Todd, T. A conceptual model of psychosomatic illness in children: Family organization and family therapy. Arch. Gen. Psychiat. 32:1031-1038, 1975.

[66] Fowler, J.E., Brudzynski, T.H., and VanderBergh, R.L. Effects of EMG biofeedback relaxation program on the control of diabetes. *Biofeedback and Self Regulation* 1(1):105-112, 1976.

[67] Thyroiditis is a condition involving inflammation of the thyroid gland. Patients are thought to make antibodies that attack their own thyroid gland.

[68] β-adrenergic blockers are drugs that sit on the receptor site of specific kinds of neurons of the autonomic nervous system. Such drugs seem to decrease the experience of anxiety, improve diabetes, and have many other effects upon the body.

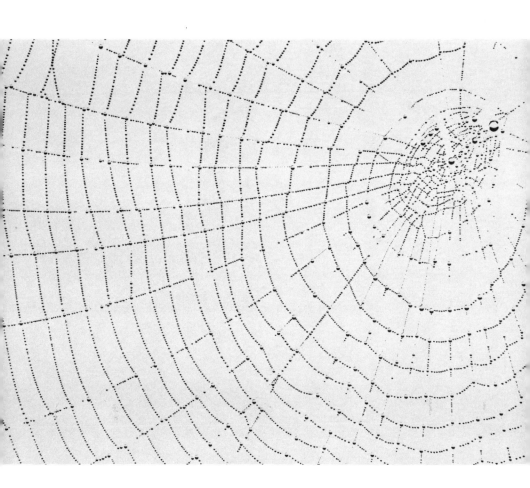

Chapter Four

Asthma and Allergies

Asthma *is a disorder* characterized by difficulty inhaling and exhaling completely. The bronchial tube bringing air from the throat to the lungs constricts and, with a narrowed diameter of breathing passageway, increased mucous secretion into that pathway, and panic at partial breathing obstruction, creates significant respiratory distress. The famous 19th century physician, Sir William Osler, observed in the time before these symptoms could be treated with drugs that asthma was a most peculiar disease, in that it was more a nuisance than dangerous. In his long clinical experience, no one had ever died of asthma, either in the acute phase or long-term. Today, most major textbooks of internal medicine[1] assert that an acute asthma attack constitutes a life-threatening emergency, and that almost all patients go on to develop fatal complications, including chronic bronchitis, bronchiectasis, emphysema, and cor-pulmonale. This change in prognosis from Sir William Osler's time to now may be related more to the ability of physicians to treat the disease, than any change in the nature of asthma. Strange as it may seem, the asthmatic patient may *need* his/her symptom in important ways. As drugs reduce that symptom, the body slowly re-calibrates itself so as to continue to have symptoms. The more physicians "battle" asthma, the worse the problem becomes because: (1) if drugs are withdrawn, the problem really is life-threatening (due to the escalation required in the face of medication), and (2) as the symptoms escalate with increasing medications, eventually they exceed the capacity of *all* medication, and since the patient has become dependent on medication which cannot be quickly withdrawn, the side effects of the medications contribute to the patient's demise.

I had never appreciated this effect during my medical training. I learned to treat asthmatic clients with a variety of drugs, changing their drug regimen until the client was symptom free. Nevertheless, clients slowly worsened each year and required more and more medication to remain symptom free. As I read William Osler's 19th century descriptions of asthma, I was amazed at how different the disease sounded. Shortly thereafter, I began to interview healthy older men and women (not in a medical, health-care context, but informally). I met several older people who had experienced asthmatic symptoms all their lives, sometimes rather severely. They had never gone to doctors but had waited patiently for the symptoms to clear. One of these was my wife's maternal Polish grandfather, age 76, who never went to doctors and had terrorized his loved ones for over 60 years with "his terrible wheezing fits."

Asthma is thought to result from a hypersensitivity of the bronchial cell lining to substances present in the air, so that small amounts of such substances, innocuous to non-allergic individuals, cause tissue reaction. Antibodies (IgE and IgA) catch hold of these small molecules while attaching themselves to the cell membrane. Histamine and *slow reacting substance* (SRS) are released (among other chemicals) and the classic wheezing response ensues. The psychosomatic theory of asthma holds that this hypersensitivity reaction originates from the central nervous system, or in other words, is a by-product of the patient's personality organization. Psychosomatic research then attempts to define what types of personality organizations and conflicts relate to asthma.

The existential approach differs in several important respects from the psychosomatic view and the biomechanical view (that no psychological factors operate for the asthmatic). First, we must separate "cause of the disease," "maintenance," and "cure." Figure 1 illustrates this.

The key element to understand from this diagram is that *there is no necessary connection between origination, maintenance, and resolution of an illness.* These are separate processes until proven otherwise. The assumption of cause and effect has led thinkers to demand that the cure of a disease be related to the "cause," violating Russell's Theory of Logical Types, which states simply, as one part of the theory, that it is not possible to compare members of a group at one level (causation) with members of a group at another level (cure). Membership of a variable in the group of variables leading to the development of an illness does not lead to that variable necessarily being a member of the group of variables leading to the cure of that same illness. Modern medicine makes this erroneous assumption by trying to link any acceptable

Figure 1.

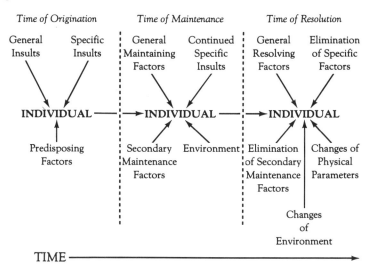

TIME ————————————————————————————————▶

treatment of illness to acceptable theories of causation of that illness. Variables may overlap in originating, maintaining, and curing an illness, but *their function differs as does their importance in each respective group.* Each of these time blocks is, in itself, a dynamic system with its own unique properties. Figure 2 illustrates this concept mathematically.

Figure 2.

GROUP 1	GROUP 2	GROUP 3
Originating Factors	**Maintaining Factors**	**Resolving Factors**
ψ_1 Specific insults	α_1 Specific insults	β_1 Specific factors
ψ_2 General factors $\neq$	α_2 General factors $\neq$	β_2 General factors
ψ_3 Environment	α_3 Environment	β_3 Environment
ψ_4 Predisposing factors	α_4 Predisposing factors	β_3 Predisposing factors
	(α_5) Secondary factors	β_5 Secondary factors
		(β_6) Tertiary factors

If we represent these as equations, we obtain a series of simultaneous, linear differential equations as in Figure 3.

Figure 3.

$$\text{Origination} = a\psi_1 + b\psi_2 + c\psi_3 + d\psi_4 + \ldots + n\psi^n$$

$$\text{Maintenance} = a\alpha_1 + b\alpha_2 + c\alpha_3 + d\alpha_4 + \ldots + n\alpha^n$$

$$\text{Resolution} = a\beta_1 + b\beta_2 + c\beta_3 + d\beta_4 + \ldots + n\beta^n$$

The various terms relate to the contribution of each of our variables in importance. This *can change*. Also, these functions are, in themselves, higher functions of more detailed *lower-level variables* which we will begin to list for asthma in Figure 4.

Figure 4 shows how many factors in varying combinations interact together to produce a gestalt situation (a whole which is greater than the sum of its parts, which cannot be understood by considering the parts separately), which under certain circumstances (to be determined experimentally and experientially) has the net outcome of symptoms which physicians label as asthma. Once the patient develops these symptoms, decisions must be made about the new perceptual experiences. The experience must be mapped to fit ongoing experience. It must be mapped onto pre-existing beliefs about the nature of the world (how things work and how he or she functions within the world). The client does this process through developing a set of belief systems to explain the new symptoms.

Such beliefs could include:

1. "I'm a sick person now."
2. "Once a person gets sick they just get worse and worse until they die."
3. "This means I'm a bad/inferior person."
4. "I've sinned, and now God is punishing me."
5. "I'll be a better person, because of my suffering."
6. "It's better to be physically sick than to manifest emotional problems."

Then clients begin to interact with other people about their symptoms. These other people have various emotional and cognitive reactions to the description of the symptoms depending upon personal beliefs about health and illness. These emotional reactions can amplify or mitigate the client's developing beliefs about the symptoms. This process of belief modification can be very hypnotic (meaning, taking place within a framework of very concentrated, focused, heightened awareness and receptivity). If a patient goes to a physician, and the physician says or implies (implications are sometimes more powerful than direct statements) the following, then the patient may create self-fulfilling prophecies:

1. "You have asthma. This will be a life-long illness."
2. "We can treat your symptoms, but we can't make them go away."

Figure 4.

POSSIBLE ORIGINATING FACTORS

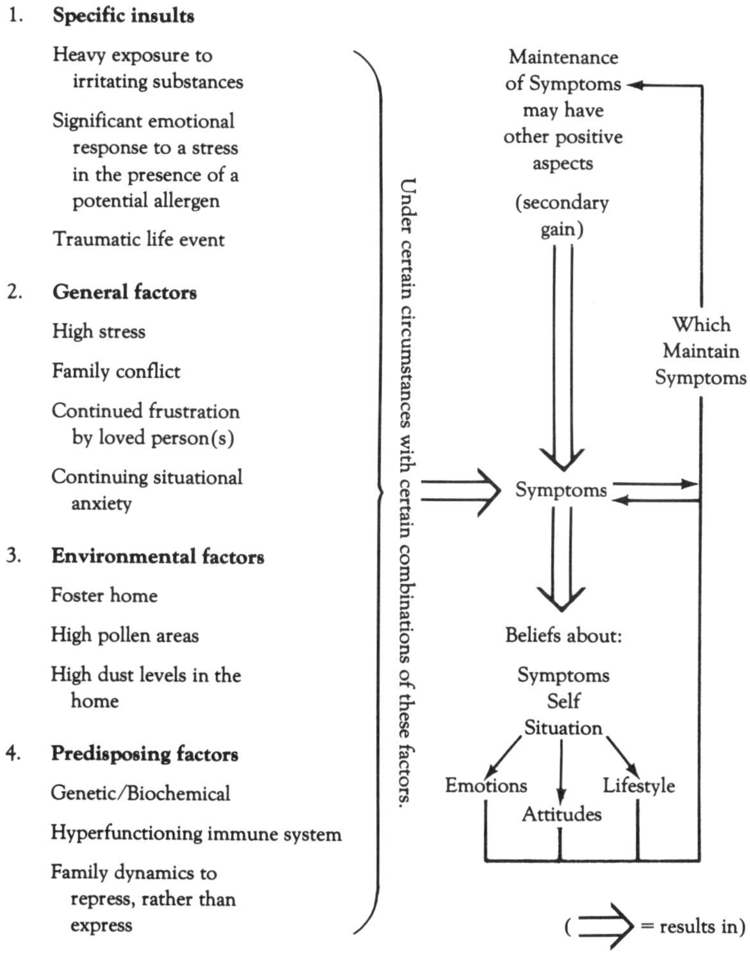

1. **Specific insults**

   Heavy exposure to
   irritating substances

   Significant emotional
   response to a stress
   in the presence of a
   potential allergen

   Traumatic life event

2. **General factors**

   High stress

   Family conflict

   Continued frustration
   by loved person(s)

   Continuing situational
   anxiety

3. **Environmental factors**

   Foster home

   High pollen areas

   High dust levels in the
   home

4. **Predisposing factors**

   Genetic/Biochemical

   Hyperfunctioning immune system

   Family dynamics to
   repress, rather than
   express

Under certain circumstances with certain combinations of these factors.

Maintenance
of Symptoms
may have
other positive
aspects

(secondary
gain)

Which
Maintain
Symptoms

Symptoms

Beliefs about:

Symptoms
Self
Situation

Emotions   Lifestyle

Attitudes

(⟹ = results in)

3. "Your disease will get worse and worse, and eventually
   it will kill you, despite our best efforts."
4. "You are a very sick man or woman."
5. "I will give you attention, whenever you have
   symptoms; otherwise, I don't want to see you."
6. "This is all due to an allergy. It has nothing to do with
   how you live."

Now, from Figure 4 it is evident, from the decisions our patient adopts about his or her illness, that beliefs develop with emotional, attitudinal and lifestyle consequences. Some of the emotional consequences of the previously listed beliefs include:

1. Depression — which can have hormonal effects, as well as a variety of other physiological consequences,
2. Repressed anger,
3. Hopelessness, and
4. Strong needs for dependency.

Longstanding attitudes or personality traits may develop from these beliefs. Attitudes are habitual emotional response patterns. Having a belligerent attitude means responding in a threatening, menacing way to another person when specific belief systems are activated that labels that other person as a threat. Some beliefs may be very dysfunctional. For example, the client may believe that anyone who wants to help has an ulterior motive leading the client to a belligerent response to people who want to offer help or love. Similar attitudes and beliefs often underlie responses leading to behavior meriting the medical label "problem patient."

Attitudes and emotions, along with beliefs, help create lifestyles. Lifestyles represent maps of the ways people live — when they get up, when they go to bed, what they eat, what they do. Depressed people, for example, tend to eat poorly (nutritionally), sleep poorly, and do very little. Lifestyle is a direct outcome of attitudes, emotions, beliefs, and motivation.

The concepts can be used diagrammatically to "explain" the asthmatic process. To do so, I will borrow from the insights of both allergic theory and psychosomatic theory. Figure 5 diagrams these concepts.

Conditioning

When patients are exposed to negative emotional situations with a special meaning, asthma attacks can be induced which are indistinguishable from attacks occurring "spontaneously" or after inhalation of allergens.[2] These situations were ones, recreated in the laboratory, which the patients had previously reported as ones in which they had previously experienced asthma attacks. An interesting conditioning phenomena was observed. Two patients who had experienced positive reactions to the inhalation of nebulized allergens, after a number of trials, began to react with attacks when only the control solution, in which the allergens had previously been dissolved, was inhaled, even though the researchers were sure that no contaminating allergen was

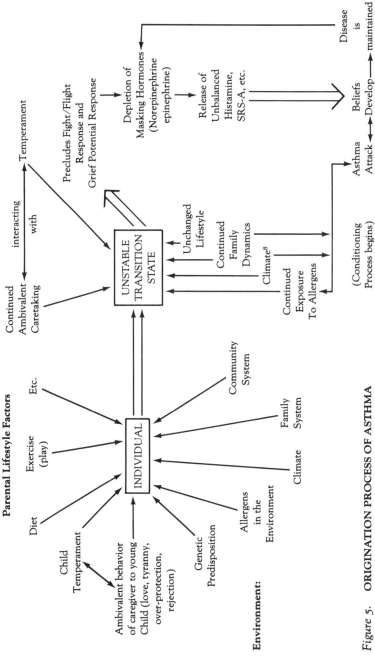

Figure 5. ORIGINATION PROCESS OF ASTHMA

present. On continuing this testing, these patients experienced attacks just from entering the same environmental setting, even when breathing pure oxygen and, later, even when only the glass mouthpiece was put into their mouth.

For the asthmatic, a constrictive physiological response can be conditioned to occur in response to certain stressful emotional situations. Without interruption, this conditioning process becomes more and more generalized.

Joannes Groen[2] has presented an intriguing theory for *how* the person becomes sensitized to allergens. This is based on studies by S. Talma[3] showing that expiratory wheezes are not produced by constriction of small airways, but by central narrowing of the trachea and major bronchi, and that many asthmatics can produce an expiratory wheeze on request. Many studies by Groen and his colleagues[4-7] have associated expiratory wheezing with active contraction of the abdominal and thoracic musculature during expiration, which (as the diaphragm is relaxed) produces high (many times normal) positive intrathoracic pressure. This, then, compresses the trachea and larger bronchi, mainly by pushing the membranous part of the posterior wall into the lumen.

Childhood Experiences

Groen theorized that asthma starts as a disturbed pattern of breathing in reaction to a frustration of the individual by a beloved but domineering authority figure.[8,9] This disturbed breathing creates the previously described effects, and hence, wheezing. From the collapse of the larger (and progressively smaller, as pressure mounts) airways, the mucous membranes swell by hyperemia[10] and edema[11] and increased mucous secretion as a result of impairment of venous drainage.[12] Part of the mucous is aspirated into smaller airways, obstructing and causing the classic expiratory wheeze of asthma. Inhaled substances dissolved into the mucous can penetrate more easily into the hyperemic basement membrane. The pressure gradient favors these large molecules being aspirated into the mucous membrane during inspiration, and pressed into the mucous membrane by the increased pressure present during expiration. The results of this penetration is contact with lymphocytes and plasma cells, which then produce antibodies to this foreign molecule. This is how Groen believes the allergic sensitization occurs — as a secondary process.

Genetics

Asthma certainly is not passed down in a simple Mendelian manner. It is very difficult to separate biological heredity from social heredity (the passing down through generations of behavior patterns and fixed interactional schemata). Joannes Groen has noted that it could be that the only genetic trait that is inherited is the predisposing personality (temperament). This might then produce symptoms only in certain combinations with the other factors we are discussing.

For example, in Israel, asthma is more frequent among Jewish immigrants from Iraq than among other groups of the population. Perhaps this represents effects of community beliefs.

Groen[2] has related that, "It is a curious fact that when the patient moves to a new climate, as from Holland to Switzerland with his family, the disease either does not improve at all in the new climate or recurs sooner or later. To obtain the best results the patient must transfer to a new environment alone; in other words, he must move to a new human as well as a new physical climate."

Temperament

Current researchers[13] on temperament assume that personality develops as an interaction between the traits or patterns and types of responses the baby brings into the world and the familial and social milieu in which the baby finds itself. The infant is born with unique ways of responding, even from the moment of birth. Problems arise when the environment and parental responses are mismatched with the baby's temperament. For example, parents of children who become schizophrenic tend to respond in a uniform way to infants and children, seemingly not noticing individual differences in those children. It has been hypothesized that children of certain temperaments are more "at risk" for developing asthma than others.[14] Adverse temperament characteristics have been shown to be useful predictive indices of behaviorally high-risk children.[15, 16]

Symptom Threshold

Given a dynamic model for the development of asthma which includes many areas or factors, next the concept of *symptom threshold* must be defined. How much of each of the factors are required to create a situation in which asthma does in fact result? After all, many people in the population are put to disadvantage by at least one of these factors, yet not all these people have asthma. Concepts borrowed from chemical thermodynamics can help us better explain who will develop asthma. If we think of a chemical reaction in which substances are placed together in a container and energy (heat, light) is added to the system, a certain minimal level of energy is required for the chemical reaction to occur and new products to develop. In baking a cake (a type of chemical reaction), a minimal level of heat is required to convert the mush of the cake batter into the texture of cake. In chemistry, as in baking, small amounts of substances called catalysts can be added to decrease the amount of energy required for the reaction to begin. For the human developing asthma, catalysts may include lowered nutrition status, genetic predisposition, and other factors. Once the reaction begins, an unstable (short-lived) intermediate, high energy step results. The product of this energized state then decomposes into the products of the reaction, meaning that no one factor alone, even if sufficiently intense, can result in asthma. We do not know if there are certain factors which must be present in minimal concentrations for asthma to be expressed.

Twentieth century Americans tend to blame themselves and feel guilty if they think their disease is anything but physical. While it is absurd to think that any process could just be physical, since people believe so, we must understand this belief. The concept of illness as punishment is what creates problems. Perhaps we can avert this process by arguing that so many of the originating factors took place in childhood that there is no blame, since children are not held responsible anyway, especially for unwitting responses (that seemed the best at the time).[14]

Resolution Threshold

Regardless of whether genetics contributed 90% or 10% to the development of the illness, genetics may not be relevant to the maintenance of an illness, a conceptually very different process from its origination. To continue the thermodynamic metaphor, much less energy is required to maintain a steady state, once established, than is required to create an entirely new situation (origination). Figure 6 diagrams my conceptualization of the maintenance process. In terms of the concepts of maintenance and cure, the relative contributions of each originating factor need not be known for cure. In fact, change of just one of the many maintenance factors may be sufficient to reach what I call the *resolution threshold*. This is the point at which improvement begins. Somewhere above the resolution threshold is the *cure threshold*, the point at which the disease is no longer present.

Figure 6 also shows that beliefs form a central core. Changing beliefs changes previous learning (conditioning), the relative importance of secondary gain, interaction patterns, communication patterns, lifestyle, attitudes, and emotions. These changes can, in turn, affect and and alter ongoing biochemical and physiological processes. They can also lead to a change of environment. This is why we emphasize changing beliefs. Changing *enough* beliefs may be sufficient to reach the cure threshold. I say *may,* because the possibility for cure must be proven each time with each individual.

Figure 6.

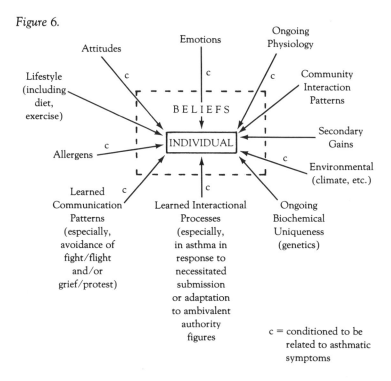

Beliefs can be altered in reverse by assisting the client to change lifestyle, communication patterns, interaction patterns, emotions, and attitudes. Physiology and biochemistry can, of course, be altered with drugs, but it seems to make much more sense, when possible, to avoid drugs and surgery — because of their side-effects and risks, and because, in clinical practice, tolerances seem to develop to the beneficial effects of drugs, but not as much to their side effects. Empirically, drugs are not always enough to reach the cure threshold. Because we want to reach the cure threshold, we must consider *more* than drugs in most cases.

Clinical experience has shown that, perhaps a 40% change in attitudes, combined with a 20% change in communication, and a 20% change in emotions may be sufficient among certain individuals for certain conditions to reach cure threshold, in spite of the genetics. This is what I find intriguing and imminently satisfying.

A transcript of a session with a client who has asthma, eczema, and allergies will further illustrate these concepts:

Deborah was a 20-year-old woman who came to me for help with eczema, allergies, and asthma. Her mother was a 47 year old graduate student with "severe back problems and nervous problem."[A] Her father was a 49-year-old business man with back problems whom she described as "emotionally out of touch." In general, initially, Deborah reported that her relationship with her mother was negative and that with her father positive.[B] She had an 18 year old brother. Deborah reported that her daily functioning was disturbed by her problems moderately at school, quite a bit at work, but not at all at home. She had completed one year of college. She felt the strengths or assets she could develop more included her "positive outlook, optimism, and idealism." She felt that her eczema was currently her worst problem and "keeps me from functioning practically." she described that her "skin dryness is a hindrance to certain activities and it itches and hurts." At its worst, the problem made her "itch and hurt. Also feel frustrated, sometimes sorry for myself." If she solved the problem, she reported that she should "feel great! (Be) freer to do what I want."

[A]   A family pattern of somatization is already present.

[B]   Reference to the diagram of Figure 4 will bring to mind the issue of ambivalent early caretaking. In Deborah's family, her mother had certainly presented such experience to Deborah.

At the beginning of our work she described the problem as present all the time and rated it as an 8 on a scale of 1–9 (9 is worst) at its worst and 5 on that same scale as an average.

Deborah had previously gone to a naturopathic, religious healer in Albany, California, who had prescribed that she use aloe vera on her rash and eat a stick of celery and one bell pepper every morning. Deborah had experienced a tremendous improvement in her symptoms while on this regimen, but had discontinued it, objecting to the taste of the celery and bell pepper. Her rash had returned with increased severity once those remedies were discontinued.[C]

At age 18, Deborah had last used LSD. She described that experience as "negativity, paranoia, evil spirit fear, and guilt.[D] She felt that I could help her eczema by "gearing me to a positive outlook."[E]

Deborah also experienced mild digestive problems including "lately having a lot of gas."[F] She reported a mild problem having orgasms and said it's "hard to rate because I have not had sex for a while, but was not climaxing except during masturbation.[G] She described minimal back pain,[H] moderate tiredness ("sleep a lot, tired most of the time") and mild lethargy ("sometimes just can't get going").[I]

[C]   An extremely important piece of data emerges. The naturopathic remedies *effectively treated* the symptoms, but Deborah discontinued them. Such behavior represents *resistance*, which I define as the situation in which the beneficial services of the symptom are not being provided in any other way and ridding the person of the symptom would only make matters worse overall. Forced resolution of a symptom leads to side effects or symptom substitution. If Deborah's symptom did not serve a current purpose, she would have continued the naturopathic remedies and not found her way to me.

Deborah restricted her diet to lactovegetarian.[J] She was overweight and over-ate when depressed, unhappy, and worried.[K] She snacked between meals on vegetables, bread, and "icky" stuff.[L]

Deborah's religion was "All One." She worked as "a student, day care worker, landscaper, gardener, and carpenter's helper."

Deborah lived alone. Her spiritual beliefs included "believing that all life is one. It keeps me optimistic. Also keeps me trying to become less selfish and more service oriented. Sometimes I pressure myself about this."[M] Deborah exercised several hours each week, mostly on her bicycle, believing that people's "outlook on life, environment, and physical activity" made them healthy or sick. Deborah's current emotional status was described as "in love, frustrated, and lonely." She turned to her best friend for support, and felt that her relationship with her parents while growing up was "mostly rotten." She was currently seeing a psychotherapist besides me. Deborah saw my function as helping her with her physical problem and her psychotherapist as helping her with her emotional difficulties. When asked about what she and her therapist did together, Deborah replied that her

[D]   Such behavior leads me to expect that Deborah has an active component of her personality which urges her toward self-destruction. I like to view the self as composed of parts — like a democratic community. The ego corresponds to the mayor who presides over the parts. If the self-destructive part of Deborah becomes very strong, it can command more votes and direct Deborah toward self-destructive acts.

[E]   Such a view begins to expose one of Deborah's major problems — her unwillingness to tolerate what she considers negative emotions — especially anger. "A positive outlook" means to Deborah being sweet and nice all the time. Her symptoms will probably improve when she can begin to learn to express anger and can recognize feelings and responses within her that do not correspond to her ideal of sweetness and niceness.

[F]   This symptom may be part of an overall difficulty with expression/elimination.

[G]   Deborah's difficulty with orgasm also points to a difficulty with expression and a tendency to block energy from extending to her periphery — to the sexual parts of her, to her breath, to therapist tried to convince her of what was wrong with her. "We talk and try to make me see things clearly."

Deborah's life stress rating was 440 within the past 2 years (300 is thought to be highly correlated with the development of physical symptoms). Within the past year her mother had developed severe back problems (44 pts), she had experienced "sex difficulties" (39 pts), she had changed to a different line of work several times (36 pts), her responsibilities had changed at work (29 pts), she experienced trouble with her father's new wife (29 pts), she had both begun and ended school (26 pts), she had changed living conditions (25 pts), she had revised personal habits (24 pts), she had experienced a change in work hours or conditions (20 pts), she had moved (20 pts), she had changed schools (20 pts) and eating habits (15 pts), and she had celebrated Christmas (12 pts). This gave her 339 life stress points within the past year. Between 12 and 24 months previously she had also been fired by her father from working at his business (47 pts), and had gained a new family member through her father's marriage to a 24 year old woman, whom she resented her father presenting as her step-mother, because of the closeness in their ages (39 pts).

her hands and feet where her eczema is most severe.

H   Deborah's back pain reminds me that back pain is the major symptom of both of her parents and points to the need to explore how she views herself as similar to each of her parents.

I   The remainder of her symptoms suggest depression, which means to me feeling the void of repressed emotion and unfulfilled meaning — in this case, probably anger, rage, jealousy.

J   Deborah was lactovegetarian because of her feeling that it wasn't nice to kill sweet creatures and because her vegetarianism affected her father, leading him to make irrational, critical outbursts about her "weirdness."

K   Deborah's food intake was a better guide to her level of emotion than her verbal expression of what she was feeling. For her, eating seemed to represent an attempt to fill her inner void, present since early childhood in the form of feeling that her parents were never emotionally available to her, that they were always at work. She reported feeling starved for love and described herself as deperately groping for any scraps and crumbs she could find — an exact analogy to her eating behavior.

She had changed her eating habits also in that period (15 pts) for a cumulative 2 year total of 440 pts. Within the 2 year to 5 years previous interval she described a change in financial state occurring when leaving home (38 pts) and an arrest for marijuana (11 pts). This gave her a 5 year total of 489 life change units.[N]

In discussing these life changes with Deborah I learned she felt as though she had much potential for gainful, meaningful work but was very afraid of failing in the world, so she would not get involved in any activity in which she could be judged on a success/failure basis. I learned that she could acknowledge a very self-critical part of herself (which we nick-named "Critic") who demanded she live up to her parents' expectations to excel in any field in which she could make much money. Critic believed she should, for the long term, take any job to please her father even if it wouldn't necessarily please her. Another part of her that we named "Common Sense" said she should do what *she* wants. We also discovered another part that Deborah named "Spite." Spite says "always do the opposite of what dad wants you to do. Run off to a commune in Northern California, take lots of drugs, and rot away. Be miserable, because it's fun in a

[L] Deborah has a strong belief in good and evil — good food and "icky" food. She's punitive towards herself when she breaks her rules which are also impossible to keep.

[M] Part of what worsens Deborah's asthma and eczema is this pressure upon herself. A consistent link that emerged during our relationship together was that between a self-deprecating attitude and the severity of her symptoms.

[N] Certainly, stressful life events associated with inadequate coping styles are correlated with the development of physical symptoms. Deborah had few effective coping styles besides acting out and repression. She would "set up scenes" to invoke her father's anger and get back at him, or she would try to deny that any of the changes in her life affected her, because "we're all one." Anger remained mostly repressed except when acted out, especially towards her father and his new wife.

spiteful way, but be miserable all the time." She recognized another part that she called "Discipline," who says "do what's good for you."

Using the Taylor Manifest Anxiety Questionnaire, I learned about Deborah's high levels of anxiety manifested by her tiring quickly, experiencing difficulty concentrating, having frequent diarrhea, blushing frequently, and losing sleep over worry with restless and disturbed sleep when it did come. She was easily upset and cried easily, sometimes obsessing so much that she didn't get to sleep. She felt useless and very nervous — at times, no good at all. Several incongruities were also noted: Deborah described herself as happy most of the time and very confident of herself. Only denial could lead her to those responses which so conflicted with her actual life.○

I used the Dyadic Adjustment Scale as an index to problem areas in relationship. I learned that the only area of disagreement in Deborah's relationship was about sex. Deborah's relationship sounded too perfect. I later learned that was true. Deborah was seeing a married man who lived next door with his wife and three children. He was experiencing incredible conflict about the relationship and had tried to make love once with Deborah,

○ Denial and repression, especially when responses proceed from such defenses, seem noticeably related to physical symptoms, especially asthma and allergies. I have learned to look for such behavioral incongruity as is reflected here.

but had been unable to sustain an erection, which he related to his guilt about an extramarital affair. Deborah viewed him as a nearly perfect man, and thought his wife was mean and vicious. She had simplistically ignored the significant issues of their arguments about childcare and accountability. Theodore, the husband, wouldn't argue. He just left the house and complained to Deborah. Deborah rated herself as happy in a relationship in which she never knew from day-to-day whether Theodore would leave his wife to be with her or would abandon her. Perhaps childhood had taught Deborah tolerance for ambivalence among significant love relationships or she had learned to deny even from herself her anxieties and anger about her lover's ambivalence.[P]

On another questionnaire I used,[17] I learned that Deborah was feeling critical of others, easily annoyed or irritated, low in energy, very blocked in getting things done, very lonely, and inferior to others. She was experiencing difficulty making decisions and felt lonely even when she was with other people.

Her responses on another section of the BICL gave all the "right" responses from the "All One, love everyone, no negativity" perspective, but clearly rang very false in terms

[P] Repressed anger and anxiety with an ideal of non-expression of anything but "positive" feelings presents itself as significant in the asthma process.

of Deborah's actual feelings about herself. More "white-washing" was occurring. Among the few seemingly accurate responses were Deborah's agreement that she was denying and depriving herself (contradictory with several other responses), restraining herself and holding herself back, and feeling that she was her own worst critic. These responses gave me some leverage to begin to get past her "everything should be sweet and nice" exterior.Q

On the Locus of Control Test, Deborah rated 16 of the 29 items as showing an internal locus of control and 13 as external. Of interest was that no real areas of her life emerged as seeming out of control. Her responses were split in each major area, again indicating to me much ambivalence.

The last test that Deborah did at home and brought back to our second session was a "Tarot Card Thematic Apperception Test." I had advised Deborah to pick cards at random to tell a story about. The cards used are from the Egyptian deck and give a further glimpse into her process.

Q   Of interest was that Deborah's affect was clearly not "sweet and nice." When she thought she was being sweet and nice, she seemed "bitchy" and caddy. There was so much anger and bitterness stored inside Deborah, that she couldn't be sweet and nice even though she tried. She wondered why friends grew tired of her even though she was so sweet and nice.

Card No. 25   "The man is standing by the castle door. He steps out into the unfamiliar countryside and his journey begins. He has taken a staff with him to help his balance and to help him climb whenever necessary. The field that he is walking in is green with low grass. It is dewy and there are beautiful little wildflowers everywhere. In the distance the grey purple mountain range looms large, shrouded in a mysterious veil of mist. The sky is bright blue and the sun is shining. It is a wonderful day to be out for a walk."[R]

Card No. 24 "This time the traveler is on horseback. She has her sun hat on to protect her nose from the rays, and is ready for action. She knows not where she is headed, only that she is on her way on a most important journey. It is dawn and the air is already warm. The eastern horizon is a lovely shade of pink above the grey purple misty mountain range. There is a large rock to her left, but seemingly no obstacles in front of her. She brings her staff for protection. It is a magical staff that she may give to someone at the end of her journey for it has special healing powers."[S]

Card No. 4 "The young woman kneels by the river and pours the water she collected on the edge of a stone. She is fascinated by its flow. Simple things hold her interest, for she is a child of nature. She spends most of her time outside, even in the rain, for she is

[R]The first card selected symbolizes to me the journey Deborah has embarked upon in coming to me. The foreground is the meadow of her sweetness and niceness. The mountains may represent the mysterious and powerful parts of her she will discover.

[S] The journey continues, but now a sense of the need for protection emerges. Does she feel she must protect herself from what she might discover about herself or from me? She may especially be afraid of feelings of a sexual nature toward me, a probable aspect of the already developing accustomed to temperature change and rarely wears clothes. Today is a beautiful day. The sun is shining and there is a slight breeze. A few clouds pass by overhead like pieces of cotton candy. A butterfly watches her and flutters around her. The woman is keenly aware of what is going on around her and can feel the air movements from the butterfly moving so close to her."[T]

Card No. 60 "Four swords hang motionless in the air. Suddenly four men appear out of thin air, each with his right hand around a sword handle. They are in motion, as if they never stopped moving from the world from whence they came. The two in front materialize in a running position, one hand up and the left hand extended back. The two in the rear appear in mid-air in a leap. They touch ground and turn to their opponents and the dance continues. The men move harmoniously, as if they were a cosmic choreographer directing their every move. They thrust in and out at each other, move from side to side, all in unison and no one is injured, nor will anyone be injured, for it is clear that this is not the purpose of this dance."[U]

Card No. 62 "Again two people appear out of nowhere, each with the right hand around

transference toward me. Would I be able to heal her with my magic wand? Could she sustain the fantasies of me as lover, especially since she could be rejected (the more so as she began to experience that sexual acting out was prohibited in the therapy).

[T] Now she retreats into positivity again.

[U] Re-emerging from her retreat into positivity, is a sense of conflict, but transformed into the nature of a dance in which the handle of a sword. The two could be a man and a woman, or two of any sex. It is late afternoon on a hot day in a barren, but beautiful, countryside. The ground is flat and there are no obstacles for some distance around the two. In the background there is a range of hills. The two stand with swords crossed for a moment, and then slowly begin to walk around each other in a counter-clockwise circle. Their movements are slow and flowing like waves on the sea. They are somehow intertwined as they continue to move in graceful circular patterns. It seems almost as if their swords were curved, so fluid are their intertwining motions. When the dance is over, they carefully lay down each sword, and come into each other's arms, where they hold each other tenderly. Their hands slip down and meet, and the two stand facing each other and looking at each other until they slowly vanish back into the dimension from whence they appeared."[V]

Card No. 1 "It is dawn, and the clouds are thick. The sun moves from place to place, looking for an opening through which to shine. It finds a small opening and shines its full morning energy through the one little hole, forcing it open with its rays. Dawn has arrived, a

no one is hurt. I use this image during the therapy to teach her the value of expressing anger — as a dance in which, performed well, no one is ultimately hurt. Hurt comes from the concealed weaponry of passive-aggression.

[V]   Now the sexual nature of the conflict emerges and perhaps her fear of being hurt through sex. She has been hurt in the past frequently through sex.

time of beginnings, perhaps the time to start a voyage. The birds open their eyes, fidget around for a bit, and start to twitter and whistle. Even the leaves seem to have just woken up and start to rustle. The little animals begin to move — nothing on earth is unaffected. The new day has begun."W

Card No. 7 "The time is long ago when most of the beings on earth lived still in the ocean. The eternal mother is nurturing them and seeing to it that no matter how brightly the sun did shine, she was there to give them water, life-giving moisture. The birds love to fly over this ocean for the vapors rise up and refresh their warm bodies. A good deal of these animals have not matured to the point of leaving this watery mother, and so they remain, slithering about in the silky mud near the shoreline. Some have ventured out of the secure wetness to see what the rest of the world has to offer."X

Card No. 11 "This woman was walking along in the jungle when this lion approached her. She did not recoil in fear, but stood her ground and regarded the handsome beast. The lion needed to satisfy his curiosity so he stuck around too. It was unusual for him to see a lone human in his forest, and stranger still that she did not run at the

W   Even the possible hurt and conflict of sexual encounter can be healed by the sun's rays, by new beginnings.

X   Perhaps this card refers to Deborah's desire for that ever-nurturing mother, or even a return to the womb environment. If this is so, rebirthing could be a helpful technique.

sight of him. She put out her hand, while smilingly looking him in the face. He cautiously approached and when it became apparent that she meant him no harm, he licked her hand. This made them both happy, for a new bond of friendship had been forged. She put her hand on his mane and caressed him and cooed while he rumbled appreciatively. He followed her back to her home at the edge of the forest where he keeps her company much of the time, even though he is rather uncomfortable indoors. They still take walks together outside and this gives them both great pleasure, especially the lion, for then she is in his domain, but he is sweet and puts his head in her lap at her house too, for he knows that his is important to her. They both benefit from this mutual love and respectful relationship — it adds to both of their strength."[Y]

Card No. 75 "This young girl is just discovering the awesome beauty of fire. She holds it at close range to better examine its qualities. She feels its warmth against her skin. She is the gentle sort, and moves lightly, smoothly and gracefully. I see that the flame in her cup came from the very tip of a divine finger. The finger is larger than her entire body. This does not strike her as bizarre for she

[Y] Unfortunately not all lions can be tamed. This face may be part of the source of Deborah's conflict — a coping style of trying to be friends when sometimes aggression is needed.

recognizes it. It is the hand of her father. He knows that she is old enough now to experience some of the mysteries of the flame without hurting herself too severely. Maybe she will learn some of its secrets, but right now she is content to watch it and let its hypnotizing dance play before her eyes."[Z]

Card No. 39   "This young man is standing out on the street. The cup is a gift from a passing stranger. He did not ask for it, but it seems appropriate that the cup now belongs to him. The apron serves to hide it from people who should not see it. This boy seems sweet and gentle and is grateful for the gift. He will drink from the cup and continue on his journey."[AA]

Card No. 3   "The night is calm. The clouds form powerful patterns in the sky and are illuminated by the full moon. One dog sleeps while the other takes in the atmosphere of this powerful night. The lake mirrors the scene above. It is summer and the serenity of the night is somehow mixed with turmoil. Could this be the calm before the storm?"[BB]

Card No. 5   "The child has grown and is on a journey. She encounters a lion who accompanies her part of the way, then a gentle bull. An eagle guides her some of the time, and

[Z]   This passageway could serve as the beginnings of a visualization to explore father issues as related to Deborah's symptoms.

[AA]   Again the belief that people are rewarded mysteriously for being sweet and nice. Deborah's life does not work this way. Rather, she seems to be trampled for these attributes — bitten by lions, burned by fire, and mugged by passing strangers.

[BB]   Perhaps Deborah is becoming more aware of her inner turmoil. Perhaps her sweetness is the calm before the storm.

on one occasion she met an **angel. The snake is watching her every move, and it seems as** though these beings are protecting her from harm, while allowing her to experience life in whatever way she wishes. She reaches the two pyramids and wonders how they got there and why. She ponders for a moment before moving on."[CC]

[CC]   There is awareness of danger, symbolized by a snake.

Card No. 28   "Country. Sticks falling from heaven to fertilize the earth. The square in the bottom half might be a house onto which the sticks may fall if the people in the house are unlucky. But the sky is blue and I imagine the sun is shining. The box on the bottom could also be sticks that have already fallen to the ground that someone has laid in a specific pattern. The sticks on top look like they would stick up like spears once they reach the ground. They also look like they could fall behind the horizontal line, and land in another domain altogether."[DD]

[DD]   Aggressive, destructive feelings again try to emerge.

Card No. 17   "Nothingness, Death. The being in the drawing has no thoughts, no soul. Alone it wanders. It makes no difference which direction it walks. It sleeps not. Yet it is aware of the bird and the wind. It takes no pleasure in the greenness of the countryside. When it finds people — as if to greet them it causes the life to leave their body. It is not cruel, for that is the nature of it, over which it has no power to change."EE

Card No. 54 "Sorrow. The knives fall upwards as if they had a specific destiny. They are in motion and it seems as if when they leave the card they would veer to the right and stick some poor individual. They might also fall to the earth and lie there for someone to cut their feet on."FF

Card No. 53 "Advantage. If I turn the card it seems that the knives would stick somebody else. This spares me physical pain but does not please me as it is at someone's expense."GG

Card No. 13 "Marriage. The couple in the card are two young people about to be married. they love each other a great deal. The man who married them is a good friend. Once married, they go off hand in hand elated that fate has set it up so that they can be together. But people cause them trouble and they must be strong to withstand the pressures from without."

Card No. 36 "Man with Position. This man is in a position to help people but is caught up in the position itself and is unable to move. He is disillusioned, but fancies himself a great philosopher. He holds an empty cup and stares into space, while the sky is blue behind him

EE   This card led me to explore Deborah's beliefs about death which are very similar to the image presented here. The sequence through the cards is that aggression leads to nothingness and death.

FF   Sorrow arises from the nothingness; sorrow that could hurt someone.

GG   This seems related to Deborah's acting out tendencies.

and he could be watching the coulds drift by. He is insecure and holds his belt, feeling the velvety texture of it because he lacks anything more substantial to give him emotional support."

Card No. 33   "Enterprises. More sticks. Someone might want to take the sticks and build a house I suppose. Turning the card to troubles nearing an end, the V shape of the nails seems to fall open, leaving the nails free for use. Maybe they could be used to build a house."

Card No. 50   "Man of the Law. This man is interested in watching the clouds go by. He looks out over the land and sees what is being done. He is a gentle sort with a good sense of fairness, however when he uses his sword to mete out justice he is doing wrong. He wrestles with this in his mind and sometimes he can find more constructive ways that educate people instead of hurting them."[HH]

Card No. 23   "A good woman. There she sits with a smile on her face listening to the birds twitter and the summer breeze. Her life is hard and she has a staff to lean on when she stands. People look up to her and give her fine clothing, but her burden is heavy. But she keeps a cheerful disposition and speaks ill of no one, helping whenever she can."[II]

[HH]   Again her conflict between aggressively sticking up for herself and being nice.

Card No. 25 "Anxiety, money. This man looks fairly paralyzed, while all this money is going to fall on his head, and could easily crush him. He stands in an impractical way with a sickle for work, and his robes falling off him so he must hold them. This makes work difficult."[JJ]

Card No. 73 "Lovers. This warrior type does not please me. One would think that with a title like lovers the drawing would be more inspirational. He looks like he's into his sexuality and not into the finer aspects of lovemaking."

Dark-haired man card. This man is playing a game. He looks out into the blueness of what appears to be the sky, but is actually just a curtain. He sits, yet his posture indicates that he is ready to spring at any moment. Actually, I don't think he's looking into the blueness at all, but straight ahead, closely observing what is going on in front of him. The round box on his lap looks mysterious. Who knows what evil lurks within it?"

Card No. 35 "Birth. The person has fallen, and is groping at the twig to help herself up again. She will make it to her feet and start again, richer for the experience, stronger. She is wary but is learning to trust. She

[II] Good women have a hard life. People look up to them, but they suffer. Most important they remain positive.

[JJ] Perhaps this refers to her fear of success.

does have a strong cynical side that must be dealt with and left behind. Perhaps when she learns that falling is not the end, merely a learning experience, she can become more positive."KK

KK   There may be some advice here for Deborah to give birth to herself.

From our discussion of these cards, we came to an understanding of some of the important parts of Deborah. These are diagrammed in Figure 7. Each boxed area represents a part of Deborah with the specific beliefs of each part listed below that part. A consideration of these beliefs reveals several sources of conflict relating to the following issues:

1. Trying versus not-trying
2. Succeeding versus failing
3. Being perfect versus being fallible
4. Pleasing others versus pleasing herself
5. Nurturing herself versus sacrifice for others.

Deborah localized the "cause" of her rash to the part she named "Conscience or Niceness." Conscience feels guilty about the battle between "Spite" and "Critic" (Critic seems a direct negative father introject), so Conscience solves the problem of guilt by forcing Deborah to be nice to others *and* sacrifice herself *at the same time*. This way she accomplishes some of the goals of both "Spite" and "Critic." The tiny parts that Deborah needs help developing are "Common Sense" and "Self-worth." Self-worth sits passively and lets all the battles rage when it could intervene (like the Man with Position of Card No. 36).

This information led to our third session which begins as follows:

Lewis: What seems right for you today?LL

Deborah: Well, I'd think I'd like to try a little bit more of your visualization, and I'd also like to try some kinesiology.

Lewis: Okay, good.

Deborah: But unless you have anything specific that you had been thinking about.

LL   Even though I've planned what I want to do during this session, I want to give Deborah a choice to minimize her resistance. My plan is the same as what she wants.

Might have to have high drama between Critic and Spite to make play (life) exciting.

Arbitrates war

DEBORAH is the Gestalt of all her parts. (Whole is greater than the sum of parts.)

CRITIC (Dad)
1. Deborah has great potential.
2. Deborah usually blows it.
3. Don't do anything that's not a sure thing.
4. It's not okay to make a mistake.
5. The purpose of life is to make money and please dad and be flashy (everyone else thinks you're doing great).
6. It doesn't matter if you like your work.
7. Try, try again.

COMMON SENSE
1. Deborah should only please herself.
2. Deborah should do what she wants to do.

SPITE (Spike) (Dark side of Dad)
1. Never please anyone especially not dad or Deborah.
2. Be a failure (drugs, commune, rot)
3. It's fun to be miserable.
4. A purpose of life is not to please anyone but me (Spite).

conflict → asthma

DISCIPLINE
1. It's not all that bad to try.
2. Long term goals are better than short term goals.
3. It will please Deborah to do what's good for her.

COP-OUT
1. It takes a lot of effort for Deborah to do what's good for her.
2. Effort is to be feared.
3. Why try, since things don't work anyway.

SELF WORTH
1. I'm usually silent and can't think of anything to say.
2. I'm very small and weak.

FUN
1. Discipline is not fun.
2. Be spontaneous.

NON-THINKING EAR
1. Exciting plays rarely ever have happy endings. (Life is usually miserable.)
2. Whatever anyone else says is true.
3. Other people define my worth.
4. Best to hang around people who think I'm great.

CONSCIENCE OR NICENESS
1. It's nice to please other people (you should please others).
2. You should be miserable if you're not being nice.
3. I can be really ruthless toward Deborah in an effort to be nice to everyone else.
4. I "cause" Deborah's rash.
5. Modern polluting devices are bad and I shouldn't use them.
6. It's nicer to starve to death so someone else can live than to live yourself.

Figure 7.

Parts of Deborah and their various beliefs, injunctions, and self-descriptions.

Lewis: No, not today. That sounds fine to me.

Deborah: That way we can both tell if things have *"loosened themselves up."*[MM]

Lewis: Ok.

Deborah: I've been sleeping a little better lately.[NN] I didn't wake up overnight. I wake up at least once. It's really weird, it's not something I usually do. It's just lately I've been waking up in the middle of the night. But this week it's only been like once a night and not really hard to get back asleep.

Lewis: That's interesting. What usually happens when you wake up?

Deborah: Well, before it was mostly I'd wake up because of noise upstairs. And that made me sleep lighter because I'd be expecting noise upstairs — wondering when he'd come home and put on his stereo or his TV. It wakes me up. You touch the same spot and after a while that spot becomes real sensitive.[OO] It doesn't matter how low — I can hear him talk on the telephone upstairs — I'm tuned into it now.

So before I was waking up to that but lately I've waken up feeling itchy like where I have my rash — burning itchy uncomfortable. Aloe vera cools it off and I can go to sleep. But

[MM] Her words and goals now reflect the hypnotic suggestion of last time, aimed at opening up her breathing passageways.

[NN] Last time many suggestions were made about Deborah sleeping better.

[OO] This sentence refers to the kinesiology process (see the chapter on applied kinesiology).

it's really strange just to wake up
to it at all.

Lewis: Ok. Why don't we try
some kinesiology?

Deborah: Should I press
now?OO

Lewis: Keep your arm straight,
your elbow up. Oh, why don't I
strengthen it up.OO If your rash
were a landscape; close your
eyes for a minute and imagine
your rash as a landscape.PP
Something that you could
actually visit as if it is a country.
Tell me what it would look like.

Deborah: Ok. The southwest
without rain. The cracks run real
deep with nothing growing. Just
dry parched earth. That's what it
would look like. Just acres of it.
There may be a few peaks here
and there but mostly it's pretty
dry earth that just flakes off. It's
real dusty too, all right along.

Lewis: Ok. That's really good.
Now, if you were to look
around what do you think could
live there?QQ

Deborah: A deer. But a deer
wouldn't have much chance of
surviving. You'd expect there to
be snakes and things that don't
need water — reptiles with
scales. And I'm seeing a lush
forest with *birds and butterflies* —
like I'm seeing two landscapes at
once — one desirable and one
that's not so desirable.RR

PP   This passage begins a
visualization technique I
playfully refer to as "creative
feature." The first step is for her
to imagine her disease as a
landscape.

QQ   The second step of creature
feature is to ask Deborah to
imagine what would live in this
land?

RR   The assumption is whatever

Lewis: If you could imagine a creature that could embody your problem or an animal that could live there, what would it look like? If you could actually look down at it yourself?[SS]

Deborah: Well, it would be shaped like a turtle — real ugly.[TT]

Lewis: Oh, ugh, describe it.

Deborah: Well, it would be a dry looking beast, like a tortoise or a horny toad lizard.

Lewis: How big is it?

Deborah: I haven't put a human in the landscape, so it's hard.

Lewis: Imagine it caught and put in a museum. How big it it?

Deborah: Like a tank, really big.[UU]

Lewis: Does it bite?

Deborah: Oh, yeah, draws blood.[VV]

Lewis: Pretty vicious, huh?

Deborah: Well, living in that dry landscape it can't really help itself. If it were *raised* in a more nurturing environment it probably wouldn't be so nasty but it's used to getting a lot of knocks so it's learned to be real vicious just out of self-defense. Sort of bite first and argue later just to make sure it doesn't get squashed.[WW]

[SS] part of Deborah that's contributing to the problem will be represented as characteristics of the landscape and the creatures that live there.

[SS] The third step is to create a creature to symbolize the problem that could live there and then to help the client describe it.

[TT] Deborah may believe that a part of her is very ugly on the inside. She may be reticient to explore the problem for fear of encountering this ugly part of her.

[UU] This description gives a sense of how big the problem is.

[VV] Deborah believes that the part of her contributing to her problem is vicious.

[WW] But that part has a reason

Lewis: Yeah, well, what would you need to catch one, to make it stand still?

Deborah: It doesn't move fast — to make it stand still?

Lewis: And not bite . . . .

Deborah: I'm trying to think of something that wouldn't be too awful for the beast itself. The obvious is to use heavy string around its mouth so it couldn't bite even if it wanted to. But, if you were nice to it and gave it a lot of water it wouldn't be inclined to bite. It would be a more humane beast.[XX]

Lewis: Lets say you wanted to catch one just to study it. You wouldn't be mean or nice to it. Just safe so it wouldn't bit you.

Deborah: First thing I'd drug it but then you can't observe it so that doesn't work.[YY] By the way, the rubbing that you're doing doesn't hurt at all so if you want to rub it harder to be more beneficial.

Lewis: Ok, so let's figure out a good way to catch it so it doesn't bite.

Deborah: So it doesn't bite, that's hard. Give it something to eat and keep it well fed. Be nice to it and make it more secure so it wouldn't have to bite.[ZZ]

Lewis: What kind of help would you need to go down,

for being vicious — because of its lousy childhood. A family system consideration is that dad spends lots of money on Deborah's rash, and Deborah can get some degree of revenge on dad by having a rash that he has to pay for. In Deborah's family money seemed equated with love and attention. Deborah has said before "I hate my father because I've had such a lousy childhood." Both parents worked long, hard hours, 7 days a week, during her childhood, so Deborah may believe that she's a victim to her lousy childhood, and that the past is more important and powerful than the present. Therapy will be directed at continuing to use and reframe the word "raise" and make the present move into the past and thereby move her forward.

[XX] Deborah seems to be saying "If people would be nice to me, I would be nice to them."

[YY] Deborah may be saying "You can use force on me or restraint, but that won't solve the problem. Drugs won't solve the problem, either." By the drugs not working, Deborah can rebel against her father, whose solution is always a new drug.

[ZZ] Deborah may be saying, "Nurture me and I'll get better." The therapy derived from this is with a camera crew, and interview it? What do you need to make it stand still?

Deborah: Well, it wouldn't run away. It would probably stand its ground.[AB]

Lewis: Which?

Deborah: Don't press so hard.[OO]

Lewis: Ok.

Deborah: You need to feed it first.

Lewis: Yeah.

Deborah: And you need a mike and some people. It's like you'd have to put your hand in its mouth for it to bite you. It's not like it would come running after you to bite you. It could only bite if it were convenient to it. So I'd feed it. I would put the mike on a stand and have it hang. If you set a few feet in front of him and asked a few questions, he wouldn't bite.[AC]

Lewis: Would that be safe enough to do it?

Deborah: I'd do it but it wouldn't be interesing to me.[AD] I'm not really interested in knowing how this beast operates. I'd rather leave him alone and just let him go somewhere else so he doesn't bother me.[AE]

Lewis: Let's say CBS is real interested in this beast and you

to increase her self-esteem and security, helping her to be secure to move about in the world.

[AB] Deborah may be saying "Part of me is open to where you are and to being helped."

[AC] The fourth step of "creature feature" is to catch the creature in preparation for interviewing it.

[AD] Another part of Deborah is not that interested in understanding her problem or to our working together. "My problem won't run away, but I'm not sure I want to face it."

[AE] The fifth step of creature feature is to help the client work for CBS and it's the only assignment they'll give you.

Deborah: Ok, I'll certainly interview the beast.

Lewis: Ok. Let's say you're driving down there.

Deborah: Well, we'd be in a van, with all the equipment — mike, mike stand, and camera.

Lewis: Okay, once you set up in front of this beast, you again —

Deborah: It looks at everybody real curiously. Actually, it's pretty docile. It seems more nasty when solitary.AF Bunch of people around it, it gets more curiosity. A "good afternoon beast. What's going on here?"

Lewis: Let's ask how it decided to come here.

Deborah: It's always been here. It swam up to the shore, through the woods and came to the deserty-dried mud spot and it's a good — it seems like the landscape looked a lot like me. Maybe it lost its way.AG

Lewis: Did it get any help getting here?

Deborah: It just walked.

Lewis: What was it doing in the sea?

Deborah: Swimming. It was probably born there. It had

imagine all the equipment and help needed to safely catch and interview the creature.

AF   "I'm more nasty when I feel lonely." In actuality, Deborah's rash seems to get worse, the more lonely she feels. When she's in the limelight, getting attention, her rash gets better.

AG   The rash may be related in some way to Deborah's current conflict of not knowing what direction to take with her life.

friends there. It used to play. It
was young. It would eat fish in
the sea. It used to hold on to
the muddy, sandy bottom and
he just wanted a change in
scenery, he was just . . . curiosity
that led him out of the water to
begin with. It didn't occur to
him to turn around. He just
walked out of the water, through
the woods to the parched
ground and settled down.[AH] I
was in a place like that once —
Nevada, hard, parched, dry
ground. And I stepped out there
and this horse fly that hadn't
eaten for a long time started
drawing blood from my leg and I
shooed him away, and he was
real insistent. I had to go back to
the car and roll up the window
to keep him away. He was real
blood thirsty 'cause there was
nothing to eat. That's probably
why the turtle became friendly
once you've satisfied his hunger.

[AH]   This seems to refer to
Deborah's life experiences to
date. It's true that asthma and
eczema served to get her
attention as a child, when other
behavior didn't.

Lewis: What did you give him
to satisfy his hunger?

Deborah: Well, meat and
what you give to a lion.[AI] It
doesn't seem like it's his natural
ocean food (but he was starving)
so he'd eat anything. He was so
ferocious he'd eat anything.

[AI]   This is significant because
Deborah is a vegetarian. Perhaps
she thinks meat leads to aggression
and is avoiding meat because
she's afraid of her aggressive side.
Teaching her how to be angry will
probably help resolve the rash.

Lewis: Ask him what he'd
prefer.

Deborah: Water and brine
shrimp.

Lewis: Is that what you brought?

Deborah: No. I thought he was a lot more vicious than he really was.

Lewis: So he's really kind of docile, it's just that he's so deprived that he strikes out at anything. It has been a long time. Does he have any sense of how long?

Deborah: No, he doesn't . . . and it doesn't rain much here . . . too much sun.

Lewis: Does he like living there?

Deborah: No, he finds it an awful place to hang out.

Lewis: Does he do anything good for like the food chain while he's there?

Deborah: There's no food there.

Lewis: How does he survive?

Deborah: He's tough. He's been there for 100 years and he just takes a bite of whatever walks by and lives on it for a long time.

Lewis: What kind of things walk by?

Deborah: Human beings. He takes a bite of someone's leg.

Lewis: I see. Does he eat the whole person?

Deborah: No, he's real slow; the person runs away. He blends in or walks around and someone thinks he won't bite.

Lewis: Well, if you were going to change him into something else, what would he like to be?[AJ]

Deborah: First of all, he needs water. Maybe a sea gull. He'd have to find a cave where it was cool, not parched and hang out there.

Lewis: How long, and how would he get out?

Deborah: He'd crawl out of his hole.

Lewis: And is there anything else there that CBS would want to know?

Deborah: They'd want to film how he was doing it — crawling out of his hole.

Lewis: It sounds like you don't think everybody lives happily ever after.

Deborah: No, I don't. I think he'd be pretty happy flying out there over the ocean. He might be lonesome for some of his turtle friends still in the ocean.

Lewis: Does he meet any birds that he'd like to meet?

Deborah: Probably, since he was lonely as a turtle.

Lewis: Yeah, of course, you wouldn't know because you

[AJ]   The next step of "creature feature," after questioning is to transform the creature into what it would like to be.

haven't talked to many birds, being a turtle.

Deborah: Maybe once he's back in the ocean he could turn back into a turtle, or just die maybe.

Lewis: Would he like that?

Deborah: It'd be an easy way out for him.[AK]

[AK] Now the part of Deborah that is self-destructive and slightly suicidal is speaking.

Lewis: What happens next to him if he dies?

Deborah: Mmm, I don't know . . . He'd become part of the air.

Lewis: Oh, that would be fine?

Deborah: Real nice. He'd not worry about eating.

Lewis: That's a problem.

Deborah: He doesn't have to eat.[AL]

[AL] Eating and overeating is a conflict area of Deborah's life.

Lewis: What would be other pleasing things about being dead?

Deborah: He'd like to be part of the land, and not have to worry about it all the time. He'd just sort of — But at the same time he'd suffer since he's just part of the air.

Lewis: How long would he stay dead?

Deborah: Forever.

Lewis: He wouldn't want to come back?

Deborah: No.

Lewis: Sounds sad.

Deborah: I suppose.

Lewis: Depends on your point of view.

Deborah: Yeah, I guess coming back would mean a lot of problems.

Lewis: I guess it would be best for him to just be done with it, in a sense.

Deborah: But he'd still be living, though. He'd be part of the air, checking things out without having to participate.

Lewis: Yeah?

Deborah: And he'd feel the wind, which is nice.

Lewis: So comfort for him comes not from participating, but his observing is pretty okay? But it's pretty hard to participate without eating. Now, anything that comes by he eats, but it could be a potential friend. A lot of trouble keeping them separate.

Deborah: It's hard to make friends if you have to eat them.

Lewis: That could be real difficult.

Deborah: He'd definitely be happier in the sea than the desert.

Lewis: Let me test your muscle,[OO] don't let me push it down, hold your arm, go, now this way, ready, okay . . . I wonder if you could relate to the problems of that creature?[AM]

Deborah: In the sense that it's unfortunate that he has to hang out in the desert. He'd rather be a human than a turtle. And turtles don't understand what's going on around him. He must be puzzled, it's unfortunate.

Lewis: Yes, what about your love relationships, what's been going on in those?[AN]

Deborah: Oh, dear, that's not something I want to talk about. I'm so much in love and all and there's so many reasons why it can't work out.

Lewis: What happened with it most recently?

Deborah: Nothing. That's the problem. It's impossible to develop given the circumstances but I feel the same way, so I feel irritated in his presence because I know it can't happen, so it's frustrating, it upsets me.[AO]

Lewis: What are the circumstances?

Deborah: He's married.

Lewis: But you still have a relationship of kinds?

Deborah: Yeah, every once in a while.

[AM] Now I try to help Deborah relate the creature to her present illness.

[AN] The creature is so lonely and needy of love, I feel compelled to ask about her love relationships.

[AO] Consider how initially her relationship was presented as "rosy."

Lewis: Does his wife know?

Deborah: Yeah, she thinks it's awful. I feel like a fool because I'd like to be friends with the family and now I've blown it.

Lewis: How?

Deborah: By being too honest and letting it go too far.

Lewis: What happened?

Deborah: We liked each other and when we started talking, I didn't know he was married until his wife and kids walked by. I just put him in the married category and that was that.

He started wanting to be friends with me, so we'd see each other every once in a while, what's appropriate. Do things that we could practically do. Nothing too classy or wonderful. And it was intense. We were in love with each other and we started thinking these crazy dreams. He wasn't exactly happy with his marriage. He had a big emotional void that needed to be filled; otherwise he wouldn't have been so receptive towards me.[AP] He wanted to sleep with me and I didn't want to sleep with him because I knew that I didn't like. . . . It was ridiculous. . . . We'd go back and forth between. . . . I didn't want him to leave his family. A burden of responsibility. I decided finally

[AP] Deborah seems to view herself as unattractive unless the other person is desperate.

to sleep with him. I hadn't had
experience with sex and he kept
assuring me it would be just
great . . . but . . . it didn't work
out. He couldn't get an erection,
because he was too nervous and
upset about all the implications
that all this would have had. It's
just as well. We tried one more
time and it didn't work and then
we'd talk more about
responsibilities, etc. By this time
his wife knew, so that's about it.
But I can't go into his house
because of his kids, because his
wife doesn't want to see me. In a
way it's good because we've got
things moving around in his
marriage.AQ

There was this other guy,
that I moved in with and lived
with and we started sleeping
together, but nothing like this —
nervous. He's been, I don't need
him any more. He's been saying
why don't you blah, blah, blah.
He sounds so optimistic and I'd
like it to happen, but he keeps
hoping I'll change in ways I
don't think are beneficial to me.
He wants me to be rational and
not emotional. Sometimes the
times I'd feel most strongly that
it wouldn't work out was when
I'd say things to him like "I
think this is true" and he'd say
"What do you have to back that
up?" and I'd say it's just a heart-
feeling, and he'd say that's
bullshit. You had to have an
expert book on it. Information
from hearsay, etc., was just no

AQ   Rather than be angry with
Theodore, Deborah decides that
she's done him a service,
sacrificing her happiness for his
(see Conscience, Figure 7).

good, not right. So that's why it didn't work out.

Lewis: How old were you when you first got the eczema?

Deborah: First time — very little. This last time? About 18, on my right index finger, I just flipped out on LSD and thought I cut my finger. Then a cut appeared and a few days later a rash spread all over my right hand and then left. Sometimes on my calves and thighs. Now it's bad on the palms and arms, shoulders, and breasts.

Lewis: When did you leave home?

Deborah: When I was 18; I got this before I left home.

Lewis: You were at home when you did the acid?

Deborah: Yeah, I lived next door to my mom, in Oakland. Then I moved 3 blocks away for about 6 months with Bernie and his old man. We didn't get along well and I didn't like him, so I moved out to that guy I talked about and lived with Tom and Sam. Now I live with 2 or 3 women but we're not getting along, so I moved out.

Lewis: So now you're 21 — who was your first love?

Deborah: I was 5 years old — does that count? But all the others on the block didn't like him as I liked him a whole

bunch. Because he stuttered. So
I just broke it off. My father
was my first love.

Lewis: Do you have memories
of him?

Deborah: We'd curl up
together and watch TV. That
was our activity together. It
wasn't very active to do. I can't
remember doing anything else
together. He used to work a lot.
My mom, too.

Lewis: What kind of work?

Deborah: They both worked
and ran a business.

Lewis: And now?

Deborah: He works 5 days a
week as an executive in SF. He
used to work 7 days a week and
crazy hours and his only day off
was Christmas Day once a year.

Lewis: Pretty crazy.

Deborah: Maybe . . . they
must have had other days off or
they just decided when to take
off. They were really into
working and not very much into
living.

Lewis: How long did they do
that?

Deborah: Till the divorce 16
years later. I don't know if they
lived that way the whole time.
We took off on a trip when I
was 4 to Boston.

The fourth session continued somewhat more by discussing Deborah's feelings about her father.

By the fifth session, we continued discussing the dynamics of Deborah's relationship with her father. I learned that the usual sequence of interaction between Deborah and her father was:

Father: I'm worried that you're just drifting, that you'll go to hell in a bucket, that you'll end up a loser.

Deborah: Quit worrying.

Father: I can't because your actions warrant that I should worry.

Deborah: Worrying can't change anything.

Father: I love you so I have to worry.

This would generate into fighting with Deborah continuing to convince her father he shouldn't worry, and he convincing her he should. I suggested Deborah truncate this fighting in this way:

Father: I'm worried that you're just drifting, that you'll go to hell in a bucket, that you'll end up a loser.

Deborah: Thank you for worrying. I'm really touched that you care so much as to worry.

Continued persistence at this level would turn the problem back to her father by acknowledging that *he* worries and that she recognized this was how he showed his love.

We discussed how her rebellion was the only tolerable response to what she considered an intolerable situation, but that, "Spite," whom she renamed "Spike," was continuing the rebellion beyond its usefulness. Trying to convince her father not to worry was not accepting him as he was, a worrier. This was the crime of which she accused him of perpetrating on her.

By the sixth session, we discovered that a kind of war was in progress between two halves of herself that she labelled "East and West." These parts took the opposite perspective on several important issues:

"East"	"West"
1. It's more important to succeed in others' eyes than it is to be happy and have fun.	1. It's more important to be happy and have fun than it is to succeed in others' eyes.

2. Happiness comes from succeeding in others' eyes.	2. Happiness is a by-product of being true to one's self.
3. Status is very important.	3. Status is not important.

The energy for this fight seemed to flow from three beliefs Deborah held:

1. The truth exists, can be found, and is absolute and applicable to everyone.
2. There's always a right and a wrong answer to every problem that applies to all people.
3. Everyone should agree and think the same about what's true and right.

We discovered that her father was merely the background for the battle between these major parts of her. Continued hypnotic suggestion was given to strengthen Deborah's self-esteem and her ability to have fun. Expressiveness training was also being done to help her express and recognize angry feelings.

The sixth session consisted of kinesiology, working with the pectoralis major clavicular and the neck muscles. After this session, Deborah agreed that a family session was indicated. I called her father, who refused. He had decided I was a quack, because I did what Deborah called "holistic medicine." He did tell me that Deborah and his son (although less severely) were both, seemingly to him, plotting and scheming to make his new wife miserable and to make him miserable. He felt he had suffered enough at the hands of his children and deserved some peace and quiet. He felt our meeting together would only make things worse. I explained to him a basic model of how family stress could contribute to eczema and explained my view that ignoring the problem was not a way to solve it, unless he and Deborah were not planning any further contact. Deborah's father disagreed. He felt that the whole problem was that Deborah needed to stay on steroids and that she was silly to worry about the side effects. He felt that all Deborah needed was a good dermatologist and a good allergist, not a quack suggesting family therapy. I thanked him for his frankness, and we parted amicably.

The seventh session was spent entirely with helping Deborah to identify and express genuinely and believably through role playing and feedback her anger at her father, Theodore, and her mother. I confronted her belief that anger was always bad by explaining to her how animals used anger to avoid violence in protecting their territory.

The eight treatment sessions were successful. At the eighth session at which Deborah terminated, she reported on a separate form (having forgotten her previous responses) that eczema was 5 on the 1-9 scale at its worst and 3 at an average now. Other parameters improved on the BICL as well. Deborah's eczema was objectively much better. The rash had disappeared from her chest, face, and legs and seemed to be only present on her hands. Deborah believed no change had occurred until I showed her the questionnaires she had filled out in the beginning. She stopped treatment, because she had decided to take no more money from her father and could not afford further sessions (her motivation was running out, too). I encouraged her to return again if she ever needed to. She had completely forgotten about her asthma and her allergies because they had not bothered her for the past month at all.

REFERENCES AND NOTES

[1] Harrison's Textbook of Internal Medicine. St. Louis: W.B. Saunders and Co., 1971.

[2] Dekker, E. and Groen, J.J. Reproducible psychogenic attacks of asthma. *J. Psychosom. Res.* 1:58, 1956.

[3] Talma, S. Über asthma nervosum. *Med. J. Geneva.* 94:337, 1898.

[4] Dekker, E. and Groen, J.J. Reproducible psychogenic attacks of asthma. *J. Psychosom. Res.* 1:58, 1956.

[5] Dekker, E. and Groen, J.J. Asthmatic wheezing: Compression of the trachae and major bronchi as a cause. *Lancet* 1:1064, 1957.

[6] Dekker, E. & Ledeboer, R.C. Compression of the trachae and major bronchi during asthmatic attacks. *Am. J. Roentgenol.* 85:217.

[7] Dekker, E., Defares, J.G. and Heemstra, H. Asthmatic wheezing and the checkvalve mechanism. *J. Appl. Physiol.* 13:35, 1958.

[8] French, T.M. and Alexander, F. Psychogenic factors in bronchial asthma: Part I, in *Psychosomatic Medicine Monograph IV.* Washington, D.C.: National Research Council; Saul, L.J. and Lyons, J.W. The psychodynamics of respiration, in H.A. Abramson, Ed. *Somatic and Psychiatric Treatment of Asthma,* Baltimore: The Williams and Wilkins Co., pp. 93-103, 1951.

[9] Jessner, L. Lamont, J., Long, R., Rollins, N., Whipple, B., and Prentice, N. Emotional impact of nearness and separation for the asthmatic child and his mother. *Psychoanalytic Study of the Child* 10:353.

[10] Meaning that the membranes are congested with slow moving blood and therefore swollen.

[11] Because of the increase in slow moving blood, fluid or edema escapes into the tissues.

[12] All this swelling worsens the congestion by putting pressure on the veins to keep them from carying away the excess blood as fast as they should.

[13] Thomas, A., Chess, S., Birch, H.G., Hertzig, M.E., and Korn, S. *Behavioral Individuality in Early Childhood.* New York: New York University Press, 1963.

[14] Kim, S.P., Ferrara, A., and Chess, S. Temperament of asthmatic children: A preliminary study. *J. of Pediatrics* 97(3):483-486, 1980.

[15] Thomas, A., Chess, S., Birch, H.G. Temperament of asthmatic children: A preliminary study. *J. of Pediatrics* 97(3):483-486, 1980.

[16] Graham, P., Rietter, M., and George, S. Temperamental characteristics as predictors of behavior disorders in children. *Am. J. Orthopsychiatry* 43:328, 1973.

[17] This questionnaire is a combination called the SCL and the BICL. I first encountered the BICL/SCL in a study conducted by Dr. Alan Gurman at the University of Wisconsin Department of Psychiatry. As a psychiatry resident, I was an occasional subject in a study of resident therapeutic effectiveness. I have used these forms since then to follow patient change.

Chapter Five

Holistic Approach to A Gynecological Disorder

The concepts of belief as applied to gynecological disorders are also best understood from a case example:

Harriet was a 32 year old woman who worked as a receptionist in a telephone answering service. She came to see me because of problems with her menstrual cycle. She was having severe cramping and a heavy menstrual flow continuing 15 days in a 40-day cycle. On pelvic exam, a large mass had been felt by her gynecologist, confirmed by an ultrasound scan and thought to be part of the uterus. The diagnosis was that a uterine fibroid of about 8 × 12 × 15 cm was present. Harriet had decided to try visualization to help her problem. I began the first session directly using visualization with a dialogue technique of having the various problem organs speak. We began by learning that her uterus and her bladder felt tension caused by her stomach.

Important elements of that first session included Harriet's stomach saying, "I've got too much to do," and "You don't relax unless you're sleeping." Her shoulders and back reported feeling very tense, and her uterus reported that it's problems were being caused by irritation from the stomach. I gave her an assignment for the next week to do an activity diary with the idea that this would help her see how busy she really was.

In the second session one week later, we again did visualization with a dialogue emerging between her stomach and uterus, with the uterus wanting the stomach to find time to take better care of it. Several levels of meaning existed in this discourse, with the most obvious being the need for Harriet to find time to take care of herself. During both of these sessions, I gave her many indirect hypnotic suggestions for her tumor to shrink and for things to readjust inside the body to their proper position.

The following week three major issues arose during our third session. One was her feelings about sexuality; the second, was unresolved feelings about a tubal ligation; the third, was her feelings about her relationship with her mother. In her visualization she discovered that the feeling part of her wanted children but the rational part of her didn't. The part that did want children was represented kinesthetically, and the part of her that didn't was represented in an auditory mode.[1] In a sense, the resolution of her internal dialogue was a "no" answer, but there was a kinesthetic backlash (tumor). Before Harriet became a receptionist, she had worked as an elementary schoolteacher, which she quit when she had her tubal ligation to avoid being around children. Her mother had had five children, not so much because she wanted to, but because she was Catholic and didn't believe in birth control. Her mother often expressed feeling trapped into having children during Harriet's childhood.

Harriet had also been involved in many sexual triangles, and had recently chosen monogamy. In these relationships, she was often the weak member of the triangle — part of unstable complexes of being the "other woman" or the woman being left. She had had intercourse with many different sexual partners and was feeling some guilt about that. She had lived in opposition to her mother's Catholic beliefs about sexuality, and as the need for this opposition was fading following her mother's death, she was finding that many of these beliefs were returning as a part of her when before they had been projected outwards as her mother's. She had just entered a relationship that she hoped would be long-term, but there were problems.

In the third visualization I used what could be called the descending tunnel approach. The idea is to help the client enter a relaxed, trance state and then "descend" into the basement of their mind to recover details they know, but don't know that they know. The person can descend on an escalator in a department store of interest to them, or in a building or by walking down into a mountain. At the bottom, they enter a tunnel through which they can go back in time. I wanted Harriet to go back in time to a time just before the beginning of her problem. An effective technique for changing beliefs is to change through imagery techniques a past event that the patient believes contributed to the problem, so that there is a memory that can compete with the actual event.[3] It's surprisingly easy for people in a trance state to go back in their experience and find out when the first seed of the problem germinated. The first seed of the problem might be 20 years before the problem will show itself. The time tunnel technique is very helpful to allow the technique of changing the past to be effective. There are as many variations on this technique as there are therapists who use it, but the basic element consists of the person going deeper and deeper into the tunnel until he or she emerges in the past. A time machine can be used conceptually the same way, and can be especially effective for the science fiction fan. One very helpful aspect of this technique is to have the client focus on very concrete details, using each representational system. It's useful, I've discovered, to have people focus on their feet first. This is perhaps because feet are universal among humans and the basic shape remains unchanged during life. We tend to ground ourselves with our feet and express our relationship to the earth with them. I began with her focusing on her feet, and then, slowly, the rest of her body. "You can, if you will, just get a sense of whether it's dark or light; are you inside a structure or outside; is it cold or warm," etc.? As soon as I'm ready for the client to make the time regression, I become very concrete, giving many details to consider and giving suggestions to experience more specific details than I (as outside the experience) could imagine. In this case, I asked Harriet to describe her perceptions of where she was. Once the client does this, he or she can be asked to follow time forward a bit to the next significant event that took place. Harriet experienced herself first at a scene in her parents' house before her two brothers were born. She was the youngest of three girls. She felt a warm sense of serenity and security and a kind of "moonlight feeling" about the house.[4] We began moving forward in time. As her brothers were being born, she experienced incredible anger toward them. She felt they upset her peace and serenity. As we continued to go farther in time, she realized she felt severe guilt about not seeing her mother in the six months before her mother died. She also felt very guilty about having moved away from home one year before her mother died (of breast cancer).

In the fourth session we began to discuss these issues, but as Harriet seemed resistant to insight at that time, I, as I often do under such circumstances, moved into a story-telling mode. I decided to use a modification of an E.B. White novel about a family of trumpeter swans at a northern Alberta lake. A young boy becomes friends with a swan that can't talk, but learns how to write. The swan comes back to Montana and goes to school and spells out letters on the blackboard. The telling of a children's story also works in the service of an age regression.[5]

The trance induction for Harriet was done by discussing the swans gliding down to their nest at the lake. I provided many family scenes: bears and cubs, deer and fawns, ducks laying eggs, because I wanted to activate the part of her brain that stored her beliefs and feelings about herself for having denied herself the possibility to create a family. I wanted to surface this issue just like the swans can dive down deep into the lake and bring a fish back to the surface and to shore. I also used images about everything inside her taking on the proper size and position as she became more and more relaxed so that everything could have a comfortable feeling, because every part of her body could be in the right position to relax. I then talked about flying and being supported by the wind. It's tremendous to see a swan with a six-foot wing-span gliding on the wind. I described that image and told her about the first time I saw an eagle ten feet above my car appearing larger than the car. The idea again is the gliding, the settling down of things into their proper position (the swan to its nest, the tumor to oblivion). Then she visited her uterus again in her mind's eye and imagined it in halves. The right side (the auditory half) had all the rational reasons for not having a baby. The left side (the kinesthetic part) had all the feelings why she wanted a baby. She dialogued back and forth from these two positions. The right side said, "It's too expensive, it takes away too much freedom from the mother." The left side talked about the warm feelings of love for a baby and how fulfilling it would be to create and nurture new life. Next, I helped her to change these *two* halves into one *visual* image. Then I suggested her arms would rise during this to give her a sense of which side was stronger and had more pull on her. Whenever a conflict involves a kinesthetic mode vs. an auditory mode, the solution is usually to create a visual mode that synthesizes both and allows them to communicate on the same terms. Thus, if Greece and Denmark are both in the common market, it's most effective to have a translator who speaks both Greek and Danish. Then both her arms began twitching. Later she told how her wrists had tingled, at the spots where I drew lines, telling her I was attaching helium balloons. Both twitched intensely. That "failure" of the arm raising suggestion was fine, because it still showed her neither side held sway over the other. Then I asked her to see herself (not just to hear herself, because her guilt was stored in an auditory mode) but to see herself *now* talking to her mother just before her mother died and hearing things that she said, but also seeing her mother saying what the pros and cons were of having kids. What stood out for her mother was the companionship children provide.

In an earlier visualization I had used the idea of her being able to visually travel down to her uterus and see a being sitting in an office off to the side with a large ledger that recorded all the events that had affected the uterus since before she was born. Then they could look back through the pages to find out when things had begun. Harriet imagined a little old man with a visor hat, (resembling Starmaker in *Oklahoma*). A curious aspect of that was that I had the same image before she spoke, but had shared no more than my instruction to see a being. I give such a general instruction so that even creatures from mythology would be acceptable. She would speak for him, saying things like "Well, I can see some smudges on the pages, but nothing shows up on this page."

For Harriet, I used a time sorting technique and we went through her entire life.[6] She began to realize that she could create an entirely new situation for her life. We especially focussed on her last three-day weekend and why that had not been satisfying. She was evaluating how to avoid overworking. She began to question all aspects of her life and began to talk about how to change things so that life was more enjoyable. She was very intrigued by what we were doing and was amazed that she had never thought to trust before that one could use a non-physical means of healing a physical problem. This was a whole new idea to her, and yet she could see her life changing. We also discussed expectations — how results in this kind of work are sometimes slower than with physical means of treatment but also can be long lasting. We discussed faith. It was significant that she had a Catholic background. Faith is something Catholics (as we all do) historically have struggled with in a unique way. James Joyce's *Portrait of the Artist as a Young Man* is a book I often prescribe to clients to understand Catholic faith and guilt. The client must have some faith (or at worst) be neutral, for any therapy to help.

In the fifth session, one week later, I used applied kinesiology. The energy meridian that was most affected was sex and circulation meridian. All four muscles related to that meridian were weak. While I massaged the points associated with making those particular muscles strong again (thereby balancing the meridian), Harriet associated to memories of herself in the sixth and seventh grade, especially as she began to menstruate. At that time she believed sex was wrong and was dirty, and of embarrassment about even having genitalia and therefore, being a sexual organism. There were obviously the transference issues that would emerge for a woman who has grown up with many sexual taboos, finding herself working with a man on those issues. I gave her many indirect hypnotic suggestions to help her feel safe and comfortable sharing those feelings with me.

In reference to those transference issues, when a woman works with a man, different issues may emerge earlier in therapy than when a woman works with a woman, but all the issues still need to surface. While the process of therapy may differ, the eventual outcome should be the same. Working with a man often elicits more issues regarding fathers, brothers, lovers, sex, sexuality, sexual attraction first. Unless the woman is gay or overtly bisexual, some of these issues may emerge later when she works with a woman, although they will emerge. This can be facilitated very therapeutically by the male therapist reassuring the woman in many ways that he is safe as is the situation. In the first visualization I told Harriet symbolically that I was safe, that she did not have to worry about me taking advantage of her. This obviously succeeded at least in part, because she seemed much more comfortable and at ease during the second session. During that first visualization, I symbolized myself as a dolphin who would make sure there were no sharks in the waters, because dolphins are very helpful to people (truism). I then told a few stories about dolphins helping sailors in distress.

Next Harriet associated to horse riding, one of her few childhood passions which she engaged in vigorously during the 7th and 8th grades.

As she continued to discuss her childhood, the overall sense was of a very constrained, restricted emotional environment. I also discovered about that time that her parents drank too much. She realized what she had really desired in her life was passion. She felt now ready for passion.

In the sixth session, it emerged that she had made many of the changes we had discussed the last week. Our problem that week was to understand how she could supply her physical needs (money, food, shelter) and still maintain those changes. She realized that meant changing her relationship, changing her job, changing her beliefs, and finding a new place to live.

In the type of therapy I am describing, the therapist helps to keep awareness building underneath the surface of waking consciousness using visualization, hypnosis, or similar techniques until the awareness is large enough to break into waking consciousness (ego consciousness). Clients may not talk much in the first four sessions. We may not talk on an ego (left brain) level at all, but engage only the right-brain. I didn't have to suggest interpretations on a left brain level. They emerged from Harriet on her own. When she had enough material that could rise up to her awareness, then she wanted help in sorting it out on a conscious level. That is important to be aware of. The therapist should not be too fast in making interpretations because jumping too fast to the talking level can fail. Resistance will then emerge; there won't be enough material to discuss. In making an interpretation, it's often much more useful to do it indirectly, perhaps by telling a story about someone else (similar to the client) who had the same problem and resolved it. I could say "That's very interesting that you should say this, because a client I saw yesterday had that same problem, and what she did to solve it was to . . ." In that say, I avoid the level of resistance that emerges to a direct interpretation. Visualization or psychodrama can be used in much the same way. An interpretation can also be made effectively using Erickson's interspersal technique[7] in which the words comprising the interpretation are emphasized within a longer sentence that conceals the interpretive sentence within itself. For example, if I wanted to help Harriet shrink her tumor I might say, "You know, the other day I was thinking about the *mass* of the earth and how if you were thinking about how *small* you really are in relationship to the earth and how in a sense the world *just shrinks down* when you communicate around *that mass* of the earth, I became very fascinated. And I don't know why I'm really talking about that, it doesn't seem to make much sense in terms of what we were talking about. But maybe *you'll find a way* that it might *make sense.*" The italicized words are emphasized with the voice.[8]

During the seventh and eighth sessions, I continued to support Harriet in making the changes she felt she needed to make to get back on course in following her life's path. More indirect suggestion was utilized with brief visualization experiences to help Harriet clarify issues in her mind. Two weeks elapsed between the seventh and eighth sessions during which Harriet re-visited her gynecologist. His examinations to his surprise revealed a normal uterus. The absence of tumor was confirmed by a repeat ultrasound scan. In the eighth session, Harriet and I discussed ways she could remain healthy — especially by recognizing her feelings and acting upon them when possible. She had quit her job and had re-entered school and had broken off her relationship. Her partner had not been interested in couples' counselling and Harriet had decided that she couldn't tolerate his low level of commitment. She had begun substitute teaching to earn extra money and was feeling excited about the changes occurring in her life.

Other gynecological problems can be approached in a similar manner, realizing that the individual circumstances and beliefs of each patient are unique. In a later chapter, I will begin to discuss some of the technical aspects of visualization in terms of how it is done. This will lead to a discussion of indirect hypnosis in a later chapter.

The following represents a transcript of my first session with
Harriet. Another chapter will discuss more of the technical elements of
visualization.

You can begin by lying down in the beach, lie in the
sand, how comfortable it is to feel the sand, the sun, just
breathing, air into your lungs, helps you to slow your
breathing down, just to begin to turn your focus, awareness, onto that beach; beginning to become more relaxed,
begin to put aside some of the pressures of the day,
beginning to put aside thinking about things, except for
thinking about the beach, maybe, or thinking about
where you feel the tension in your body; but there's no
need to think about things from the day. There's no need
to carry any extra thoughts right now. Just the sun, the
bright yellow sun in the sky, the warm sun warmth on
skin, breathing deeply down into the lungs you could
also breathe into the space behind your eyes, your
sinuses, kind of breathe deeply into your sinuses, breathe
the tension out, or at least begin to wash the tension
away, and let yourself begin to breathe out some of the
tension that has been collected in the sinuses. PAUSE.
Breathing into that space behind your forehead, behind
your eyes behind your nose. Just like the water washes
up gently onto the beach, kind of rolls onto the shore.
By the time it gets there, and how the beach is so
smooth, warm to walk on, to swim in, comfortable water
letting you float on the surface without a lot of effort, if
you want to, or you can dive down deeper into the
water, say, if you have the proper equipment, you might
dive down to find buried treasure boats that were sunk,
maybe even things that weren't worth very much then
would be antiques now, and will carry a high price in the
city. Or just the pleasure of diving, down into the clear
blue water, diving down to find the bottom of the sea, to
see the coral, the bright colored fish . . . this is a real safe
ocean . . . we've sent some dolphins out to keep out anything that isn't safe. Nothing dangerous about this ocean.
The dolphins are real helpful, they'll make sure everything that is there is only something that really should
be there. Just like you do for yourself sometimes. Relaxing
your forehead, relaxing your eyes; smoothing out the

lines on your eyes, just like the water smooths out the
sand; very smooth, beginning to relax your nose, your
cheeks, the lines and folds that don't belong there, can
just begin to disappear, just move over on your face;
that's right, I can see it happening, some line that just
isn't there anymore, your chin and your neck and your
shoulders, like someone that you care about is rubbing
your shoulders, massaging them, helping them to let go
of tension, to begin to let go of tension, from the
daytime, from the past, just like your neck, just like a
waterfall, a tropical waterfall in Hawaii and the water
starts out, and it comes down in steps slowly, and the
steps begin to get larger, and the water goes deeper
down, toward wherever it's going, the steps are broader,
deeper, like coming down the back of a mountainside, of
the hillside; coming down the middle of the mountain,
the middle of the hill, down to the lower parts of the
hill; and splashing down into a pool of water at the base
of the hill. Sometimes you can find a waterfall that is just
the right height to stand under; and it's so refreshing, to
do that, you can just feel the water coming down on
your scalp, just washing away some of the tension that
you've held onto, onto your scalp, coming down, down
onto your neck, just relaxing your shoulders onto your
back and the middle of your back, low back, and then
you might turn around and feel that fresh, calming water,
coming down the front of you, all the way down,
washing down your thighs, your legs, down into the pool
of water that is so clear. And not very far from where the
water comes in, it is very quiet and relaxed in the pool of
water. If there are trees nearby they send their rootlegs
into the ground, down, to tap that water, to use it to
grow with, to use the nutrients in the water to nourish
themselves. All the way down to the tiniest feet rootlegs
of the tree, that can fill up with that water, here. You
might imagine how a tree might feel warm inside, kind of
a full, expanded feeling, as it took in the water that it
needed from the earth, just like you might feel if you
were lying in the sun, on the beach; you might feel the
warmth of the sun's rays touching you, the sand, you
might smell the nice smells of the beach . . . PAUSE and
you might begin to turn your focus down, into yourself,

too, down, to your uterus, if you like, or any other part
of your body that you feel needs your attention. It's
possible to begin to become more relaxed as you do that
even as I continue to talk or you talk. You can do just
what you need to do here or anywhere. That's possible.
If you would like to begin to see your uterus, just move
one of the fingers of your right hand. All right, good. Let
yourself begin to feel or touch or see your uterus in
whatever form it presents itself to you. It might not
make sense at first, but that's all right. There's no need
to try to figure everything out, in the beginning. And
when you've really got a really good picture or feel of
your uterus, you can move one of your fingers of your
right hand again. Good. Now, you can choose to,
Harriet, tell me about how it looks, or you can just
experience it without talking. If you'd like to tell me
about . . . you could again move one of your fingers of
your right hand, okay, good. Tell me how it looks to
you, then.

The relaxation induction has been rendered prose-style almost like
poetry, to give the reader a feeling from the visual appearance of the
flow of consciousness effect which the induction produces in the
listener. I begin by giving Harriet suggestions that she can begin to
relax — she doesn't have to be relaxed immediately. The reference to
buried treasure refers to her self-discovery of the treasures of Harriet's
inner world. These are the treasures she can use to cure herself and are
the ones I hope to help her find. The reference to dolphins is my way of
telling Harriet that I will do my best to make her journey safe, that she
can trust me as the sailor trusts a dolphin. I lead Harriet through a
relaxation process from head to foot by linking various parts of her
body to images of nature — the back of a mountain, a tropical waterfall,
a pool of water at the base of a hill. I have already learned from Harriet
that her favorite place in all the world is Hawaii, which directs me to use
Hawaiian images. I also know that she enjoys skin diving.

Harriet: . . . It just sort of
looks like a pear shaped. . . .
Pink-looking, cold . . .
(inaudible).

Lewis: Any other details that
seem important?

Harriet: Oh, I guess that's all. I'm not sure if there are any ovaries or not.

Lewis: Ok. Would you like to imagine now a little office, now, near there, with a little person who's kept a history, a long, detailed history of everything that's changed in your uterus?[A] Does that fit into your image?

A   I give Harriet the choice of taking a different course than what I have suggested, thereby allowing her to feel as though she's choosing the visualization, which she is.

Harriet: Mmmm

Lewis: Ok. Imagine yourself, if you like, going into that little office, sitting down before that being who's kept the history, and asking that being, if you want to, to turn the book back in time, to a time just before that problem began to develop, that lump. Let me know when he's got the right page, or she, or it.[B]

B   Turning the pages of a book backwards represents a kind of time regression procedure.

Harriet: He can't find it.

Lewis: What's making it hard?

Harriet: Well it's just kind of hard to tell when it really began, because it just could have began years ago, but not a few months ago; but it seems like the very beginning was years ago, but it's so hard to pinpoint.

Lewis: If you ask them to turn the book back to a time that they were sure it wasn't there, could they do that?[C]

C   The exact time of onset is more difficult to locate than a time preceding the onset when the problem was definitely absent.

Harriet: Oh yes, yes.

Lewis: Ok. Ask them to turn the book back to a time, the latest time they can, where they're sure that it wasn't there. Ok., just ask them to tell you some things about that time, keeping in mind that their perceptions may be real different from how you might have perceived it on the outside.[D] What do they say?

D   I'm attempting to give instructions so that Harriet's evaluative side can relinquish analysis of what's being said by other parts of her.

Harriet: They say they are sure it wasn't there, they're sure it wasn't there in the early 20's, but I still don't know whether it was there last year. I'm confused.[E]

E   It's important that I distract Harriet from being too concrete and analytically accurate.

Lewis: Well, it's really good to know a time when it wasn't there. That's real important, even if they don't know when it started. It's really good to know when it wasn't there.[F] Could you ask them if they know any things that are different about you in your early 20's and now? Could they tell you some of the differences that they've noticed in you?[G]

F   If once it wasn't there, it's possible to imagine some time in the future when the tumor will also be gone.

Harriet: Um. It seems like. . . . The things that they know that I don't know?

G   Our level of detail in age and origin of the tumor is sufficient to begin the more important work of ferreting out which life changes Harriet has made since her early 20's that are related to the growth of her tumor.

Lewis: Just their perceptions whether you know them or not or even would agree with them, because they might take a different look at you than even you would.[H]

H   Further instructions are given to avoid judging whatever comes up, thereby allowing repressed material easy access to surface consciousness.

Harriet: Well, the only thing that comes to mind is that I

seem to have more problems
and who am I kidding, even that
seems like a lot. Well, nothing
that seems more specific than
that. But my periods were
different then, around then. Just
that they were not heavy, just
sort of easy, and I didn't have
any cramps or anything.[1]

Lewis: Is there anything else
there of significance recorded?

Harriet: I don't think so.

Lewis: Now, let's imagine for
a minute, if you like, that your
uterus could speak as well.
Could you ask it how it feels
now, just how it feels to be a
uterus now?

Harriet: Like it's going
through some changes. It doesn't
like it too much. It feels like it's
too tense, touchy . . .
sometimes. Right now it's fine,
but I'm relaxed, but other times
it gets too angry, 'cause it feels
tense.

Lewis: What are some of the
things that happen outside of it,
you know, outside of anything
that it has control over, that
contribute to it feeling tense?

Harriet: It sort of seems like
sometimes the whole area
around it, my stomach area,
whole area around it gets very
tense, solid, sort of makes it all
tense.

Lewis: Uh-huh. And when it
becomes tense and angry, how

[1]   Too concrete . . . I'll try a
different approach.

can it let go of those feelings; what can it do? What does it do now?

Harriet: Well, it sort of doesn't know what to do so it just gets so angry and after a while it makes it feel sick; where it feels sick it makes the person relax; because they're sick, they have to lay around and relax.

Lewis: Would you be interested now in travelling to the stomach? To see what the stomach would say about what are the things that make the stomach tense?

Harriet: Ok.

Lewis: Ok. Then let yourself see yourself, feel yourself in the neighborhood of the stomach, becoming aware of it, and imagine that just for a minute it can also speak. And what are the things that make it tense?[J]

[J] The technique utilized here represents an organ dialogue approach, similar to the gestalt dialogues between parts of the self as developed by Fritz Perls.

Harriet: Too much to do. Too little time and too much to do.

Lewis: How long has it felt that way?

Harriet: Off and on since August or so. Didn't get too bad until September.

(long pause)

Lewis: And what does it do when it becomes really tense?

Harriet: Feels nervous and sends jittery messages to other parts of the body.

Lewis: Are there any other parts of the body that are feeling tense besides the uterus from those messages?

Harriet: Yes. Sometimes it feels like, my bladder feels like that way too, partly because it gets filled up easily, but also because it gets nervous, I think. It just feels nervous, I think. It just feels nervous in that whole area.

(long pause)

Lewis: I can at least imagine that someone is saying inside there that there needs to be less to do and more time to do it in and more time just to relax. Does that fit for you, too?

Harriet: Yeah.

Lewis: Once you've really allowed that to permeate your awareness, look around and see if there is any other information you need to take from inside you before you come back into the room where we began.

Harriet: I'm not sure what's in the back, but something there needs my attention.

Lewis: So they need the attention just as much as the rest of you. . . . Ok., well, you've

heard that, those parts of you;
now imagine yourself back on
the beach in Hawaii, that restful
place in the warm sun, and let
me know when you're
completely there. Ok. Give
yourself a minute to really
enjoy that place and then, at
your own speed, then let
yourself come back, into the
room that we began in.
Sometimes people feel refreshed
and invigorated, sometimes they
feel a renewed sense of energy
and sometimes they feel
something different, when you
come back, which you can do by
just opening your eyes when
you're ready to.

REFERENCES AND NOTES

[1] This refers to the areas of the secondary cortex of the brain in which the feelings were represented. Harriet would feel her desire to have children and then talk herself from doing so. The resolution was to help her see both positions visually. For more information on representational sensory modalities, see Reference 2.

[2] Cameron-Bandler, Leslie. *And They All Lived Happily Everafter.* Cupertino, California: Meta Publications, 1979.

[3] In addition, returning to a time before the problem reinforces the suggestion that there will be a time when the problem is gone.

[4] "Moonlight feeling" is a good example of synesthesia.

[5] *Stuart Little* is also a useful book for helping people change beliefs. One passage from *Stuart Little* that can be very useful in giving people the suggestion to change beliefs is a discussion of realism. Stuart Little (a mouse) is the teacher and it's time to make up rules. Several present want a rule that you can't take things from others. Others argue that it's not possible to make such a rule work. Stuart then orders one child to go over and take something from another and run with it. He does and the others all run and catch him and make him give it back. (Of course, he was just following instructions.) Stuart Little then presents to the group proof that such a rule can work, since it was just tested and did. The rule is adopted that "we have to be nice to people and not take things from them." What Stuart Little did was to challenge a belief some held and were resistant to relinquishing, in a way that allowed them to change their belief by providing an experience consonant with their new belief. Visualization serves the same function. It provides an experience consistent with the new belief.

[6] Distortion of language is used to help "contaminate" the client's beliefs. For example, if one is walking up a hill with a friend, one could ask the question, "Should we keep walking down this hill or should we turn around and go back up?" The same style distortion can be used to advantage. The reason is one of changing orientations. Many people do orient themselves differently. For example, it's difficult for people to relate to others with different orientations. Consider the comments of one of my students as I discussed disorientation. "That's, that's you talking about up and down and down and up. It's really, it's a very personal kind of orientation, because it drives me crazy when people talk about going up to Los Angeles or down to Tahoe or something like that, when my orientation is you have to go down. South. To Los Angeles. And up in the mountains to Tahoe. And it's like those things just really bug me if it's out of orientation. Downtown and uptown. Some people say they're going downtown and some people say they're going uptown. It's things like that that drive me wild." The point of her comment is that down and up are relative concepts. Problems occur when people make the assumption that relative concepts are absolute. In doing this with time, we have the person stuck in a problem, turn around their concept of time and go backwards in time as if they were going forward. This is done by having them describe the events they see as leading to the problem, in backwards order. Or put them all on cards and throw the cards into the air and let them fall down. Then the client picks up the cards and tells their story seriously as though it happened in that order. We think this works because people get locked in certain time sequences that are just as "illogical" as the exercise. Having them create a new time sequence, even an absurd one, helps them to see that they've locked themselves into a linear time-dependent process that doesn't have to be how they think. For example, if a person believes they have to own a house to be happy and they can't own a house until they are 34 and have been working 8 years, then they can't be happy until 34. But, since the conclusion of owning a house being equated with happiness is potentially erroneous, the card exercise might serve as a hypnotic message that our client can be happy first, then buy a house. The fact that this altered sequence does make conceptual sense makes it believable. A common problem with patients such as Harriet is that they may have developed a certain dependence on one system of doing things or upon a certain pattern of behavior. First came learning and then came situations

in which that behavioral response was successful; then came situations in which that response only made the problem worse. The old coping style doesn't fit.

[7] See the chapter on indirect hypnosis.

[8] Another example of the concepts illustrated in the work with Harriet involved a very intellectual woman who proudly announced that she had never been hypnotized. I worked together with Gayle Peterson to help her since she seemed too resistant for just one therapist to be effective. She had severe insomnia. I read an article on Paleobiology with very emotional emphasis into one ear and hypnotic instructions were given by Gayle to the other ear. We did the hypnotic induction together, but I did mine in an auditory mode and Gayle did hers in a visual mode. When we were done, the woman was very confused, but had entered a trance. Several weeks later, I saw her and her husband together and he said that session had really helped with her problem. She said, "What problem? No, it didn't help me at all; it didn't help me at all!" And he said, "Well ever since that session you've been sleeping fine." And she said, "Sleeping? I haven't had any problem sleeping." She had even forgotten she had had a problem! In this kind of therapy, it's important to get used to the fact that when we've done our job the best, the client may give us the least conscious appreciation. The better one works the more the client should feel they did all the work and the therapist did nothing except sit there and tell stories and engage their interest. Questionnaires and symptom diaries are useful in this respect to document how much the client is changing, because the client *won't* remember how severe their symptoms once were. If they forget they had a problem, they may say "I didn't change at all. In fact, I don't even remember why I came in." So before- and after-questionnaires will make clear to the therapist what actually changed without relying on the client's capricious memory of the past. I like to evaluate progress once every 8 weeks in such a manner.

Chapter Six

Philosophical Considerations

The approach to medicine that I am proposing can well be called existential, meaning that it promotes multi-leveled well-being in a personal accountability context. Therapy involves movement toward well-being. Personal accountability means that the emphasis is on the question "what can I do to help myself?" The client needs to be active in promoting his or her own well-being, as getting well usually requires a change in the quality of life experiences of the individual. Medical management can influence the quality of life. Life experiences change as a result of interactions with health practitioners.

The concepts of existential medicine mean a change in the role of the traditional American provider of health care. The provider's function is not to take care of the patient; to make decisions for the patient; to pick from a wide range of possible treatments which the provider (physician, nurse, etc.) considers most appropriate, but rather to form a cooperative relationship ("therapeutic alliance") with the person in which the provider of care endeavors to explain the particular diagnosis, its possible range of errors, the alternative methods of treating such a condition, and the research which has been done to evaluate such treatment alternatives. Then the provider needs to step back and allow the individual to choose the particular treatment most appropriate to his or her way of experiencing life.

The health care professional needs to know what his or her own values are, and how acceptable it is for the client to hold different values.

Carl Rogers[1] has listed some characteristics which distinguish his client-centered approach from other points of view. Some of his points can be paraphrased to characterize the client-centered approach of existential medicine:

1. The provider holds a continued belief in the client's responsibility (given the knowledge of diagnosis, prognosis, and treatment alternatives explained at the client's own level of understanding) and in the client's inherent capacity to choose the treatment alternatives most consonant with his or her own experience of reality. Every therapeutic procedure has particular side-effects, particular psychosocial consequences, which alter in unique ways the client's experience of the quality of life. The client or consumer of medical care is the only one with the potential to know fully the correct alternative for himself or herself. The health care provider need not necessarily agree with every choice that the client makes or participate with the client toward effecting that choice.

In most physician-patient encounters, the physician has already decided on a treatment paradigm for a given diagnosis, regardless of the personal attributes or desires of the patient. This paradigm is usually based upon the physician's past experience, or upon the fears and decisions relevant to his or her own life, but not to the individual coming for consultation. It is perhaps equally important to dispel the notion in the minds of consumers of health care that there is one "right" method of treatment for any disease, and that the particular physician consulted should immediately know that method. The relationship is two-fold. If the client expects to be taken care of in a mindless way with the physician making all the decisions, then the physician will come to believe all clients expect such treatment and will consistently render it.

The client also needs to respect the needs of the health care provider. *Mutual respect* between client and professional is part of the goal. If the client does not respect the health care worker nor feel that the professional has any help to offer, whatever help *is* offered may not be very effective.

Our goal should be to help the person experience reality in the framework he or she has chosen, and to assist him or her with health care within personal belief systems.

2. The professional needs to maintain a continued focus on the phenomenal world of the client and attempt to see the individual's world from the inside. This is a kind of intuitive empathy. The more intuitive the health care provider can be to the individual client's needs and the client's particular mode of being-in-the-world, the better alliance the two can form.

Our goals as health care providers should be to develop accurate descriptions of the people who come to us, in order to develop a plan most consistent with their own uniqueness. Preconceived notions must be discarded in the exciting process of discovering a new person.

3. The same general principles of provider-client interaction apply to all situations, regardless of the diagnosis or condition. In the case of unconscious patients, these principles should apply to former desires made known by the patient, or to the doctor's interaction with the family.

These general principles apply to the attempt that the health-care provider makes to understand persons as who they are, in their own contexts, as sentient beings.

4. The health care provider needs to maintain a view of the practice of medicine as one specialized example of all constructive interpersonal relationships. Just as physical or pharmacological methods of medical treatment benefit individuals, there is also a direct benefit from a warm and caring provider-client interaction. A negative client-provider relationship can detract from the efficacy of any therapies being applied. In psychotherapy these factors have been described as the "non-specific interpersonal factors" so important for the success of the therapy. Considerable work on the placebo effect has shown this to be true for general medicine, as well.

Mind and Body

So called non-specific factors may actually be key elements in explaining healing. To separate general medicine and psychology is to maintain the mind/body dualism and to claim that events in the body are unrelated to the psyche. A complex interaction clearly exists between the psyche and soma, as we have seen in the preceding chapter. In a more metaphysical nature, Nobel prize winner in neurophysiology Sir Eccles has gone the further step to lecture that the soul may control the body by manipulating chemicals in the brain; altering electrical transmissions across synapses, thereby altering the body.[2] The learned helplessness theory of depression gives us another model which relates a disorder (depression) to both mind and body.

The learned helplessness theory asserts that the depressed person has learned that he or she can do nothing to control his or her environment or situation. The catecholamine hypothesis claims that depression is associated with a deficiency of the neurohormone norepinephrine at specific neuronal receptor sites in the brain limbic system.[3,4] The catecholamine hypothesis is based in part upon the evidence that imipramine, a drug which increases the amount of norepinephrine available in the brain (probably by blocking its reuptake by the neurons) improves depression more than placebos.[5,6] Drugs which inhibit the actions of the enzyme monoamine oxidase (which breaks down norepinephrine), thereby increasing the levels of norepinephrine in the brain, also improve depression.[6,7] Reserpine, a drug which depletes norepinephrine levels in the brain, produces depression in man.[6,7]

The pharmacology of learned helplessness within the animal brain resembles the proposed pharmacology of depression of the catecholamine hypothesis. When an animal is shocked with no chance of escape, it is taught "learned helplessness." Then the animal is put into a situation in which it can escape shock by an action (either by jumping over a barrier within 10 seconds after a green light appears, or by pushing a lever within 10 seconds after the sound of a tone). Once trained to the state of learned helplessness, these animals do not learn quickly to avoid the now escapable shock. Rather, they display many of the attributes of depressed humans, including a lowered tendency to initiate new responses, lack of aggression, loss of sexual desire, and a tendency of the symptoms to improve with the passage of time. Rather than escape the shock, these animals huddle in the corner and passively accept the shock, even though it can now be avoided.

One solution to the mindbody problem is Wolfgang Köhler's principle of isomorphism: that for every physical event for which there is a psychological correlate, there must be a physiological correlate in the organism. Kohler states: "Any actual consciousness is in every case not only blindly coupled to its corresponding psychophysical process, but is akin to it in essential structural properties." Thus, if a physical event occurs in the outer world (such as a fight with a lover), we have thoughts and feelings (psychological correlates), certain patterns of excitation in the brain (psychophysical correlates), certain body processes, such as increased pulse rate, release of epinephrine, increased stomach secretion of acid (physiological correlates), and an anamnestic response, triggering the release of similar memories, which then add fuel to the psychophysiological processes already underway.

Constitution

Some concepts from clinical philosophy can help us to develop a better philosophical base for existential medicine. Constitution refers to the ways in which we organize our perceptions into a system of beliefs. Once a system of beliefs is constructed, it serves as a series of windows through which to see the world and to respond to the people around us. Constitution begins with the first sensory experience. To the infant, perhaps at first a mass of stimuli presents itself. The infant must learn to make sense of that stimuli so that it can respond to the world and get its needs met. This process can be frightening, or it can be exciting, as many adults will verify who have been helped through hypnosis to remember their experience of being an infant. In a very short time, the infant develops a fairly sophisticated conceptual system. Perhaps its early categories are organized kinesthetically into "feels warm," "feels wet," "feels cold," or "not connected to feelings." Then perhaps it expands these categories by making additional distinctions within each category. The category "no feeling" can be subdivided into auditory, visual, and olfactory categories. Auditory may be further differentiated into "sounds that precede being touched," "sounds that scare me," and "other sounds." The process obviously continues until the child has enough categories so that any given event that confronts it can be contained within one of them. Eventually enough events are categorized so that the child has a coherent world model. The beliefs about how events fit together in this world constitute the client's personal belief system.

This world view can be shared with other people through communication and language. When two people communicate, they develop a shared world view in terms of the beliefs they agree upon. These two people have begun a group. As more join their group, consensual validation becomes available for beliefs held in common by members of the group. Similarly, Don Juan believes that each person's experience of the world is individual and unique, often organized quite arbitrarily into personal belief systems about reality. The *way of the warrior* involves the recognition of the capricious nature of these representations of reality.

The process of constitution is the process of constructing a belief system that orders an individual's perceptions. During childhood, we learn to consensually validate the beliefs of our parents in order to fit into the world views of our family. The thereby constituted world view must be maintained in order for us to preserve a sense of order. Schizophrenia is the result of complete *de-constitution*, in which all cathexis to order is abandoned, and perception exists unchanged in its raw, unfiltered, unrefined form. Constitution implies a sometimes conscious and sometimes unconsicous, sometimes deliberate and sometimes passive, decision of the self or ego about how to organize the data of experience. Certain constitutions or belief systems are more common and traditional than others. The sense data which move together — like a running animal or a flying airplane — are usually organized as one object, whereas the background against which they move — the forest and the clouds — becomes a separate object or series of objects. There are many other ways of organizing these perceptions. For each common and traditional organization, there are realities that reflect other possible organizations. These other realities or belief systems can be said to exist parallel to the dominant or common organization which the person utilizes. An altered state of consciousness allows us to see these other realities and to draw ourselves toward change.

To understand change, we need to understand how a person has created the world they wish to change. There is a remarkable interplay between the freedom and power of the inner self and the environment and situation within which a person may find himself or herself.

The change process — regardless of the symptom or manifestation — is a process of de-constitution; of helping the client to take apart his or her world view in those areas where it is problematic (meaning incongruent with the client's actual goals). This may involve helping the client to become more open to the experience of pain, joy, or love. It may involve helping to push the client toward a decision-making crossroad where the choice of what to de-constitute and how to re-constitute it becomes completely conscious. In other words, the client is faced with the decision — should I keep my beliefs or should I discard them? Richard Bandler[9] tells an interesting story about such decisions and crossroads:

> . . . A professor I had . . . in college, Melvin Stewart, [was a] biologist *par excellence.* Melvin's main interest in biology during my college days was the study of desert terrain. He would take groups of young, flourishing biologists down into the desert for intensive study. Most of the time these trips were uneventful, although they did serve an educational need. However, one summer, miles from civilization, the Land Rover broke down. It was therefore necessary for Melvin and his young crew to set out on foot to find their way back to get help. They took with them only the essentials for survival — food, water, and maps. According to the maps they would have to hike for about three days to reach the nearest signpost of civilization. So the trek began. Marching, resting, then marching again, this solemn and determined group proceeded through the hot wilderness. On the morning of the third day a tired and worn out group reached the summit of a huge sand dune. Thirsty and sunburned, they began to view the terrain about them. Far off to the right was what appeared to be a lake with small trees surrounding it. The students jumped and screamed for joy,

but Melvin did not. He knew that it was only a mirage. He had been here before, he said to himself. He presented the bad news (as would any professor) as facts that had to be accepted. His students, however, rebelled and insisted they knew what they were seeing. The argument continued until Melvin was worn to a frazzle. Finally he conceded to let the students go out to the mirage, after obtaining a promise from them that once they discovered it was a mirage they would sit down and not move until he returned with help. Each student swore they would wait and not wander any further. Melvin went his way ... and the students went theirs. Three hours later the students arrived at a plush new desert resort which had four swimming pools and six restaurants. Two hours after that they set out in a Land Rover with the rangers in search of Melvin, who was never found.

Melvin and his students each faced a perception and a choice. Did Melvin actually see the "mirage" or was his faith in the constancy of the accuracy of his historical knowledge so great that he only saw desert where the students saw water? One cannot know. Melvin would not deconstitute his belief that no water existed in that spot. The students would not deny their perception that they saw water.

If I have a constituted belief that other human beings are dangerous and will hurt me if I let them get too close, that belief will affect my behavior. From my behavior and my perceptions of others' behavior, I may attract to myself people who will hurt me if I let them get too close to me. By deconstituting my world view and by changing my belief system, I can begin to open myself to the possibility that others can be friendly, and that not everyone is out to hurt me. Then I can experience more happiness than I previously allowed myself to feel. When my belief system changes, I can begin to open my world to those who can give me the love I need without hurting me. When I do this, my body may relax to the extent that bothersome physical symptoms can disappear. Clear communication between people depends upon a consensual uniformity of constitutions. Language is an important "bank," "pool," or reservoir of constitutions (belief systems), and the primary way that people have to understand each other's beliefs.

Physiological problems can result when constitutions (belief systems) fail to perform their expected pragmatic tasks in a reasonably efficient manner. Some belief systems seem to succeed for their holder, but only at a high price. Therapy does not necessarily change the patient's reality, but changes the way he or she creates and maintains a world view. Therapy is a systematic, supported, deconstitution and reconstitution process. Before new belief systems can allow for better functioning at a smaller price, deconstitution must take place. Deconstitution separates an organized world design into its various constituents. Insanity is anxiety-produced deconstitution, and can serve as an unexpected opportunity for the deconstitution-reconstitution process. The British psychiatrist, R.D. Laing, believes that psychotherapy consists of allowing, in a supportive environment, the self to reconstitute.

The world is similar to a puzzle that has an infinite number of ways for the pieces to fit together. It is unique in that no right or wrong way exists by which the pieces must fit. A unique world design is created each time the puzzle pieces are fit together to produce a mosaic. This is the process of constitution. To teach children the already accepted forms of constitution is to socialize them. To deconstitute is to dissemble the pieces. Reconstitution is to create a new order, a new mosaic with the same component pieces. The constitution-deconstitution-reconstitution cycle is natural art, similar to the cycle of seasons from summer through spring.

Cathexis — also called identification or fusion — is an indicator of the attachment or commitment that the self makes to one particular way of organizing and creating a world view. The term usually refers specifically to one area within the entire organization of experience. For instance, I may have a strong cathexis or commitment to a certain way of breathing. This results from the way I organized the data present in my world as a child. Perhaps because of my experience with childhood anxiety, I learned to breathe very shallowly and to retain some of the air in my lungs. This could have been because of a certain fear of emptiness. When they are young, children may be particularly unaware of the differences between experience created by internal states and the experience created by others impinging on them. I have remembered through hypnotic procedures the need to have something to hold onto as an infant. A very anxious feeling, a feeling of emptiness could be compensated for, by holding in the breath and becoming constipated. As a child I had early asthma and was overweight. Later I could de-cathect from this commitment and experience the world without such symptoms.

The philosopher Peter Koestenbaum, believes that the reason we do not remember our earliest childhood experiences is not for any lack of memory power, but for the lack of organization in those experiences when they occur.[10] We can only recall experience that is organized in a manner similar to how our experience is organized today, and when we go very far back into childhood, we uncover experiences that are completely disorganized by our current standards of perception.

In order to remember such early experiences we must enter an altered state of consciousness in which both nonverbal and unorganized experiences can be remembered. Then the conscious, remembering mind can process this previously unprocessed experience. Age regression techniques are effective because much of this early data has never before been subjected to processing by the adult, conscious ego.

An example will help clarify how this material on constitutions and categorization is clinically important.

Imogene, a 24 year old woman of Boston Irish Catholic background came for therapy because of chronic recurrent vaginitis. She had been married for 15 months, during which time she had experienced vaginitis most of the time. She loved her husband and no marital conflict existed on surface examination. Imogene had been sexually active with one partner other than her husband before marriage. Occasional vaginitis during that time had responded promptly to treatment by her primary care associate. After marriage, no drug seemed to help. Other underlying diseases had been ruled out. She was referred to me for further help.

By our second interview, the nature of her problem had become more clear. With the help of her parents and the church, she had developed a categorical system in which being raped, making love, and having an abortion all fit into the same category for her. This category could be called "events involving penetration of the vagina by others." She did not resolve the contradiction with her belief system that was caused by making love with her husband because it immediately evoked the idea that she was being raped or having an unwanted abortion. She had experienced one abortion which she had felt pressured into having and felt guilty about. Intercourse reminded her of that guilt. Her problem existed in her mechanistic conceptual system — a common problem in this society.

Therapy consisted of helping her to see that the way she conceptualized experience was inadequate to her needs. She quickly developed three different categories of perception:

1. forcible penetration of the vagina against the will,
2. acceptance of having her husband inside her body as an act of love,
3. necessary (but not emotionally desirable) penetration done with her consent (her abortion, pelvic exams).

Thus, she discovered that emotions (as well as mechanics) were valid dictators of categories of experience. After more discussion and resolution of her guilt feelings about the abortion (plus allowing herself to grieve), she terminated therapy. Her vaginitis had completely resolved itself without medication and did not recur within the next two years. Premarital sex, unlike sex during marriage, had not led to as severe symptomology. In the context of her childhood family beliefs, premarital sex was not "real" sex until consummated by marriage. Therefore, Imogene did not have as rigid a categorization problem for premarital sex.

Phenomenology

Phenomenology means the study of phenomena; "the things themselves," or "the things as they present themselves." In practice, it refers to a method of study or learning about patients that emphasizes the uniqueness of each individual case. In this method, *no* assumptions should be made. Observations are begun with simple description. Then the descriptive material, in a sense, organizes itself into useful categories of perception. Pre-existing theories are not used to organize the data; rather, theories are derived from the data itself.

The holistic health practitioner can gain great insights from the methods of phenomenology in working with the individual patient. In each case, the uniquely individual psychology each patient displays must be discovered anew. Traditional scientific medicine holds that a condition need only be diagnosed so that one particular, specific treatment can be instituted for all patients. In treating all individuals with similar symptoms the same way, errors of categorization can be made. Treatment needs to be individualized to be maximally effective. This is the goal of holistic assessment, evaluation and treatment.

Phenomenology can help us immensely by stressing the importance of beginning the learning process anew each time we need to know about a person. This is not to say that we do not have some vague notions about the inner landscape of our patient from previous experience with patients. We do. But we must discard even that. We must become *pre-suppositionless* about the client we are assessing. Forget the fact of the diagnosis. Remember that many paths lead to one final common outcome. Discard beliefs about the condition and the person. Rediscover anew in each person the reasons for their problem. This is a truly individual psychology. The psychic terrain is mapped and remapped in each investigation.

Mind-Body and Eastern Philosophy

Since some holistic practices are reportedly derived from Eastern philosophy, it is interesting to examine how Eastern philosophy handles the mind-body problem.

Sankya yoga philosophy holds that mind and body are one and inseparable. A mind-body dichotomy does not exist. However, it holds that man has two natures, one physical and the other spiritual, and that each struggles to dominate the other (rajoguna and tamoguna). The struggle occurs in the context of an artificial dualism. If the struggle between the spiritual and physical continues, each aspect threatens to dominate the other and the net effect may be inertia. When rajoguna and tamoguna battle, inertia emerges as the victor. Integration of physical body process and spiritual process potentiates growth. (On the other hand, we could question the Eastern belief that the mind and the body necessarily have to battle.)

In Hatha Yoga, physical exercise has the effect of helping one to recognize the unity and harmony of physiological and psychic forces. Dr. Rammurta Mishra, an Indian student of yoga psychology, states that "every psychological activity has its physical significance, which is expressed by various attitudes and moods of the body."[11] He states, "Mind is like an engine which impels the body to adopt a specific posture." Western bioenergeticists and the gestaltist Wolfgang Köhler have taken similar positions. Eastern philosophy is so tied to a religion that it does not seem helpful as the basis upon which to organize a philosophy of medicine, although its concepts can be helpful in showing us how another culture organizes its perceptions.

Encounter With Other Selves

The experience of encounter which occurs in meditation or reflective states has suggested to some a kind of "cosmic mind" or "inner subjective transcendental ego" rather than pure or lonely subjectivity. It is an issue with which we need concern ourselves because of its emergence in clinical practice. Who or what are guides? When Wanda experiences herself in a past life, is that *real*, or only a mental construct? How do we decide?

Some conclude that this experience of other existences (guides, past lives, higher selves) gives credence to the concept of a Transcendental Ego. A careful scrutiny of this sense of internal encounter with another Self supports Hocking's view that the universe is a vast person, self, or mind and that it is not quite true that *I* am that mind. This is the experience of the Universe as a living, feeling gestalt of "All That Is." Such encounters suggest that the observer of the plane of existence on which I currently live is not just me, but that I am a miniscule part of a larger whole. I like to imagine a pyramidal structure in which many separate smaller selves on a "physical world" can be summated over space and time to create what would be called a Higher Self. Summation can continue among selves at this level to arrive at progressively greater levels of organization and inclusion. Summation can continue among selves at this level to arrive at a final gestalt which could be called "All That Is." "All That Is" could be described mathematically as the limit (in the sense of calculus) as the Universe converges toward Infinity.

Body Relations

In our experience of reality on the physical plane, our bodies are never separated from our minds, yet the body has been described as a "physical object to the ego," e.g. an object like a table. This represents a lack of integration between the mind and the body such that the body is seen as a separate entity. Clients who experience dying in a "past life" provide some fascinating accounts of decathexis of themselves from the physical body. Therefore, there may be some transcendental element that comprises us. Interestingly, people who report deaths in past life experiences find themselves continuing to experience themselves in a body. They are not an isolated, separated pure consciousness in their reported experience.

The body is our most intimate expression of ourselves. Our experience is always filtered through our body. From birth, we are obviously inseparable from our bodies, and they are our most unique and individual form of expression. We are totally committed to our bodies in a rather complete and total way.

Some people who feel very separate from their body (and therefore emotionally decathected) may react adversely to the psychophysiological view of illness. For these people, as long as they can view their problem as existing only in their body (and they do not see themselves as the same as their body) the body can be separated in their view of themselves as not really a part of them, but existing outside of them. These people have developed a relationship to their body such that "it's out there," instead of being considered a unique part of them. They don't have to feel responsible or that they need to change if their problem is "out there," as opposed to within themselves. Physical existence requires a certain total commitment to being "in-the-body" and to being integrated in a physio-emotional sense to this body existence. People who tend toward self-blame or low self-esteem may find acceptance of the psychological and lifestyle aspects of illness more troublesome than believing in external forces. This difficulty poses further problems in their ability to view illness as a positive force for change and growth. In accepting a psychophysiological view of health and disease, we must first dispel the notion that illness is bad or negative.

Many people define distances of various objects in physical reality from what they consider their essence to be. Traditionally inert physical objects are considered furthest away, then other people, their body, and finally, their essence. Indirect experience, however, (even imagination) must have a context and a vessel for the essence that is the self. That essence is usually an imagined representation of the body. Even the person who imagines himself or herself as pure consciousness experiences invisible containers. Otherwise that consciousness would stretch to infinity. I have never heard a description of an experience of identifying with or being part of a vast greater consciousness that does not include some sense of separation of the essence of the self from that greater consciousness. Defining and experiencing boundaries may be an important constitution related to health. When the boundaries of the self are set too small, then adequate feedback to permit growth and change is not received. When "my body" is not really a part of "me," I have more difficulty realizing that minor physical symptoms — aches, pains, etc. reflect relevant feedback that something is truly wrong. Instead of looking within or viewing the environmental context of his or her life, the person goes to a doctor to get rid of these minor ailments. When feedback is ignored, most systems have adaptive mechanisms to increase the intensity of that feedback so that it will be noticed by control centers. For the human being, if the ego (waking consciousness) completely ignores the early warning signals of body dissatisfaction, symptoms intensify. If ignored for long enough, tissue changes occur. Then doctors may make a diagnosis. Drugs can reduce the intensity of symptoms, but, as long as life events, stress, and beliefs remain unchanged, forces within the body continually increase the pressure for symptoms to worsen. A vicious cycle of increasing drug dosages begins with dosage continually rising to reach the same effect. This phenomenon is labelled drug tolerance by pharmacologists.

Every illness can provide a stimulus for tremendous personal growth. Each person chooses whether or not to use that opportunity. Symptoms, including fears (especially the fear of death) may reflect a philosophic crisis resulting from the patient pursuing a different direction from what is best to continue on a path of growth and development. There are innate feedback mechanisms designed to help us understand when we are "off-course." Just like the warning that occurs in the navigation system of an airplane when the course has been disturbed beyond the capacity of the automatic pilot system, the body signals to the ego when a new course must be plotted.

General Systems Theory

Systems theory has much to offer for a philosophy of holistic health. General systems theory had its 20th century origin in the biological observations of Victor von Bertalanffy, and has been most widely applied in the fields of family therapy and psychiatry. The gestalt statement that "the whole is greater than the sum of its parts," is a basic statement of systems theory. A system is an entity which is more understandable in its gestalt (wholeness) than it would be if it were broken down into components. If the behavior of a mass or a crowd could be explained by looking at the individual characteristics of each individual in that mass, there would be no need for a theory of systems. Unique, definable properties of groups exist such that working units or composites of relationships can be described that can best be termed systems. Systems appear to have a life of their own; a kind of energy, motivation, set of rules and guidelines, and direction of their own that may often exist independently of the motivations, rules, guidelines, directions, and personalities of the individual members of the system. Systems are layered upon each other like the multiple skins of an onion, beginning with very simple systems and moving to the more complex in a stepwise inclusive fashion. This complexity can be illusionary in that it actually represents the movement from micro to macro process, even though the elements of each level can be equally complex. The biological system posed by the human body in comparison with the ecosystem or a sociocultural system represents increasing layers of complexity. In each of these systems, the component elements differ, but the nature and concept of "the system" remains constant.

Any system has a series of rules governing relationships and interactions within that system. A study of these rules is properly termed the study of meta-rules.

Mathematically, the notion of systems is easily understandable. The idea that the whole is greater than the sum of its parts can be expressed by a series of simultaneous linear differential equations such as:

$$\frac{d\psi_1}{dt} = f(\psi_2, \psi_3, \psi_4, \ldots \psi_n)$$

$$\frac{d\psi_2}{dt} = f(\psi_1, \psi_3, \psi_4, \ldots \psi_n)$$

$$\cdots$$

$$\frac{d\psi_n}{dt} = f(\psi_1, \psi_2, \psi_3, \ldots \psi_{n-1})$$

This series of simultaneous equations elegantly illustrates the nature of systems. For any change in one variable, because that variable affects all others, a change results in all other variables. When all other variables change, since all variables feed back to affect the original variable, the first variable that was altered originally is altered again and the process continues until a more or less steady state is reached. This steady state is very tenuous and easily unbalanced. This delicacy is useful, in that it allows the system to quickly respond to the environment and to be very adaptive.

If there were no system relatedness, a change in one variable would have no effect on the others. Then this series of simultaneous differential equations could be reduced to one simple mathematical expression called a Taylor series, rather than many different differential equations which must be solved simultaneously. Systems theory and analysis is based upon a simple mathematical truth: when variables are interrelated, any change in a given variable will affect all other variables, which then results in a change on the initial variable. This constant process continues indefinitely, and explains the property of systems to grow and change (called their morphogenic aspect). Problems such as disease or social problems occur when this fluidic feedback-change process breaks down and rigidity occurs.

Feedback is an essential element in systems. Feedback can be positive or negative. Positive feedback tends to amplify differences, whereas negative feedback tends to diminish differences. In any system, both positive and negative feedback exist, and give the system the ability to change.

Systems are both morphogenic and homeostatic. If change and adaptation do not occur, stagnation results and the system becomes unable to function. Systems have a tendency to resist change. This tendency is called the homeostatic aspect of the system, and has been especially studied among families. In psychology, family systems theory and therapy arose from the observations of Don Jackson and his colleagues at the Mental Research Institute of Palo Alto that schizophrenic patients who experienced marked improvement when treated in a hospital setting suffered complete relapse on return to their families. In studying these families, Jackson and his colleagues discovered a tremendous pressure from other family members for the identified patient to return to the schizophrenic symptoms and behavior that had previously led to the hospital admission. The family did not *know* they were encouraging the patient to get worse. Rather, in the nature of the homeostatic properties of systems, they tried (unconsciously) to keep things the same. This is similar to the behavior of netted lobsters. In New Orleans, the Creoles, upon netting lobsters, put them in buckets of water and nonchalantly leave them at the edge of the shore. Any lobster attempting to climb out of the bucket is immediately dragged *back* by his companion lobsters. The same process happens in other systems, such as families of schizophrenics or families in Harlem.

Virginia Satir is one family systems theorist who has paid special attention to the morphogenic aspects of family systems. Morphogenic refers to a tendency for growth, change, and successful adaptation. She found that normal families (normal systems) are families in which growth and change is the norm. From a survival perspective, any system, be it a body, tribe, or culture, will need to develop new response patterns and to maintain a wide set of response patterns, given constantly changing (in unexpected and unpredictable ways) demands from the environment, along with constantly changing conditions. A constantly changing environment (such as the planet Earth) requires systems to be capable of constantly altering themselves to be prepared for new environmental conditions in which the system may find itself. Cultures that cannot respond to new conditions may die out. The Hindu culture of India provides a good example of a culture that has adapted many times to changing conditions (invasions) and incorporated the invading culture. Other cultures have not accomplished this so well and have disappeared.

Virginia Satir's philosophy of family systems therapy rests on a brief-term model in which families are viewed as having been (for a multitude of possible reasons) blocked in their normal process of growth and change. Therapy consists of finding and removing those blocks so that the family can continue to grow, change, and adapt. It would be wrong to emphasize either the homeostatic or the morphogenic aspect of systems at the other's expense since they are equally important.

One of the most valuable contributions of systems theory is the elimination of the concept of initial causality and hence the need for blame. Medicine and psychology are replete with theories based upon the unit theory of causality (meaning that one specific, historical cause can be identified) with blame being placed on either biochemicals, parents, germs, or fate. For example, a biochemical etiological theory of schizophrenia would hold that schizophrenia is a biological defect with its genetic components. A systems etiological theory of schizophrenia would be much more complex. It would include many contributing factors. In particular, a phenomenological-based systems theory would not place primary emphasis on any given factor without a careful investigation of all factors in order to understand which are important in a given clinical setting.

More importantly, there may not be a cause in the narrow sense of one cause leading to one effect. The following case illustrates this, and gives the example of a man whose illness can best be understood within the context of his family.

This 48 year old man presented to me with complaints of severe shoulder pain for the past year and a half. Neil complained of severe pain in the shoulder and pain if he attempted to move his shoulder in some specific ways. In his medical history no explanation or identifiable "causes" of the pain could be found. Neil had tried almost every treatment known to medical science.

He worked as an administrator of a large State office. I began by trying to explore what had happened in his life in the years prior to the onset of his pain. One and a half years before the pain began, he had bought a house. He reported having put in a sprinkler system one year prior to the pain. Six months prior he had done cement work on his house. All his answers were phrased within a belief system that only some physical trauma could have caused his problem. Even though my initial question related to life events of the past, he answered only in concrete physical terms related to skeletal muscle movement. Then he related that two years prior he had moved to Northern California from San Diego.

I asked him about his marriage. He had four children and had been married for the past 22 years. I inquired about stresses in his life. The first stress he mentioned was with his son, who had just turned 18. He had had trouble with this son for the last five years, but said that now this son was out of his house. He reported having had problems with his son's lack of control and his son's attempts to assault him both verbally and physically. Neil had obtained a court restraining order to keep his son from ever visiting his house. They day before visiting me his son had arrived at Neil's front door and Neil had called the police, who took the son away. His son had not created a disturbance, but Neil reported that he had finished with that son "and did not want any further communication or to see him again." Then he reported he had the standard day-to-day stress of marriage, family, and work. He quickly went on to describe his job. Budget cuts were being made and there was a movement afoot to abolish his whole department on the grounds that it was unnecessary in the organization. The final stress he reported was that he had bought his home partially uncompleted and finishing it had become half way between a hobby and a worry. He said this was stressing but not critically so.

I was curious about the standard stresses he had glossed over, so I asked him about those. He said that he and his wife bickered about things and that they weren't getting along well. He had filed for divorce three months previously. His wife had begged him to stop the final papers and said that she would change. He decided to give her a trial period. He said his wife had problems that she alone needed to resolve, although she kept arguing that her problems were symptomatic of a family problem. He was very upset that his wife had continued contact with the older problem son. Neil said that sometimes she would do and say what he believed to be correct (no contact with the son), but then would encourage the son to stay in contact with her and to visit. He said he would take the children if there was a divorce because he didn't feel his wife had a good relationship with the other three children.

We can immediately observe that it would not be possible to understand this man without some knowledge of his family. Individually, his son might be seen as a scoundrel and his wife as a weak, ineffectual, paralyzed decision maker. Yet the members of this family fit together in a much more dynamic, *real* way than through such stereotyped roles. We have a strong-willed, decisive man who makes important decisions at work and tends to view the world in an all or nothing, right or wrong manner. His wife complements him by seeming to have a weak, indecisive nature as does his son, by being decisively evil, wrong, and bad. The wife mediates between the father's position as the "right one" and the son's position as the "wrong one."

It seemed significant that his shoulder pain should occur in the arm that he used to write with or to use scissors with. Neil seemed to have a pattern of cutting people off when they weren't as he wanted them to be. It also seemed significant that in his job he was facing the threat of being cut off, just as his wife was facing the threat of being cut off from him. If he couldn't move his shoulder, then it would be harder for him to "cut off" people (e.g. sign divorce papers, court orders, etc.) and he would more likely be dependent on others and less decisive in an all or nothing manner. He might spend more time with his family, rather than working on the house when at home. I felt very sad to think of the relationship among he, his son and his wife. It seems common in families for the mother, father, and oldest child to form a kind of explosive triangle with the other children as the background chorus. Another common pattern is for the two oldest children to take opposing sides with the warring parents. The first pattern happened in my own family, in which I was seen as the "cause" of problems between my parents. The second pattern occured in my wife's family in which she sided with her father against her mother and her older brother sided with her mother against their father. This was stable until her father moved out, at which time her mother and brother could still war with her, but she was left without the support of her father.

Systems and the Nature of Holistic Practice

In the past century, medicine has become progressively more differentiated and specialized. The need for specialization is implicit in the philosophical assumption that the best way to gain knowledge is to continually reduce a phenomenon to smaller and smaller parts in order to study each part in greater depth. Such constant reduction results in a proliferation of specialists, each with more specific interests and expertise. While reductionism and specialization can be useful and important to the extent that a phenomenon is divided into arbitrary distinctions to increase the understanding of components within each distinction, an increasingly progressive loss of comprehension of the interrelatedness of the parts occurs. This loss of gestalt comprehension is especially relevent to understanding body health.

Categorization schemes used by scientists may be capriciously arbitrary. Michel Foucault has written eloquently about the arbitrary nature of these schemes.[12] In one Chinese categorization scheme there were eleven groups of animals. Among these were pigs, animals that fly, animals that slither low to the ground, furry animals, and the Emperor's animals. This classification system was satisfactory since it reflected all the needs of those using it. Anyone who killed the Emperor's animals would be killed himself. Therefore it was only necessary to know that an animal belonged to the Emperor. Further curiosity might get one in hot water. This classification system was as useful and valid as modern categorization systems based on zoological research, since it met all the needs of its users. Categorizational schemes are very representative of the way a given culture organizes perception and consciousness. Eskimos have 27 different words to describe the subtle nuances of the one English word "snow." Since there was no general word for snow, they would have to discriminate between each of the 27 types of snow before speaking, whereas an English speaker could first report that it was snowing or that there was snow, and then, if needed, look closer to describe it in more detail. The categorization system of modern medicine provides certain recognizable bases for understanding the perceptive ability and consciousness of its users. What seems to happen is that when a process of sensations and experiences are given a name (a diagnosis), there is a pattern by which the client is locked into the attributes of that name. The client can go home and read all about this "named entity" which he now has. The doctor can predict what will happen for the next ten years from the name.

Mary Seemans[13] has written a very interesting account of the relationship between names and identity. She concludes that, in part, names represent the intensions, hopes, desires, and traditions of the namers of a child, and, in part, the temperament of the child influences its namers' choice of name. Her example of the name choices of patients with multiple personality syndromes follows:

> Different aspects of identity are sometimes compartmen-talized. . . . One patient whose given name was Leila . . . had two other identities, Lola (from the song *What Lola Wants, Lola Gets*) and Lilith (from the Hebrew Lilith, "night monster," female demon of Jewish folklore). As Lola, the patient went to bars in an attempt to meet older men who, she hoped, would indulge her as her father had done. As Lilith, she engaged in unsavoury criminal activities. Both Lola and Lelith, phonetically so similar to Leila, were totally repressed and, superficially wholly unlike the personality of Leila.
>
> Another patient with this syndrome, Violet, was in many ways the prototype of a "shrinking violet." She had two alter egos: Viva — her vivacious, aggressive self and Violaine (after Mallarme's fictional heroine) who, in a dreamlike automatic writing state composed poetry.

Ursula Le Guin[14] describes in her *Earthsea Trilogy* a process of a binding spell (in a magical sense) invoked by the naming of names. Diagnosis has such a magical effect upon many patients, binding them to what the doctor believes will happen to people with that particular disease.

By ordering diseases by organ systems according to specific patho-logical anatomy, a system is established that perceives illness and people narrowly by what is wrong anatomically or structurally. Through increasing specialization, the ramifications of anatomic change upon other systems is appreciated less. The possibility for improved understanding and treatment through simple description and perception is lost, because all new research tends to support the classification system, *because it is done within the perceptions of the system it is treating.* A study may compare the MMPI (a psychological test) profiles of ulcerative colitis[15] patients and normal patients and find no differences. A conclusion may be made that psychological factors do not play a role in ulcerative colitis. The fallacy is that there are discrete anatomical (structural) processes in personality that can (or should) be correlated with physical disease. The *structure* of personality as *specifically objectively* measurable is thought to be able to correlate with the structure of the bowel. Instead there really is no reason why both should not be non-specific outcomes of a more basic *process* which specialization misses.

Through such conceptualization systems, doctors ignore the more subtle factors operative in affecting health and illness. This is especially relevant in the problem of random, controlled studies. Nine out of ten recent randomized, controlled studies, although tremendously expensive, prove the null hypothesis.[16] This means that the treatment that is being compared to inactive drug does not show any effectiveness. This contradicts the knowledge of clinicians that these treatments do seem to help patients. One specific example, reported recently in the *New England Journal of Medicine* illustrates this.[17] The role of the drug cholestyramine was studied in preventing mortality from heart and arterial disease through its effects upon lowering blood cholesterol. The effects were not significant. There were significant differences when patients who religiously took their medication (whether active drug or placebo) were compared to patients who did not. The compliers (those who took medicine) experienced a significant reduction in mortality regardless of whether or not their medicine was an active drug. Was the reduction in mortality due to their belief in the power of the medicine or their motivation to get well (as measured by the adherence to the medication regimen)?

Another excellent example concerns the treatment of minimal amounts of high blood pressure with medication.[17] Random, controlled studies showed approximately 20% reduction in mortality from the recognized complications of high blood pressure following treatment with a diuretic medication. (Diuretics cause the kidneys to excrete more salt, and, therefore, water.) More difficult to explain, however, was a similar reduction in mortality among the drug treated patients (compared to controls) in deaths from car accidents, cancer, and suicide. How did blood pressure medication affect car accidents, cancer, and suicide? Did these patients adopt a different attitude toward themselves as a by-product of treatment that affected other areas of their life? These questions deserve to be studied.

Foucault[18] believes that the arbitrary division of the human body into subsystems arose with the philosophical notion that there was a location in the body for all diseases. This was first seriously proposed by the Frenchman Bissault, one of the first pathological anatomists of the 16th century. In order to find the "seat" or "cause" of disease, his philosophy was to progressively divide and then to further divide.

Holistic practice takes an entirely different standpoint. To find the basis for disease, we must abandon the search for specific structural cause. We need to look at the natural groupings of events in don Juan's way of actually seeing the inter-relationships. This means abandoning prior belief systems. Holistic health practice as a specialty includes the whole body and the whole family, and is based on an entirely different conception of medicine from that of specialists. To understand the person and the problem, everything must be understood. In some ways every view contains some truth even if distorted. There are no necessary facts, perhaps only patterns and groupings of data.

Medical Phenomenology

Phenomenology is an epistemological method. This means that it is one method or approach for learning about the world and the individual's relation to it. The basic technique is to use the phenomenological *epoché* which consists of making a presuppositionless detachment from my position in the world to achieve a view of things as they really present themselves. This is the Western equivalent of Eastern meditation. It is very important to realize that the experience gained in the meditative state may bear little resemblance to the words used to describe that state. The Christian may speak of the experience of the presence of God or the personal touch of Jesus Christ. The Buddhist may describe the feeling of bliss or nirvana from the meditative state. The philosopher may speak of the experience of the transcendental ego. If unenlightened as to the nature of language, these three could argue for hours about who was right. The best way to be "right" is to simply describe with the expressed caveat that even basic words have different meanings to different people. A given word or sentence evokes what Bandler and Grinder[19] call a "transderivational search," in which the listener matches up the heard word with his experiences connected with that word, which might not relate to what is being said.

The phenomenological *epoché* or reduction can be made several times, one step at a time deeper into the meta-realm. In the first phenomenological reduction, I step out of the concrete, everyday world into a position from which I can look at myself and others and my relation to myself and to others. This is the level of meta-communication, of analogic thought, and of body language.

At the next phenomenological level, I can look at myself looking at myself looking at the world. This can proceed indefinitely, and may be symbolic of reaching out to deeper levels of consciousness. Suspension of prior beliefs is important. Throughout our lives we gain beliefs and assumptions about the world around us, about ourselves, and about our relationship to other people. These assumptions begin from the moment of birth. Anna Freud[20] describes the state of the early infant as a "prepsychological, undifferentiated, unstructured state, in which no division exists between body and mind or self and object." It is from this state — which is a state of emotional cathexis and attachment devoid of concretized, objectified relations — that we develop concrete assumptions about the world. This description is also exactly how the meditator might describe the meditative state or a phenomenologist might describe the process of viewing the world without assumptions. How, we might ask, does Anna Freud know this about infants. She doesn't. She *imagines* it to be true from her own experience. This experience could include recovered memories of her own infanthood (obtained spontaneously, through psychoanalysis, or through hypnosis), descriptions by others of their memories of being an infant, "scientific" research on infant perception and cognition, or her personal experience of being an infant. One of the most interesting of my personal experiences is how infants will look at what appears to be nothing and will laugh and laugh.

One criticism that anyone can level at most descriptions (especially those of psychoanalysts and others who are deeply invested in a particular theory) is that the description of the experience is too closely intermingled with the theoretical interpretation of that experience, or is presented in terms that assume one interpretation. We need to avoid doing this as much as possible.

A knowledge of the method of phenomenology can be an invaluable tool for the holistic health practitioner. An empirical science of medicine is insufficient to explain the wide variety of phenomena that exist in medicine. An adequate philosophy of medicine must explain the reason why there, in fact, exist cancer cases purportedly cured by laetrile in spite of the lack of efficacy of laetrile to treat cancer in double-blind, controlled studies. It must explain healing in all its many and varied forms. In the spirit of Hamlet, when he spoke to Horatio, we must realize that a better theory of medicine must explain "the more things in earth and sky than your philosophy has ever dreamed of." In the spirit of Hamlet as phenomenologist, who relinquished his prior assumptions about the world to accept the reality of his father's ghost, to experience that reality and to act upon it, we as phenomenologists must give up our prior learned beliefs about the world and be willing to incorporate all pieces of experience into our perception. This is incumbent upon the holistic practitioner and upon the unified generalist, to an extent that might not be so to the specialist.

The specialist has a clearly, albeit arbitrarily defined, bailiwick. A specialist is reponsible for a specialized set of problems. The relationships between those sets of problems, although complex, since they must be complex to require a specialist, are also limited in definition and scope. The specialist in endocrinology is not an epidemiologist, is not a psychiatrist, is not a sociologist. The unified generalist or holistic practitioner must be all of these. He or she must have a philosophical background from which to integrate these different disciplines.

In viewing the patient's process, the holistic practitioner needs to have a different point of view. He or she, by definition, is interested in all problems pertaining to the person and to the family, but to a limited scope of complexity. This, however, opens up a new level of complexity, which only the holistic practitioner in the health-care team can appreciate. This is the level of inter-relatedness between the various components of the person. Whereas there is a complexity of diagnosis and treatment for any given organ system treated by a specialist, there is an equivalent, if not greater, complexity regarding the relationships among organ systems, body, mind, and environment.

Holistic practice offers a chance to break out of the specificity determined by the pathological-anatomical mode[18] of disease, and to open ourselves to the creation of a new description of the process of living. That this process of living is sometimes deteriorative, and that the being who is deteriorating requires intervention, creates the demand for the profession of medicine. The holistic practitioner as phenomenologist becomes responsible for understanding the relatedness of the whole patient and of the patient's environment. In approaching a given process, he or she as phenomenologist lets go of prior assumptions about the patient, the patient's family, the patient's sociocultural system, the patient's prior problems, and his or her understanding of those problems, and describes what can be "seen." He or she describes in accurate detail everything initially perceived about the patient. From this initial level of accurate description, simple as it may be, the supra-structure of holistic medicine can emerge, well-supported on its foundation of descriptive knowledge about the individual.

REFERENCES AND NOTES

[1] Rogers, C. *Client-Centered Therapy*. New York: Basic Books, 1974.

[2] Eccles, R. Neurophysiology and the Soul. Lecture given at Indiana University, April, 1972.

[3] Schildkraut, J.J. The catecholamine hypothesis of affective disorders: A review of supporting evidence. *Am. J. of Psychiatry* 122:509–522, 1965.

[4] Cholinergic stimulation (release of increased levels of acetylcholine in the brain) may also stimulate depression, while drugs that block the action of acetylcholine sometimes alleviate depression.[8]

[5] Klerman, G.L. and Cole, J.O. Clinical pharmacology of imipramine and related antidepressant compounds. *Pharmacol. Rev.* 17:101–141, 1965.

[6] Cole, J.O. Therapeutic efficacy of antidepressant drugs. *J. Am. Med. Assoc.* 190:448-455, 1964.

[7] Davis, J. Efficacy of tranquilizing and anti-depressant drugs. *Arch. Gen. Psychiatry* 13:522–572, 1965.

[8] Janowsky, D.S., El-Yousef, M.K., Davis, J.M. and Sekerkelyi, H.J. Parasympathetic suppression of manic symptoms of physostigmine. *Arch. Gen. Psychiatry* 28:522–547.

[9] Bandler, R. in Gordon, D. *Therapeutic Metaphors*. Cupertino, Calif.: Meta Publications, 1978.

[10] Koestenbaum, P. *The Vitality of Death*. Newport, Conn: Greenwood, 1975.

[11] Mishra, Rammurta, *Yoga Sutras*. New York: Bantam, 1976.

[12] Foucault, M. *The Order of Things*. New York: Springer-Verlag, 1975.

[13] Seemans, M.V. Name and Identity. *Canadian Journal of Psychiatry* 25:129–137, 1980.

[14] Le Guin, U. *The Earthsea Trilogy*. New York: Bantam, 1976.

[15] Ulcerative colitis is a disease characterized by periods of severe diarrhea and ulcers in the large intestine.

[16] Personal communication, Dr. Bill Brown, Stanford University School of Medicine, Division of Biostatistics, 1981.

[17] Personal communication, Dr. Harold Goldberg, Robert Wood Johnson Clinical Scholars Program, Stanford University School of Medicine, 1981.

[18] Foucault, M. *The Birth of the Clinic*. New York: Springer-Verlag, 1970.

[19] Bandler, R. and Grinder, J. *Patterns of the Hypnotic Techniques of Milton H. Erickson, M.D.* Vols. I & II. Cupertino, California: Meta Publications, 1977.

[20] Freud, A. *The Ego and the Mechanisms of Defense*. New York: Academic Press, 1969.

Chapter Seven

Empirical Evidence of Mind-Body Connection

Psychoanalytic Research

It is not surprising that psychoanalysts have long been interested in the relationship between mental processes and the physical body. The need for study of the relationship between biology and psychology is implicit in the theoretical foundations laid down by Freud. Much early psychoanalytic research studied the relationship of biological sexuality to psychological sexuality.

The psychoanalyst Otto Fenichel wrote that "every fixation necessarily changes the hormonal status."[1] By fixation he loosely refers to psychological conflict or neurotic fixation. By this he meant that thoughts and feelings are related to hormones within the brain. Once habitual patterns of response are developed (fixated) in the personality, Fenichel would argue that these represent specific hormonal pathways within the brain that subsequently have effects upon the body. This belief has led to research upon both men and women. For men, correlations have been found between hormone production by the testicles and the sense of urgency of male sexual impulses.[2] Psychoanalysts argue that hormonal influences determine the emotional experience. The belief that hormones and behavior develop *simultaneously* is more consistent with the available data of experience. My title, *Mind and Matter*, suggests this. The mind does not override the body (mind over matter), nor does the body determine emotions (as many biological psychiatrists argue), but through simultaneous interaction, both arrive at a location in which each reflects the other. This is reminiscent of Soviet experiments in which two hearts beating at different rhythms are placed on a table with mirrors reflecting each heart's image to the other. After several minutes, the hearts are observed to synchronize and beat at the same rate.

In one analytic study, women kept records of their body temperatures each day. Cells from the lining of their vaginas were gently removed with a swab and examined under a microscope. Hormone levels were determined from the shape and appearance of the vaginal cells. These biological records were compared with notes made after each therapy session by the psychoanalyst (who did not know where the women were on their menstrual cycles). Either set of data (analytic notes about the women's sexual behavior or the temperature charts) could be used to chart the menstrual cycle, and both coincided almost exactly. The analytic researchers concluded that female sexual behavior was at least partially determined by hormonal changes in the ovarian cycle. This presents a statistical error because all that is known is that sexual behavior and hormones are somehow related — not that one causes the other. Two parallel cycles were found — an emotional cycle and a hormonal body cycle. Perhaps health results when these cycles are integrated, and disease is more likely to occur when they are out of synchrony. Such data can help explain how emotions affect physiology. For Harriet (whose case is discussed in Chapter 5), it is conceivable that her hormones were chronically out of balance with her behavioral cycles. Perhaps an imbalance of hormones contributes to the development of fibroids.

Other observations from this study effectively demonstrate the interactive nature of emotions and physiology. For example, when the women began to produce more estrogen,[3] the psychoanalytic notes revealed the women's tendency toward an active, extroverted, heterosexual orientation in their sexual contact. With the progestin phase, the notes indicated a more internal direction of energy with less tendency toward active pursuit of sexual contact.[4] During the time between the end of the menstrual flow and ovulation, the psychoanalysts reading the sessions recognized active sexual tendencies in the women's behavior, dreams, and fantasies. An increased alertness seemed to exist in the extroverted activities of each individual woman.[5] The increase in estrogen seemed to parallel observations made during the session that the women tended to organize and integrate various areas of their lives more so than during the time of estrogen decline.

At the time of ovulation, estrogen production has reached its maximum and is being surpassed in intensity by a later occurring rise (during the menstrual cycle) of the hormone, progeterone. During the time around ovulation (when both estrogen and progesterone have reached their peak production, unless conception occurs), the session notes showed an increased emotional tension and a strong tendency for the women to actively seek sexual contact. After ovulation, the emotional tension seemed to decrease and a period of relaxation was observed to follow. The effect was a generalized eroticization. The desire to make love exhibited a more conscious and romantic quality, rather than the seemingly more driven quality of pre-ovulation desires. Whereas before ovulation the women tended to initiate sexual contact, after ovulation they seemed to enjoy being the more passive recipient of their partner's erotic desires — enjoying sex, but usually waiting for their partner to initiate.[6]

If pregnancy does not occur, the production of progesterone declines along with the production of estrogen, and the ensuing low hormone level characterizes the premenstrual phase of the cycle. During the premenstrual phase, the psychoanalytic notes showed an increased emotional tension with a "driven" quality in the women's activities of these days. At the same time an urgency of sexual desire occurred which the same women might not experience in other phases of the cycle. During the menstrual flow, emotional tension relaxed and excitability decreased.

In the same series of observations, emotional factors seemed to have an important influence upon the menstrual cycle. Emotions could cause a delay in the menstrual flow. Gratifying or exciting heterosexual intercourse could facilitate ovulation, while frustration or fear could inhibit it. The number of ovulations, the frequency of the ovulatory cycle, and the symptoms of the pre-menstrual phase (more so in some women and less so in others) were also influenced by emotional factors. Many readers can no doubt recall instances of this in their own lives or the lives of friends or lovers. I have frequently observed that women who are afraid they may be pregnant experience a delay in the onset of their menstrual cycle. (On the other hand, perhaps some of them were pregnant and their desire not to be changed their hormonal level such that a spontaneous, early miscarriage occurred.) A brief case example will serve to illustrate this.

Kathryn was a 24-year-old nurse, living in Cheyenne, Wyoming. She had stopped having menstrual periods, and went to her gynecologist when six months had elapsed since her last period. He took a careful medical history and ruled out the possibility of structural pathology in her body. Then, being sensitive to issues of emotions and the body, he took a careful psychosocial history.

For the past nine months, Kathryn had been working the 11 p.m. to 7:30 a.m. shift on the postpartum unit of her hospital. She had begun this shift because it assured her of always being able to work 40 hours weekly. There were many nurses competing for the shifts with more desirable hours, and such assurance was not possible. She had also been involved with a man whom she both cared for and felt was not meeting her emotional needs. She wanted to end their love relationship, but was unsure how best to do so. She felt generally unhappy and dissatisfied with her life at that time.

Her doctor told her that he could do an expensive hormone investigation, but that it might be more cost effective for her to use the money to take a month's vacation. She decided that this was just what she needed. She gave notice at work and left with a close woman friend for a four-month vacation to Britain. One month after her arrival on British soil, she experienced a menstrual period. She has continued to have normal periods since then, even after returning to Wyoming and resuming work. When she returned, she did not re-enter the relationship from which she had extricated herself. She worked on rotating shifts, and allowed herself to be comfortable with the uncertainty of whether or not she would be able to work fulltime. She discovered that her new perspective was such that she didn't always want to be required to work fulltime. The uncertainty of available hours had become very congruent with her desired lifestyle.

Perhaps genetic or familial factors led to stress which affected Kathryn's menstrual cycle before it affected other organ systems. Perhaps it was symbolic. Certainly if she did not menstruate (meaning she was not ovulating) she did not have to risk the psychic trauma of conceiving a child with a man whom she was trying to leave. This could protect her from the trauma of an undesired but perhaps necessary abortion, should such a pregnancy occur. Perhaps the added stress of work made it possible for her emotional conflicts and incongruencies to be expressed in her body.

Kathryn's doctor made a very important intervention. He gave her the permission she needed to take care of herself. Because her doctor had prescribed a vacation, she could use this prescription as a way to end an undesired relationship and to separate from work. The doctor lent his support as an authority figure to the part of Kathryn that knew what she needed, but had not previously had the strength to convince Kathryn's other parts. In the Senate chambers of Kathryn's inner self, her doctor's oration as a respected foreign dignitary convinced enough of the undecided Senators (parts of Kathryn) to vote in favor of the vacation. Then the bill carried. Without the doctor, it could have been hung up in committee for months, with various factions endlessly debating its pros and cons. Doctors should never underestimate their power in situations such as Kathryn's.

Amenorrhea

It is commonly accepted among many gynecologists that psycho-logical factors can affect the menstrual cycle to the extent of causing amenorrhea such as Kathryn experienced. Unfortunately, most gyneco-logical writers mention anxiety as a frequent "cause" of amenorrhea, but do not carry the concept to the point of training medical students, resident physicians, and other clinicians how to use this knowledge to help their patients.

Many beliefs, attitudes, and conflicts can affect the individual woman's menses. The culprits for one woman may bear no resemblance to the problematic issues for another woman. If we can eliminate the word "cause" from our vocabulary, our words will more accurately describe the true, complex, interactive nature of emotions and phys-iology. One or two single "causes" never exist. Likewise, if we can accept the uniqueness of each individual, we can stop trying to generalize our findings about one woman to fit all women. For example, in the psychoanalyst Therese Benedek's clinical practice, common factors contributing to amenorrhea in young women were anxiety and role conflict related to their feminine sexual identity. This anxiety and fear could be so strong that their ovarian cycle could be completely sup-pressed. Most of these women had no lack of sexual desire, but they strongly believed that menstrual periods were "dirty, painful, and disagreeable" and wished to be rid of this "curse."

Resolving such issues helped these women to regain normal men-strual cycles. Regardless of this, if I adopt the attitude that San Francisco Bay Area women of 1980 who experience amenorrhea and contact me for help have the same underlying emotional conflicts as New York women of 1940 contacting Dr. Benedek, I will have made a serious error. Some may be similar, others will not be. I must discover the problem with each woman *independent* of what I learn from all other women with the same physical symptom. This is why research which attempts to link psychological traits or personality types with specific symptoms frequently fails.[7]

Psychophysiology and Infertility

Rubenstein,[8,9] another psychoanalyst interested in the relationship between biology and sexuality, compared the physiological events that occurred during the ovarian cycle of a group of infertile women to a description of their behavior obtained from notes of psychoanalytic sessions. Among many of the infertile women, a shift in the menstrual cycle had occurred so that ovulation occurred during menstruation, a time when these women did not normally engage in intercourse.

Many clinicians have observed that pregnancy often occurs during intensive medical investigations of infertility.[10-12] Many have theorized that the process of the medical investigation of infertility breaks down possible psychological barriers to conception.[13] The cerebral, thinking, feeling part of the brain has many pathways to send information to the hypothalamus, which regulates ovulation.

Psychoanalytic Views of Infertility

Traditionally, in psychoanalytic terms, the infertile patient has been thought to consciously and obsessively verbalize the wish for a child, but unconsciously to reject pregnancy, childbirth and mother-hood.[12,14-19] This is probably one small subset of the emotions and beliefs which may relate to physiological infertility. Other psychological issues that have emerged in my work with women include (1) a firm conviction on the part of the woman (sometimes conditioned by prior hypnotic suggestion on the part of a health care professional) that her body is incapable of bearing children, or (2) excessive conflict between the woman and her mate. I have worked with several women who have tried to conceive a child in an effort to repair a stressful, unsatisfying marital relationship. Their fallacious thinking was that a baby would create a focus of sharing that would lead the relationship to higher levels of closeness and intimacy. The opposite usually occurs. After ending these unsatisfying relationships, several of these women quickly became pregnant with new partners in better relationships, much to their surprise. For this reason, it is useful for doctors to encourage women to be very careful with birth control when entering a new relationship, even if years have been spent in an old relationship with no contraception or conception. Relationship conflict and stress theo-retically encourage the woman's body to produce antibodies to the man's sperm which would attack the sperm early in their trek to fertilize the egg. Perhaps some part of the body has the wisdom to know that the relationship is not ready to add a child. Many happily married couples separate and divorce after the birth of a child. The first two years of a child's life are perhaps the most stressful years of its parents' lives. In this context, I have worked with infertile couples to improve their relationship. When this work is successful, conception often occurs.

Dr. Earl Warren reported a case similar to those of some of the women I have worked with. In his discussion of amenorrhea at the

1978 Annual Meeting of the American Medical Association, he described a woman who had not ovulated for a considerable time and, surprisingly enough, re-established normal ovulation immediately after she divorced her husband. Dr. Warren began his discussion by stating that the reason she had re-established ovulation was completely unknown to him, jokingly saying that the divorce was probably the cause. It was fascinating to see how quickly he and the other members of the audience perceived the very real relationship between emotions and body processes.

Psychoanalysts have long thought that there are situations in which an organ, such as the uterus, comes to manifest the symptoms of an underlying emotional conflict. When this involves the hypothalamus, pituitary, ovary and/or uterus in such a way as to prevent conception, fertility may result when the underlying conflicts are resolved. Such emotional issues include fear of pregnancy or of the baby taking over the mother's identity. General overall stress can result in chronic non-adaptation which depletes body resources necessary for conception. When the stress is removed, fertility is restored. Some women have a deep fear of sexuality, equating sex with rape. The psychoanalyst, Helene Deutsch, sees this as a female counterpart to male castration fear.[14] Each attempt at intercourse can reinforce this fear and eventually produce frigidity. The woman becomes conditioned to be afraid of anything passing into or out of her vagina. Giving birth, perhaps because of the size of the baby or the associated pain, becomes associated emotionally with fear of self-destruction.

Infertility — Psychological Testing

Psychological testing has failed to differentiate between infertile women and fertile women.[20] An existential model would have predicted such findings. Each person is unique. No necessary relationship exists between two individuals with the same physical symptom. In cases of infertility, 300 factors can contribute toward infertility, and a given individual may experience a contribution of 0.03% to 99% from any individual factor. The reader can quickly see why psychological testing results would be inconsistent or negative. The model from which psychological tests appear valid assumes that each infertile woman would have the same percent contribution from the same psychological factors. This means that conflict about motherhood might be thought to contribute 20% toward infertility for *all* women, or it would not be thought to be a pertinent factor. This is why so little is learned about emotions and infertility. Studies using a battery of tests, such as the MMPI, Rorschach, TAT, and Figure Design test have been more successful.[21] A greater distribution of responses indicating emotional disturbances was found among infertile patients on the Rorschach test compared to fertile women.[22] Infertile men and women have been found to regard themselves as being extremely controlled from the outside as compared to the outlook of fertile persons.[23] (A Rorschach test is a projective test consisting of black-and-white and colored ink blots about which the client tells stories regarding what sense they can make of the pattern.)

Psychological tests, especially non-projective tests, suffer from the limited quantity of their information. Since so many factors can contribute to infertility, an objective psychological test would not be expected to distinguish an infertile group from a fertile group. Rather than discussing causes, it may be better to talk about areas of significance that relate to the illness under consideration. What about physical tissue scarring leading to infertility? A depressed woman with low self-esteem could lead a lifestyle involving frequent intercourse with many partners. Depression may lower her body resistance and when she contracts a predictable case of gonorrhea, it becomes full-blown pelvic inflammatory disease. It would be difficult for a simple, pencil and paper psychological test to predict such events.

Life stress has been related to infertility.[24,25] In one series of tests performed on 500 infertile patients, 24.4% became pregnant after making a significant change in emotional attitude.[26] Many observations have been made of infertile patients who conceive successfully after the first or second consultation with a physician for the purpose of resolving an infertility problem.[27]

In another study from France, 19 patients who had been diagnosed as infertile had been completely evaluated medically and were without pathological findings. These patients then received psychotherapy, and in some cases relaxation therapy also. Seventeen of the 19 patients became pregnant.[20]

Pregnancy After Adoption

The apparent frequency of pregnancies after adoption — sometimes in a matter of days — has been used to support the relationship between the "mind" (whatever that is) and infertility.[28] The relief of tension and anxiety occasioned by adoption has been reported to lead to spontaneous pregnancy and to lead to a disparity in pregnancy rates between patients whose infertility was most likely stressful in origin, and those with organic findings.[29] Another study reported 37 couples who conceived in a brief period around the time that their applications for adoptions were accepted.[30] Others have found no difference between infertile couples who adopt and those who do not.[31-33]

Such conflicting findings are consistent with an existential approach to health and disease, as has been previously discussed. Table 1 shows how emotional and structural factors can work together. The table illustrates how the same physical endpoint of infertility can have different physical body pathways, each with different possible emotional correlates. Mind and body always work together, but in as many ways as are imaginable in their interaction together.

Table 1: Possible reasons for psychophysiological infertility.

Physical Endpoint	Emotional Coorelates
a. Tubal obstruction.	1. Depression and low self-esteem leads to lowered body resistance, more severe infections, tubal scarring, and finally, tubal blockage.
	2. A belief in the fragility of the body leads to lowered body resistance, more severe infection, tubal scarring, and tubal blockage.
b. Hormonal-axis disturbances.	1. Mediated through cerebral-hypothalamic influences from underlying psychological conflict from stress, and desire not to be pregnant.
	2. Mediated through effects upon the hypothalamus from conflict about sexuality.
	3. Mediated through the hypothalamus from other sources of conflict.

Menopause

Menopause has been observed to begin earlier and with more intense reactions among women who have not had children than among women who have.[4] According to the analyst conducting this study (Therese Benedek), the better the personality was integrated and the less the woman's personality was affected by the hormonal changes of the menstrual cycle, the more easily she went through menopause. These women quickly became independent of hormonal stimulation for creating the sexual excitement previously related to the menstrual cycle. Women who were unable to adapt to the monthly premenstrual hormone decline and had premenstrual depression and dysmenorrhea (menstrual cramps) were more apt to suffer from discomforts during menopause. Benedek reported a case of dysmenorrhea in which she isolated the emotional correlates.[4]

> The young married woman had no menstrual difficulties before marriage. She became pregnant easily, and she had two children (age difference between them 1½ years). When her second child was about 1½ years old, she suddenly felt strong, aggressive impulses toward her children. She became panicky; she fought her panic with phobic reactions. Along with this, she developed severe dysmenorrhea. She equated her feeling about menstruation with abortion and felt that she suffered because she did not want more children. Her emotional cycle had shown the fight against motherhood. Thus we assume that, corresponding to and in response to her severe state of anxiety, a regression took place. In this case, we assume that the anxiety and guilty feelings increased the tonus of the autonomic system and at the same time disturbed the balance of the hormonal cycle; the two factors together are responsible for the dysmenorrhea.

Methodology of Mind-Body Studies

The connection between psychosocial events and biological conditions depends upon a psychobiocultural model of medicine which believes there is a link between the social and psychological experience of a person and his or her internal physical state. A good example of this may be provided by studies about risk factors for heart attacks.[34] Recent research has shown that individual heart attack risk factors that were previously thought to be important are not as important as assumed. Rather, specific individual risk factors are important only in interaction with overall lifestyle.[35] The theoretical perspective underlying the search for specific risk factors may be misguided. Chronic disease mortality may be caused at least in part by the depletion of "adaptive energy," primarily through the effects of stress.[36] Even risk factor research needs to move away from the level of specific risk factor studies to a more systematic view of lifestyle and emotions. Heart attacks are not "caused" by cholesterol or by hypertension as isolated variables. The process of becoming susceptible to a heart attack results from a history of psychological and physiological experiences which lead to a breakdown of the entire individual and his or her body.

The search for individual specific risk factors as causes of disease rests on the assumption that humans are like machines, and that the "death" of the machine can be scientifically traced to the malfunction of specific parts. Just as societies are not the same as biological organisms, the life of a human is more than a sum of various bodily functions and parts.

Fallacy of Case-Control, Double-Blind Experimentation

In most scientific circles, many of the studies and case examples I have been discussing are discounted as invalid since they are not double-blind, controlled studies.[37] The case study approach is nevertheless a very valid method of science. Some phenomena are best approached by the case-study method, which utilizes first-person experience to understand the phenomenon under study. Double-blind, controlled studies can never tap the full richness of human experiences.

Current beliefs about what constitutes proper science and proper methodology are hindering our progress. One example is the insistence on double-blind, controlled studies before acceptance of a result, and the non-acceptance or disavowal of any result or area of investigation not amenable to treatment in a double-blind, controlled manner.

In recent years the double-blind, controlled experiment has become a controlled double bind. The method is actually misleading. Other approaches are more valid to understand people rather than to actually believe it is possible to create random groups equal in every respect except for one treatment they are receiving.

The rationale for double-blind, controlled studies comes from the belief that it is possible to control for the individual variation among people by simply assigning every other person to a different group (treatment or non-treatment). This *assumption* has never been *scientifically* proven. The contribution of all factors involved in an illness except one factor cannot be cancelled out by randomization, because of their interactive nature. All factors are related. Such a method denies, from the onset, the uniqueness of each individual. Theoretically, in randomized studies, neither the treaters nor the recipients are aware of which group they are in. This is often very difficult when active substances are being used which produce side effects. It is often easy for clients to discover to which group they belong. For those who misjudge which group they are in, there have been side effects from both placebo and treatment.

The double-blind, controlled study is predicated on the belief that the researcher really can isolate one active ingredient of the healing process, and that it is an active biological substance. The implicit assumption is that other active processes (including the placebo effect) can be controlled or eliminated by a random method of assigning people to arbitrary groups. Such a random assignment is thought to result in a normal distribution of all other factors which may affect healing. If we believe that 300 possible factors exist for any illness, how can all these factors distribute in some even way across 200 people.? When the random distribution hypothesis has been tested in other fields (anthropology, for example) it has not been found to be true.

There have been many reports of drugs or herbs being used to treat conditions and proved satisfactory initially, but are ultimately shown to have a minimal or no effect in double-blind, controlled studies. This has caused considerable consternation and debate regarding the relative merit of these substances. An existential model can explain why such events occur and why the double-blind, controlled study is, in general, inappropriate. The individual variation in response to drugs must be tremendous. This follows from our experientially based understanding of how tremendously different individual people really are. In clinical practice an incredible range of variation exists among individuals and their responses to treatment. Why should this not be true for research? The most crucial issue, however, is that our emphasis upon the importance of the individual — of individual beliefs, attitudes, and emotions; of one's own family and not all families — is entirely outside the philosophy that gave us the double-blind, controlled approach. If everyone is individual, it is impossible to randomize. How can 200 very different, very unique people be randomly assigned to two groups such that the groups are equivalent? The theory is that the healing effects of beliefs and attitudes will be evenly distributed, yet not one has ever measured beliefs and attitudes in double-blind studies to be sure that they are indeed distributed so as to cancel each other. The beliefs behind this approach to science are completely unproven.

Edwards[68] describes a case study from which we can learn a great deal about the individual uniqueness of the factors that contribute to or detract from health. It would be hard for me to conceptualize how to randomize the important factors in this case:

An older, objectively very beautiful single woman is sitting in my office. She is recovering from an operation where she had a silicone implant put in each breast. She is worried because one breast is healing normally but the other is forming scar tissue, growing hard and rock-like. I ask her to talk to her breasts, to ask them why this is occurring, and then give them a voice so they can respond. I trust her body knows the explanation for her symptoms.

She speaks for the breast that is healing well. 'I feel happy, like I look good, better than ever, I feel confident.'

The other breast says in a whisper, 'I feel torn apart, ripped away, invaded, rejected. I'm not good enough for you the way I was. I'm angry and rebelling.'

The woman moves deeper into herself. 'I suppose I've never really felt totally good about how I looked and thought if I could just fix my breasts I would look fine.'

'Do you suppose,' I say gently, 'that your breast wants you to listen more to your own values, to live more from the inside out?'

'Well, I am under a great deal of pressure to look good,' she responds. 'We are very critical of each others' appearance where I work, and in my field you really have to look good, all of the time. You are constantly being judged. I'm tired of the pressure.'

'Ask your breast what it needs to heal correctly,' I say to her. She closes her eyes and goes inside herself, speaking for her breast.

'I will heal correctly if you like yourself better. You need to take some of the pressure off at work and do more what you want to do. Be yourself more there.'

With further psychotherapeutic work, this woman's breast did heal correctly and she was able to feel better about herself and be more herself.

Importance of Psychological Factors on Physical Process

A 7-year-old child with congenital heart disease whose parents were having severe marital difficulties can introduce us to the importance of psychological factors to physical health.[38] The child died, for reasons unclear to the operating surgeons, one month following a second surgical intervention for congenital heart disease (ventricular septal defect and pulmonic stenosis). In a play therapy session preceding the operation, the patient had described a defect "too big" to repair in his doll's heart, and had concluded that the doll "would have to die." The authors hypothesized that "continued parental fighting during the critical post-operative period may have led to Bobby's 'giving up' his futile hope for a more relaxed home atmosphere, as well as life itself."[38]

In Selye's terms, the parents' fighting may have led to the depletion of adaptive energy with the resulting creation of a state of exhaustion in Bobby, thus preventing successful coping with the physical process (in this case, post-surgical congenital heart disease). The ensuing compensation leads to clinical deterioration and death.

Obviously Bobby's parents are not "to blame" for Bobby's death. As has been discussed in Chapter 1, blame needs to be eliminated as a clinical concept. In over-reacting to the problem of blame, the clinician could ignore the powerful benefits that couples' therapy with Bobby's parents could have had for Bobby. If the parents were having relationship problems before Bobby's death, imagine how much these increased after his death. The incidence of divorce is very high after the death of a child. Even if couples' therapy could not have helped Bobby, it might have allowed his parents to cope much better with his death. They could have improved their relationship to the point of being able to find support and solace in each other. For fear of "laying trips on parents," some clinicians neglect to recommend the interventions that could prove most helpful.

Stress can be another important contributor to physical illness. Stress has been intimately related to many disease conditions, including hypertension and heart disease. A necessary level of the "will to live" may exist for healing also. Given Bobby's congenital heart disease, an incredible number of possible scenarios existed, ranging from death to successful life-giving surgery. The inner psychic landscape helps to determine whether external conditions will lead to resolution of illness or to decompensation and death. Psychological stress, just as any stress, can overload the "will to live" mechanism and convert it to the "will to die" mode. The Simontons found that this will to live or commitment to life is very important in successful recovery from cancer, as it must be with other conditions.

Reducers – Augmenters

A neurophysiological phenomenon that improves our understanding of the ways in which emotions and mental processes (neurophysiological processes) affect the body is that of the reduction or augmentation of perception. A brain area has been found in several research efforts which has been termed the Sensoristat. It seems to be located in the general region of the reticular activating system (below the limbic system), and acts as a kind of thermostat to determine the intensity of stimuli reaching the cerebrum (i.e., awareness).

Asineth Petrie, a British psychologist, first discovered this phenomenon in her experiments with patients who had undergone lobotomies. Each of her subjects was presented with a long, tapering wooden bar and three short bars — narrow, medium, and wide. The subject was blindfolded and asked to feel the medium-width short bar (the test bar) with his or her right hand, and the tapered bar with his or her left. He or she was then asked to judge at what point along the tapered bar its width was the same as that of the test bar. Next the wide bar was presented for the subject to rub with the right hand, moving the hand back and forth in time with a metronome (to make the amount of stimulation constant). After two minutes he or she was again asked to judge the width of the test bar by finding the appropriate corresponding width on the tapered bar. Petrie found that patients who had undergone lobotomies usually judged the test bar to be smaller after rubbing the wide bar. She called these people reducers, theorizing that they tended to reduce the magnitude or intensity of a stimulus. Augmenters were those picking a width on the tapering bar which was wider than the test bar, meaning that they had increased in their mind the intensity of the stimulus. She found in other tests done on "normal" people that reducers were able to endure more intense experimental pain, while augmenters had a low pain threshold.

This concept of pain reduction has been used to greatest advantage in the childbirth arena.[39] The woman anticipating labor is faced with the challenge of needing to enter a reducing mode regarding the pain of her labor. To do this she must consciously re-interpret the early pain of labor as inconsequential, knowing that the pain will only become more intense. Paradoxically, if she knows that she does this in order to decrease her experience of pain, it will not be effective because she will not *really believe* what she is telling herself. Clinically this is handled by *telling* the woman hypnotically during childbirth classes (or during individual sessions) that as long as she can debate the question of whether or not she is in labor, she is not in labor. As long as she can question whether or not hard or active labor has begun, then she is, *by definition*, still in *early labor*. She is helped to learn on an emotional level that the pain of hard labor is perhaps 50 times more intense than early labor. She is helped to prepare for an intense, painful labor. While being given indirect suggestions for a short labor, she is helped to prepare for a long labor. She is prepared so that her coping mechanisms

are ready for long, intense pain. Sometimes women with such preparation (when it has been very successful) will call their doctor or midwife
to examine them in order to determine if they are in hard labor yet, and
will be found to be almost fully dilated (i.e., in the late stage of labor).

The hypnotic trance is another example of the reducing mode.
During the hypnotic trance, the client has "tuned out" all other stimuli
and reduced perception to a limited area surrounding the messages of
the hypnotist. Meditation is similarly effective in eliciting a reducing
mode. Since acute schizophrenics are very much in an augmenting
mode, meditation may help schizophrenics by teaching them how to
break the habit of augmenting perception while under stress.

The most technological way of determining if one is in an augmenting or reducing mode is by a computer-averaged evoked potential (EP)
technique. Several flat disc-like electrodes are placed on the person's
scalp. His or her brain waves are amplified and fed into a computer. As
the subject relaxes in a darkened room, a computer program controls
flashes of light so that four random intensities of light ranging from
intense to dim are presented rapidly. Electroencephalographic (EEG)
brain wave voltage is measured, and the information is fed into the
computer every 4/1,000th of a second. After four minutes the computer has gathered enough EEG responses to the light flashes to calculate
four average evoked brain wave potentials, one for each light intensity.
Another computer program measures the size of each of these four
evoked potential waves and mathematically determines if the size
increases from the dimmest light to the brightest (this happens with
augmenters), or begins to fall off as the bright intensities are reached (as
with reducers).

Manic-depressive patients are usually augmenters. Treatment with
lithium tends to make them reducers. A brain "sensoristat" may
control sensory input, such that, when it is functioning properly, the
person is kept optimally alert and interested in his or her environment.
When environmental input is low, a shift toward greater augmenting
can admit sensory stimulation that would ordinarily be unnoticed, and
thereby maintain alertness. At high sensory levels a shift toward reducing can help prevent sensory overload. Acutely psychotic patients,
shortly after hospital admission, tend to be augmenters especially if
they have not been symptomatic long. Those who continue to be
augmenters, perhaps because of difficulty evoking protective inhibitory
mechanisms against sensory inundation, are less likely to recover by
the end of a four-month hospital stay compared to schizophrenics who
become reducers. In fact, those with the strongest reductions from
augmenter to reducer are shown to improve the quickest.

The reducing-augmenting control mechanism may play an important role in many diseases. An augmenter may decompensate toward the somatic expression of stress at much lower levels of stress than a reducer. This may explain the frequent observation that people under great stress often do not become ill until that stress is removed. The large amount of stress may have forced them into a reducing mode in order to cope. When the stress lifts, they return toward an augmenting mode and become ill as their newly achieved augmenting mode admits more stress than their body can successfully cope with. A disease then results.

Such a sensoristat mechanism is necessary because conscious experience is limited in terms of the number of perceptual distinctions the individual can make at any moment in time. Research seems to indicate that conscious experience is limited to about 7 ± 2 "bits" or "chunks" of information at any moment in time.[40] David Gordon[41] presents a useful explanation of this concept.

> A "bit" of information is determined by the level at which a discrimination is made. For example, when learning a seven-digit telephone number for the first time, each of the numbers is a bit/chunk/unit of information. Once the phone number is known, that string of digits becomes one bit/chunk/unit of information. As information is "chunked" at increasingly complex levels, generalization is gained at the expense of resolution (detail) — (for instance, consider the following levels of information: telephone ➜ page of telephone numbers ➜ a line of numbers on the page ➜ the digits on that line.[41]

Without the sensoristat reduction/augmentation mode, there would be no regulation of sensory input and we would be completely overwhelmed with stimuli. The development of belief systems serves to formalize that function by creating rules for what information is to be attended to as "meaningful" and what is to be ignored as "background noise."[42]

Regulation of sensory input seems to be tied to the concept of representational systems. Representational systems represent the sensory modes in which we relate to the world — visual, kinesthetic, auditory, olfactory, and gustatory. Many people have a primary mode which they use more often than the other modes. Development of a primary mode can provide an advantage by giving us the opportunity to develop specialized skills. The more one particular system is developed and used, the more readily subtle perceptual distinctions can be made. The disadvantage is that the person with an overdeveloped representational system may always respond from the standpoint of that system. An example will clarify this. An artist friend has a very well-developed visual system, but has not developed her auditory system. While she draws exquisitely and does beautiful paintings, she sometimes misinterprets what her friends say to her, because she is not in the habit of listening closely and accurately. She does not fare well in arguments, because she does not listen exactly to what the other person says. She also has trouble *listening* to lectures, because she becomes confused at so much talk.

Resolution is the ability of a perceptual system to discriminate detail. Perceptual range is the variety of perceptual experiences discriminated. A "narrow" range might include only the printed word (visual), while a broad range could include music (auditory), art and literature (visual) and gymnastics (kinesthetic). In don Juan's teachings, the way of the "warrior" seems to involve the development of each perceptual system to such a highly evolved level that some new perceptual systems are attained, specifically those of "seeing" and "knowing." This increases the perceptual range to include data from realities usually "tuned out" by common cultural belief systems.

A reduction of perceptual range can create problems, in that the person can feel stuck in experiencing little about how to respond to feelings that arise or to the situations encountered. A person who approaches everything visually may have problems learning to dance, since dance involves all three modalities — seeing the movement, feeling the movement (especially in dance before a mirror to couple the visual line with the kinesthetic feel), and finally, telling one's self how to move and counting the movement or combining it to music (e.g. Rellever ... 2 ... 3 ... 4 ... plier ... 6 ... 7 ... 8 ... Porte-bras ... etc.). Simply asking the person to observe himself or herself before a mirror as he tries to copy a movement can serve to combine the visual and the kinesthetic, as he or she must pay attention to how his or her muscles feel as they create the proper line.

Over-utilization of one sensory system can contribute to a person's ignoring, losing, or not attending to information available only in different sensory systems, thereby potentiating problems. An older couple, married for 29 years, provides a good example of this mismatch of sensory modalities. The wife was planning verbally for a complete separation from the husband. The husband was experiencing significant anxiety because the wife was still physically affectionate after a glass or two of wine (even to the point of sexual intercourse), even though persistent in her discussion of the plan to separate. The husband was predominantly kinesthetic in his processing of this information. He placed much more emphasis on their occasional physical contact than on the message of the wife's words. Therapy consisted of helping the wife to match her behavior with her words in order to help the husband to have a clear sense of her feelings. Once the husband realized in his own terms that the wife really *did* mean to leave, his anxiety reduced and he could begin to cope more successfully.

A final disadvantage of overutilizing one representational system (perceptual system) is that the person doing so may not recognize significant aspects of his internal emotional experience. When an experience occurs for the first time, learning results as the person copes with that experience. This experience (for example, a girl friend leaving) presents itself in all modes (kinesthetic, visual, auditory) and could be perceived dominantly in any of those calibrated ways that determine by previous experience how the client reacts to communication in the present. Even though our client's first two girlfriends had similar facial expressions to the third, the third *meant* what she said as she said it, whereas the first two did not. Can our client "re-calibrate" his communication such that he can truly listen to the girlfriend's statements about what she really means? The problem arises when our client pushes his girlfriend away before she leaves him, even though she's not planning to leave him.

If, as in another example from our patient's past, people praise him and tell him they like him and he later learns that they have said the opposite to others, he may develop a coping style characterized by "Be careful when people tell me they like me; they probably mean the opposite." If he then meets a woman who tells him that she cares for him and that he is valuable and important to her (and she really means it), the visual cues (her facial appearance when she speaks), the kinesthetic clues (how she touches him), can make him draw an erroneous conclusion about her interest and level of concern. Such a conclusion may mitigate against success in love, since his woman-friend will grow tired of constantly being asked to prove (verbally) that she means what she says. To her, the evidence is apparent in her touch and her manner. Our client is not tuned into visual and kinesthetic clues. His dominant mode is auditory and he's learned not to trust what he hears. We must teach him to perceive in a kinesthetic-auditory-visual gestalt (e.g., "I know I can believe her because her touch and her body language matches her words").

Neuroregulators: Neurotransmitters and Neuromodulators[43]

Recent information on neuroregulators may be useful in developing a holistic theory. The intimate connections involved in the body-mind interface could lead us to wonder about the physical regulator substances somehow involved in communication between parts of the brain and the various physical organs.

Neuroregulators may be subdivided into those which convey information between adjacent nerve cells (neurotransmitters) and those which amplify or dampen neuronal activity (neuromodulators). The concept of neuromodulation is still new and incompletely developed. Biological chemicals present in the brain affect communication between nerve cells in a manner similar to the way hormones affect other parts of the body. Two potential types of such neuromodulation are being considered. These modulator substances could be released from neurons, glia, or true secretory cells to amplify or dampen, (that is, to set the tone of local synaptic activity[44]) by altering the effectiveness of the neurotransmitter. A neuromodulator might affect neurotransmitter synthesis, release, receptor interaction, re-uptake, or metabolism. For example, adrenal glucocorticoids (stress hormones) influence the steady state level of tyrosine hydroxylase, an enzyme in the brain affecting the activity of one type of neuron (catecholaminergic). Neuromodulators such as the adrenal stress hormone can be released either within the brain or from other parts of the body, and can act directly on large numbers of neurons at great distances from their site of release.

Although the formation of catecholamines (one type of neurotransmitter and a category of stress hormone) involves only a few enzymes, regulation of the formation is immensely complicated. Some of the steps in the formation of catecholamine are affected by feedback inhibition, and others are influenced by endogenous inhibitors or activators. The rate-limiting (slowest) first step involving tyrosine hydroxylase can respond both to stress and to neuronal activation. With stress over a period of hours, an increase occurs in the number of enzyme molecules, thereby enhancing the amount of catecholamines which can be formed. With such short-term activation, a several-fold increase in activity of the enzyme can occur, with no concomitant change in the enzyme molecule itself.

Individual neuroregulators respond differently to stress. Such individual differences in the stress response may be associated with differences in the degree to which a rate-limiting step can be controlled by activation or dampening.

It two rats are given aversive stimuli so that they will fight one another, the resultant neurochemical changes are quite different from those occurring if similar animals are given the same amount of aversive stimuli in isolation. Thus, profound neurochemical differences separate the effects of escapable versus inescapable aversive stimuli.

Certain stresses, such as exposure to aversive stimuli, seem to alter the re-uptake mechanism for the neurotransmitter norepinephrine, a finding that suggests changes in the function of neuroregulators at the synapse, with potential alterations in responsivity of receptors during stress. A behaviorally induced change from chronic stress or lifestyle factors could facilitate long-lasting changes in the brain. Perhaps the change process readjusts behavior at the synapse as the individual's behavior in the world changes.

Do genetic factors influence some aspects of neuroregulators? The levels of the catecholamine synthesizing enzymes in mouse adrenal glands and brain may be under some degree of genetic control. Genetic factors may also affect other critical neuroregulatory processes such as release, metabolism, re-uptake, and receptor interaction. High levels of certain forms of aggression may be inherited in mice. These more aggressive behaviors correlate with higher levels of adrenal catecholamine synthesizing enzymes and high concentrations of brain cyclic AMP. Do these mice learn to be aggressive from their environment — family, mother, playmate? If so, are these changes induced rather than inherited?

Endogenous Opioids as Neuroregulators

Thus far, two independent endorphin (endogenous opioid) pathways have been delineated in the brain — a beta endorphin system with a single cell group in the hypothalamus sending long axons to innervate midbrain and limbic structures, and an enkephalin system with multiple cell groups throughout the spinal cord and brain stem, having relatively short axons. (Endogenous opioid refers to the property of these chemicals to mirror morphine in some respects. Endogenous means "made by the body.")

The endorphins are found in high concentrations in brain areas involved with pain transmission, respiration, motor activity, endocrine control, and mood. Connections between the endorphins and ACTH (a stress hormone) have been suggested from observed increases in the concentration of endorphin in blood and brain during stress paralleling increases in pain tolerance. If they are a part of the basic system modulating responsivity to pain and stress, endorphins may play critical roles in behavioral and emotional responses to the environment. Endorphins are known to decrease pain, acting upon the same brain cells in a similar manner to morphine. Narcotic antagonists decrease pain tolerance of volunteers especially resistant to pain; these volunteers also tend to become more augmenting of all stimuli (in the reducer-augmenter pole discussed previously).

Techniques of releasing endorphins may also induce the reducing mode of stimuli processing, to help coping abilities in an over-stressed individual and contribute to an increased capability for problem resolution.

Other Aromatic amines such as the phenolics[45] have been identified in brain tissue and may also serve as neuroregulators. Cerebral concentrations are less than early discovered neurotransmitters such as catecholamine and hydroxytryptamine. In common with other neurotransmitters these arylalkylamines are distributed within the brain in a heterogeneous fashion, are present in a synaptosomal fraction after homogenization, possess a high turnover or clearance rate after their intracerebral introduction, and are synthesized in-vivo by dehydroxylation of catecholic precursors and by hydroxylation of beta-phenylethylamine as well as by decarboxylation of their parent amino acids. Most of these noncatecholic amines are behaviorally active, are potent pharmacological agents, cross the blood-brain-barrier with ease, can release and/or replace the classical neurotransmitters, and mimic the stereotypes of amphetamine. They have been variously shown or claimed to be excreted abnormally in the urine of patients with migraine, Parkinsonism, schizophrenia, and depression. They are all synthesized in one way or another from the essential amino acids, phenylalamine and tryptophan.

Synesthesia

David Gordon[41] has developed important neurophysiological principles into a clinical strategy in the concepts of sub-modalities and synesthesia. Each representational (sensory and encoding system) system discriminates among stimuli according to specific submodalities. For four of these systems, the submodalities as defined by Gordon are:

Vision	Audition	Kinesthesis	Olfaction
Color	Pitch	Temperature	Frangrance
Brightness	Loudness	Pressure	Concentration
Saturation	Timbre	Texture	Essence
Shape	Patterning	Form	—
Location	Location	Location	Location

These submodalities have been established to be experimentally equivalent, moving horizontally, across the table. This is particularly true for the relationships between color and pitch,[46] color and temperature,[46,47] brightness and loudness,[48] and location[49] across all four modalities. People consistently match more intense sounds and brighter lights to increasing pressure. Colors at the lower or red end of the spectrum are perceived as warm, while those tending toward the ultraviolet (blue) end of the spectrum are perceived as cooler. The red end of the spectrum is usually perceived as being associated with lower auditory tones and the blue end with higher pitched tones.[48,50-53] This fits our everyday experience. Buttons connected with heat are usually red, while "quiet" blue colors may adorn an expensive hotel lobby.

Gordon states that "a 'cross-over' occurs when a submodality in one class becomes associated with a submodality in another class." Examples include a *tight* stomach becoming associated with a *loud* noise or a *high-pitched* tone with a *bright* light. "Those pairs of equivalent and cross-over submodality distinctions which demonstrate such experiential correspondence" are grouped together in what Gordon calls patterns of *synesthesia*. "Synesthesia refers to the ability of sensory discriminations originating in one sense modality to evoke patterned perceptual experiences in another sense modality." Knowledge of such patterns can assist in therapy by helping the client to gain access to personal experience in a new and different way. Gordon gives an example of how this can be done using a technique he calls *Intradimensional shifts*.[41]

> Deborah, who was thoroughly acquainted with submodality strategies, had as a client a young man, Steve, whose problem was that he felt lonely and unwanted when alone. Deborah had Steve specify exactly how he knew he was "lonely and unwanted" by having him check through his representational systems while recounting his last such experience. The submodality distinctions that appeared were that he saw himself 'standing, bent over a little, arms hugging his chest, and not moving at all.' His picture was in 'black and white,' and in it he looked and felt 'cold.' He also felt 'empty' in his stomach. As a check, the counselor took Steve back, using his 'empty' stomach feeling, to a number of other experiences, all of which turned out to be isomorphic. She then had him carefully watch his picture of himself and pay attention to his feelings, then instructed him to (at her signal) turn the picture into a *color picture*. As soon as he added color

to his picture his image of himself immediately began spinning and dancing. Steven's body feeling also changed, and he realized that he had 'a million things to do,' and that those times when he was alone were his golden opportunity to do any of the things he enjoyed doing. For a short while afterward, whenever he felt unwanted and lonely, he would suddenly realize that he was seeing that old black-and-white picture of himself. By changing it back to color he immediately felt better and ready to do something. Soon the colorful change he had made generalized sufficiently so that he no longer felt lonely or unwanted, unless he specifically wanted to.

[In this account] Deborah has Steve *specify* his 'problem' in terms of submodalities, then uses the kinesthetic component of his experience as a lead into past experiences. That all of those experiences were isomorphic with his 'problem' was assurance that Steve's constellation of submodality distinctions was an accurate representation of his experience.

Deborah then selected the submodality in which to make the change (color), effecting the transformation by having Steve monitor the rest of his modalities while he changed the picture of himself from 'black-and-white' to 'color.' The result was that he was put in touch with new personal choices regarding his emotion/behavior. Over the following days this experience generalized as he generated new behavioral experiences for himself and as he regenerated past experiences.

Environmental Stress
and Disease: Hypertension[54]

Henry and colleagues have been using complex population cages stocked with CDA mice to study the relationship among psychosocial interaction, aversive behavioral conditioning, and high blood pressure. Animals are raised together from birth with minimal emotional arousal, despite social interaction. Experimental group animals consist of adult males and females isolated since weaning, and placed together in an environment conducive to sustained competition for territory. Repeated confrontations among animals lead to repeated arousal of the sympathetic adrenal medullary gland, and of pituitary-adrenocortical neuroendocrine response patterns. The experimental group, which is not spontaneously hypertensive, develops sustained elevations of blood pressure. Significant aortic arteriosclerosis,[55] heart disease and kidney failure result. These adverse physiological changes (including high blood pressure) persist, even when the animals are returned to isolation.

Arousal of the sympathetic "fight or flight" reaction is triggered by the urge to protect access to valued goals (territory) and is dependent on the integrity of the amygdalar nuclear complex in the brain. Perception of the loss of valued goals (territory, money, status), dropping status, and social role expectancies leads to hippocampal arousal. The withdrawn, depressive, "hopeless" response that ensues stimulates the pituitary adrenocortical system.[56] When two rats fight, an exposure to foot shock will not induce as severe an injury as it would if the shock occurred when they were isolated. Aggression itself may serve as relevant feedback such that the animal perceives itself as achieving its expectations.

The withdrawn, depressive stance increases the intensity of the hypothalamo-adreno-cortical response which leads to stomach ulceration. The hypothalamo-pituitary-adrenal dysfunction that results in elevated cortisol that occurs in primary depressive illness is not found in secondary depression. Elevation of plasma cortisol is a sign of increased functioning of the adrenal gland, a biological sign of stress. Many experts believe that the stimulus for primary depression is the failure to achieve relevant feedback regarding one's position in the environment in an immediate manner. When we can control our environment we do not feel as stressed. Biological changes occur more readily when we are stressed and cannot control our environment. Rhesus monkeys who can control high intensity noise show no significant elevation of their plasma cortisol, but those exposed to the noise without any possibility or expectation of being able to turn it off showed significant diminuation of social contact and a marked elevation of cortisol.

Each of us has had experiences with stress and control. Recently I was called for an IRS audit. Mistakes were being made by the IRS. My file was lost many times, transferred to the wrong office, and audited without my being invited. When I was paying an accountant to handle the case, although I was less involved, I felt more stressed, because I felt that I had no control. When I took over the job from the accountant, I worked harder and had more direct contact with the IRS, but felt less stress because I was more in control *and received more direct relevant feedback* about what was going on. Dealing with IRS auditors in the flesh, though stressful, was less stressful than receiving vague messages from my accountant. (And ultimately more quickly gratifying as I had three "no change" years.) Each reader may discover similar personal experiences regarding feedback, control, and stress.

Animals that are deprived of using a control method that they have successfully learned respond to a now uncontrollable stimulus with aggression and an even greater biological stress response. Such data have led to theorizing that the hippocamus and the remainder of the brain related to the stress hormone ACTH plays a role in depression among people presently coping with stress by withdrawal without hope of success. Previously discussed learned helplessness is obviously very similar. Depression results when the only perceived choice is to withdraw. A very different physiological process occurs among rats responding aggressively to stress (the amygdalar fight-flight arousal response). Their expectations of success had been so recently denied that these rats still continued to expect to regain control over the noxious aspects of their environment.

The limbic system response patterns of a challenged, dominant animal seem to differ from those of a defeated animal who never expects to regain control. When formerly isolated mice are placed together, a sympathetic adrenal-medullary, "fight versus flight" response begins, highly activating the renin-angiotensin-catecholamine system. As these mice age in a socially abrasive situation, a gradual behavioral shift occurs in their behavior, from aggression toward avoidance. The neuroendocrine changes correlated with this shift are very similar to those changes found in the human condition of low-renin essential hypertension.

Changing from actively aggressive behavior in the competition for territory and position to an avoidance mode of passive subordination or learned helplessness, could predispose in part to low-renin hypertension. Such behavioral shifts can occur as readily in Western society as in mice cages. From the age of 20 to 40, active struggles usually occur for a place in life, a position, a sense of territory, similar to the adolescent struggling for a sense of identity within the self. When a position is reached, if it is unfulfilling (even if positions on the social hierarchy are open to advancement) or if the sense of territory is inadequate ("There is not enough room for me to be me"), or if there is no relevant feedback to anchor oneself in the world, a learned helplessness position can develop with hypertension trailing in its wake.

Stress and Hypertension

Recently, increased attention has been paid to the roles of stress and psychological factors as sources of risk in the development of hypertension and coronary heart disease.[57] Individual coping style (either internally through psychophysical manifestations, or externally through interpersonal networks) are also being recognized as important factors.

Smoking and drinking are both common "coping mechanisms" and stress or tension relievers.[58] Hypertension may be an internal coping behavior, while drinking and smoking, as well as illicit drug behavior, are external behavioral coping mechanisms.[58,59]

A.F. Brunswick and P. Collette studied eleven indicators of psychological well-being in a group of urban black adolescent males, including feelings of depression, worry/anxiety, loneliness and isolation, direct self-report of a "nervous/emotional problem" and physician-report of the presence of a nervous or emotional problem in association with high blood pressure.[60]

Adolescents with two or three high blood pressure readings on three separate tests scored in the "less well" direction relative to the normals in seven of eleven items. The consistency of this finding supported the concept of depression being more prevalent among adolescents with consistently elevated blood pressures.

Two groupings of the studied variables considered statistically significant accounted separately for about 20% of the variance of high blood pressure in black males. This means that these two factors could predict 40% of the changes in blood pressure, leaving all other factors (including those not measured or thought about) to account for the remaining 60% of the changes in blood pressure. The first factor represented a general psychophysical health factor. Physician-rated obesity and the boy's own subjective rating of his overall general health were the strongest components of this factor. This was followed closely by two subjective indicators of emotional well-being, more specifically of depressed mood. These were the ratings of whether or not this was the "best time in my life" and what "sort of time [the youth tested] was having," ranging from very good, through pretty good, to not good. This psychophysical health factor discriminated most strongly those with "any high" blood pressure (labile and consistently high) from those with "no high" blood pressure readings.

Evidence of Neural Control of the Adrenal Cortex

Neurophysiologically, higher brain centers modify the body's response to stress. Early and recent research has suggested that the hormone norepinephrine is somewhat specific for anger, and the hormone epinephrine somewhat specific for fear. When the fight response is aroused, the resulting behavior suggests anger more so than fear. A concomitant increase in norepinephrine levels occurs. Increases in epinepherine are generally associated with arousal situations and especially with the threat of loss. Such threats can include loss of social status and access to territory, including the good things that animals and humans work to get (primary reinforcers) and the others to whom animals and humans become attached (love).

People can create fantasies of danger and/or stress to which their adrenal gland responds. There may be no "real" danger or stress (meaning apparent to an outside observer). Yet this "imagined" stress is as real to the adrenal gland as the "real" thing. The evidence for direct nervous connections from cerebrum to adrenal gland includes observations that the production of one important adrenal stress hormone, cyclic AMP (adenosine 3′, 5′-monophosphate) is reduced following cutting of the nerves in the splanchnic plexus, the source of most of the autonomic nervous fibers to the abdomen. In studies of important adrenal (cortical) enzymes regulating the production of stress-related hormones, it has been found that there is neural control of the production of cortico-steroid hormones, so important in stress states, by the autonomic nervous system. These enzymes include both PNMT (phenylethanolamine N-methyltransferase) and dopamine-beta-hydroxylase, another enzyme which produces stress hormones. The production of steroid hormones and the delivery of glucocorticoid hormones to the adrenal medulla could depend upon the action of a neural receptor at the synapse of the nervous system upon the adrenal cells which allows ACTH to regulate corticoid synthesis. Active innervation of the adrenal cortex by the autonomic nervous system to modify control by ACTH of steroid synthesis may provide a mechanism by which other diseases can develop, especially with a chronic change in nervous activity. Low-renin essential hypertension may be one of many such diseases.

Mind and Breathing

Bioenergetic therapists have emphasized the importance of breathing and breathing patterns in maintaining chronic muscular tension and helping the body become susceptible to disease. There is ample evidence that the parts of the nervous system that control breathing are intimately connected to other parts of the brain that affect processes such as blood pressure. The lateral part of the nucleus tractus solitarius (a collection of cell bodies in the brain, also referred to as the nucleus parasolitarius) has been indicated as the place where the cell bodies of nerve fibers from the lungs reside. Neuron fibers from this nucleus travel upward to the cerebral cortex to give it the information necessary to affect respiratory function. The nuclei of nerves going to the lungs to affect breathing travel from higher brain levels to reside in the nucleus parasolitarius. Breathing and breathing exercises are an important aspect of psychotherapy, especially of relaxation training, anxiety reduction, and bioenergetics. It is interesting to speculate about the connection of the various parts of the nucleus tractus solitarius to each other. Another part of the nucleus has a controlling function over the baroreceptors which control blood pressure. There may also be connections between these two parts, such that alterations of breathing patterns may alter baroreceptor functioning and hence, blood pressure. This could be mediated through inhibitory neurons which also receive input from the cerebral cortex through direct electrophysiological connections, or through neuroregulators. This would also imply that chronic abnormal breathing patterns could help to create a hypertensive state, and that altering these patterns might be a part of the therapy for hypertension. Axons from the perikarya (cell bodies) of the nucleus tractus solitarius (NTS) can be followed into different parts of the reticular formation, for example, to the nucleus ambiguus. From the reticular formation these projections can rise to the cerebral cortex or to the limbic system, especially the hypothalamus. Through these projections, breathing could affect emotion (which is mediated by the limbic system) or hormone production (mediated through the hypothalamus).

Many potential ways exist by which stresses upon the organism produce hormonal and physiological changes. Assume that a person becomes acutely angry. A variety of physiological-hormonal mechanisms are activated through nerve connections from the central nervous system. These include the amygdalar fight-flight response, inducement of cortisol production, etc. Blood pressure rises. The heart beats more rapidly. Breathing changes. The cerebral cortex monitors all these changes through incoming nerve connections. A complex feedback-activation loop exists. If the person does not discharge the anger and maintains burning resentment, physiological effects occur. Baroreceptor tone may be modified to keep blood pressure high. A state of continued stress may be maintained by the adrenal glands. Just changing breathing patterns could begin a change in the other system by decreasing the intensity of nerve firing in one part of the brain (nucleus tractus solitarius) and thereby helping other brain areas to relax.

Obstetrical Studies and Stress

Stress results in increased production and excretion of catecholamine hormones. Environmental stress and catecholamines adversely affect labor. Among mice, environmental stess is associated with higher proportions of pup mortality at birth. Both alpha and beta adrenergic receptor sites are present in the blood vessels of the uterus, to respond to catecholamines.[61-65] Stress which increases catecholamine production in the mother (fight or flight response) decreases the flow of blood to the uterus and therefore to the baby. This causes the oxygen level of the baby's blood to fall, and can chronically stress the baby over time. A baby who has used its adaptive energy to cope with stress prior to labor may not be able to tolerate the added stress of labor. When this occurs, the normal stress of labor may transgress into distress.

No significant change occurs in the mother's blood pressure with increased doses of norepinephrine until a decrease in uterine arterial blood flow of greater than 30-40% occurs.[63,64] Stress can adversely affect the baby before the occurrence of any untoward outward effects upon the mother herself.

Among pregnant ewes between 85 and 140 days of gestation, a 39% decrease in uterine blood flow occurred during systemic infusions of epinephrine ranging from 0.2 to 0.4 micrograms per minute per kilogram.[64] The addition of either epinephrine or norepinephrine to the blood in concentrations found in commonly occurring stress states can, then, produce significant vasoconstriction in the uterine vascular bed, thereby reducing blood flow and oxygen distribution to the baby.[65]

The blood supply to the kidney is also sensitive to the vaso-constricting effects of norepinephrine.[66] Norepinephrine causes the blood vessels to become very small in size (vasoconstricted) and there-fore not deliver as much needed blood and oxygen to the kidneys. Thus, stress which produces more norepinephrine can also have nega-tive consequences for the kidneys. Chronic tightening of the blood ves-sels in the kidneys can decrease blood flow and thereby contribute to creating high blood pressure through altered hormonal response in the kidney. Kidney disease could also result from damage to the very sensitive blood filtering apparatus (the glomerulae) in the kidney from lack of blood and oxygen. Infusions of norepinephrine mimicking physiological stress causes reductions also in the amount of blood flowing to the thyroid gland.[67] Such a chronic reduction of blood flow could impair thyroid function.

Psychophysiology of Cancer

Caroline Bedell Thomas, a Johns Hopkins researcher, provides an example of the empirical basis of the mind-body connection through her cancer research. She found a correlation between how close a child is to his or her parents and the type of relationship he or she has with them to the likelihood of developing cancer many years later. 1,337 Johns Hopkins Medical School students representing the classes of 1948 to 1964 were studied. 1,185 were white males. One hundred seventy-nine of these white male students developed significant disease in one of five major categories: hypertension, coronary heart disease, mental illness, cancer, or suicide. Students who had low scores on a close-to-parent scale developed more cancer and more mental illness, and had a higher incidence of suicide than those who had higher scores. Those with higher closeness-to-parent scores were more likely to develop hypertension and coronary occlusion. The differences held true regardless of whether the interaction measured was sibling to parent, parent to sibling, or parent to parent. Dr. Thomas felt her findings were consistent with the "three-hit" theory of carcinogenesis, in which it is postulated that to develop cancer in the absence of a clear-cut, relatively biological insult, there must exist a genetic predisposition to the disease, adverse emotional factors (of which closeness to family could be important), and a breakdown of socio-biologically integrated systems.

Summary

From this preliminary discussion, the reader may quickly discover that laboratory and statistical evidence for the mind-body approach is rapidly accumulating. This progress is limited only by the sophistication of both our thinking and our methods.

REFERENCES AND NOTES

[1] Fenichel, O. *The Psychoanalytic Theory of Neurosis.* New York: W. W. Norton & Co., Inc., 1945.

[2] Pratt, J.P. Sex functions in man. in Allen, E. (ed.) *Sex and Internal Secretions,* 2nd Edition. Baltimore: The Williams & Wilkins Co., 1939.

[3] Estrogen is a "female hormone" produced by the ovary that increases from the cessation of menstrual bleeding until ovulation occurs. It prepares the lining of the uterus to be able to accept an egg. Estrogen also aids in the preparation of the egg for release from the ovary.

[4] Benedek, T. and Rubenstein, B.B. The sexual cycle in women. *Psychosom. Med. Monograph,* Vol. 3, Nos. 1 & 2. Washington, D.C.: National Research Council, 1942, Benedek, T. Sexual functions and their disturbances. in Alexander, F. *Psychosomatic Medicine.* New York: W.W. Norton & Co., Inc., 1950.

[5] Unless conception had occurred.

[6] The psychodynamic concomitants of lactation have been found to be similar to those of the progesterone phase of the cycle.

[7] For examples of attempts to link personality traits with specific symptoms see Anestasia, A. *Psychological Testing.* London, McMillan Co., 1968; McAndrew, C. The differentiation of male alcoholic outpatients from non-alcoholic psychiatric outpatients by means of the MMPI. *Q.J. Stud. Alcohol* 26: 238-246, 1965; Hedberg, A.G., Campbell, L., Weeks, S., et al. MMPI (mini-multi) to predict alcolics' response to a behavioral treatment program. *J. Clin. Psychol.* 31:271-274, 1975.

[8] Rubenstein, B.B. Functional Sterility in Women. *Ohio State M.J.* 35:1066, 1939.

[9] Rubenstein, B.B. The vaginal smear-basal body temperature technique and its application to the study of functional sterility in women. *Endocrinology.* 27:843, 1940.

[10] Pennington, G.W. and Atlay, R.D. Some surprising results in the investigation and treatment of the infertile woman. . *Obstet. Gynecol. Brit. Commonw.* 79:651, 1972.

[11] Benedek, T., Ham, G.C., Robbin, R.P. et al. Some emotional factors and infertility. *Psychosomatic Medicine,* 14:484, 1953.

[12] Ford, E.S., Forman, I., Wilson, .R., et al, A psychosomatic approach to the study of infertility, *Fertil. Steril.,* 4:456, 1953.

[13] Some of the procedures used during infertility work-ups are obnoxious enough that anticipation of these tests could provide some motivation to conceive.

[14] Deutsch, H. *The Psychology of Women.* New York: Bantam Books Edition, 1972.

[15] Rubenstein, B.B. An emotional factor in infertility. *Fertil. Steril.,* 2:80, 1951.

[16] Rothman, D., Caplan, A.H., and Nettles, E. Psychosomatic infertility. *Am J. Obstet. Gynecol.* 8:373, 1962.

[17] Fischer, K. Psychogenic aspects of sterility. *Fertil. Steril.* 4:466, 1953.

[18] Marsh, E.M. and Vollmer, A.M. Possible psychogenic aspects of infertility. *Fertil. Steril.* 2:70, 1951.

[19] Denber, H.C.B. and Roland, N. Effect of Tybamate on psychosomatic symptoms in a group of infertility patients. *Fertil. Steril.* 20:373, 1969.

[20] Denber, H.C.B. Psychological factors and infertility. *J. Reprod. Med.* 2:285, 1969; Karahasanoglu, A., Barglow, P., Growe G. Psychological aspects of infertility. *J. Reprod. Med.* 9:241, 1972; Reboul, J. Sterilites "Psychogenes." *Presse Med.* 4:743, 1975.

[21] Eisner, B.G. Some psychological differences between fertile and infertile women. *J. Clin. Psychol.* 19:391, 1963.

[22] Platt, J., Fischer, I., and Silver, M.J. Infertile couples: Personality traits and self-ideal concept discrepancies. *Fertil. Steril.* 24.972, 1973.

[23] Sandler, B. Emotional stress and infertility. *J. Psychosom. Res.* 12:51, 1968.

[24] Sandler, B.L. Infertility of emotional origin. *J. Obstet. Gynecol. Br. Commonw.* 68:809, 1961.

[25] Stone, A. and Ward, M.E. Factors responsible for pregnancy in 500 infertility cases. *Fertil. Steril.* 7:1, 1956.

[26] deWatteville, H. Psychologic factors in the treatment of sterility. *Fertil. Steril.* 8:12, 1957.

[27] Orr, D.W. Pregnancy following the decision to adopt. *Psychosom. Med.* 3:441, 1941.

[28] Sandler, B. Conception after adoption: A comparison of conception rates. *Fertil. Steril.* 16:313, 1965.

[29] Andrews, R.G. Adoption and the resolution of infertility. *Fertil. Steril.* 21:73, 1970.

[30] Weir, W.C. and Weir, D.R. Adoption and subsequent conceptions. *Fertil. Steril.* 17:283, 1966.

[31] Tyler, E.T., Bonapart, J., and Grant, J. Occurrence of pregnancy following adoption. *Fertil. Steril.* 11:581, 1960.

[32] Banks, A.L., Rutherford, R.N. and Coburn, W.A. Fertility following adoption. *Fertil Steril.* 12:438, 1961.

[33] Banks, A.L. Does adoption affect infertility? *Internat. J. Fertil.* 7:23, 1962.

[34] Johnson, A. Sex differentials in coronary heart disease: The explanatory role of primary risk factors. *Journal of Health and Social Behavior.* 18 (March): 46-53, 1977.

[35] Intersociety Commission for Heart Disease Resources. Primary prevention of the atherosclerotic diseases. *Circulation.* 42:155-195, 1970.

[36] Selye, H. *The Stress of Life.* New York: McGraw-Hill, 1956.

[37] A double blind, controlled study is one in which individuals are randomly assigned to treatment groups, for example, and no one knows (investigator or patient) who is getting what treatment.

[38] Cline, F.W. and Rothenberg, M.B. Preparation of a child for major surgery. *J. Am. Acad. Child Psychiat.* 13:78, 1974.

[39] For more information on paradoxical pain reduction through lowering the pain sensoristat by preparing the woman to expect pain, see Peterson, G. *Birthing Normally: A personal growth approach to childbirth.* Berkeley, Cal.: Mindbody Press, 1981.

[40] Miller, G.A. The magical number seven, plus or minus two: Some limits on our capacity for processing information. *Psychol. Rev.* 63:81-97, 1956.

[41] Gordon, D. *Therapeutic Metaphors.* Cupertino, CA: Meta Publications, p 150, 1978.

[42] Karl Pribam has written about the limitations on the ability of each of us to be aware of our perceptions. Interestingly, our ability to encode and store data of experience as long-term memory far exceeds our ability to be aware of that information being processed. This is one of the helpful aspects of hypnosis and visualization — the memory can be recalled and experienced whereas, the first time it was experienced it may not have reached awareness. For more information, see Pribam, K. *Language of the Brain.* Englewood Cliffs, N.J.: Prentice-Hall, 1971.

[43] Much of my discussion of neuroregulators was learned at seminars and conference presentations given by members of Jack Barchas' research group in the Department of Psychiatry at Stanford University. Interested readers can locate and follow Dr. Barchas' work for the newest information on neuroregulators. Studies mentioned in this section were performed by his group.

[44] Synapses are the connectors between neurons. Neurotransmitters cross the synapse to activate other neurons. Neurotransmitters are manufactured in the cell of the neuron wishing to communicate with another neuron. An electrical impulse flowing down the neuron facilitates the release of the neurotransmitter into the space between neurons. Then the neurotransmitter must reach a receptor on the neuron with whom communication is desired. Enzymes break down the neurotransmitter to clear the way for further communication much as snow plows clear mountain roads of snow. The neuron initiating communication may also have a reuptake mechanism to recover unused neurotransmitter once communication has been successful. Neurotransmitter release, successful activation of another neuron, and reuptake all involve delicate, graceful, and subtle events on the level of the cell membrane just as successful ballet requires movements of fine muscles

quickly forgotten by all but anatomists. The synaptic area resembles a way station for the communication process of the Pony Express. A rider races into the station, quickly refreshes himself and grabs a fresh horse to race out again. Then the tired horse is cared for. Through several such linkages the continent of the body is traversed.

[45] The various isomers of tyramine and its derivatives are included as phenolics (phenylalkyl, beta-phenylethylamine and its derivatives and indolylalkylamines such as tryptamine).

[46] London, I.D. Research on sensory interaction in the Soviet Union. *Psychol. Bull.* 51:531-568, 1954.

[47] Podolsky, E. *The Doctor Prescribes Colors.* New York: National Library Press, 1938.

[48] Stevens, J. Marks, L. Cross-modality matching of brightness and loudness. *Proc. Natl. Acad. Sci.* 54(2): 407-411, 1965.

[49] Held, R. and Freedman, S. Plasticity in human sensory motor control. *Science* 142:3591, 1963.

[50] Pedley, P. and Harper, R. Pitch and the vertical location of sound. *Amer. J. Physiol.* 72:447-449, 1959.

[51] Stevens, J.C. and Rubin, L. Psychophysical scales of apparent heaviness and the size-weight illusion. *Perception and Psychophysics* 8(4): 225-230, 1970.

[52] Payne, M. Apparent weight as a function of color. *Amer. J. Psychol.* 71:724-730, 1970.

[53] Payne, M. Apparent weight as a function of hue. *Amer. J. of Psychol.* 74:104-105, 1971.

[54] Interested readers may find the references for studies described in this section by locating and following the work of Dr. Henry and his colleagues.

[55] Arteriosclerosis is commonly known as hardening of the arteries and is a precursor of heart attacks and strokes.

[56] The pituitary adrenocortical mechanisms seem to be able to function independently of the amygdala and the limbic system in terms of active avoidance of shock or noxious stimuli. This implies that there is independence of the pituitary adrenal axis of hormones from the amygdalar complex, which leads to complex fighting responses.

[57] Glass, D.C. Stress, behavior patterns and coronary disease. *Am. Sci.* 64 (Mar/Apr): 177-187, 1977.

[58] Selye, H. Some Introductory remarks. In. Dunn, Jr., E.L. (ed.) *Smoking and Behavior: Motives and Incentives.* Washington, D.C.: Winston and Sons, 1973.

[59] Brunswick, A. Health and drug behavior: Preliminary findings from a study of urban black adolescents. *Addict. Dis.* 3(2): 197-214, 1977.

[60] Brunswick, A.F. and Collette, P. Psycho-physical correlates of elevated blood pressure: A study of urban black adolescents. *Journal of Human Stress.* 3(4): 19-31, 1977.

[61] Greiss, F.C., Jr. The uterine vascular bed: Effect of adrenergic stimulation. *Obstet. Gynecol.* 21:295, 1963.

[62] Greiss, F.C., Jr. Differential reactivity of the myoendometrial and placental vasculatures: Adrenergic responses. *Am. J. Obstet. Gynecol.* 112:20, 1972.

[63] Ladner, C., Brinkman, C.R., Weston, P. et al. Dynamics of uterine circulation in pregnant and nonpregnant sheep. *Am. J. Physiol.* 218:251, 1970.

[64] Rosenfeld, C.R. and West, J. Circulatory response to systemic infusion of norepinephrine in the pregnant ewe. *Am. J. Obstet. Gynecol.* 127(4): 376-383, 1977.

[65] Rosenfeld, C.R., Barton, M.D. and Meschia, G. Effects of epinephrine on distribution of blood flow in the pregnant ewe. *Am. J. Obstet. Gynecol.* 124:156, 1976.

[66] Gombos, E.A., Hulet, W.H., Bopp, P., et al. Reactivity of renal and systemic circulations to vasoconstrictor agents in normotensive and hypertensive subjects. *J. Clin. Invest.* 41:203, 1962.

[67] Hoffbrand, B.I. and Forsith, R.P. Regional blood flow changes during norepinephrine, tyramine and methoxamine infusion in the unanesthetized rhesus monkey. *J. Pharmacol. Exp. Ther.* 184:656, 1973.

[68] Edwards, M.E. Clinical philosophy and the meaning of physical symptoms. Paper presented at P.S.I. Graduate School of Professional Psychology, Phenomonology Symposium. Ms. Edwards is in private practice in Los Gatos, California.

Chapter Eight

Visualization

Visualization and mental imagery techniques can be very useful in general psychotherapy and in psychophysiological psychotherapy. Imagery techniques can be used for a variety of clinical goals, including reducing anxiety, bypassing resistance, preventing obsessive defenses from thwarting therapy, and changing physical illness. Imagery techniques can be very helpful with psychotic clients as well as with clients with many other problems. Several brief examples illustrate the use of visualization:

Penny was a 32 year old woman, 7 months pregnant with her first child. Penny had a history of chronic isolation and difficulty in relating to other people. She had been hospitalized once in the past for a psychotic episode. She tended toward strong paranoia, heard voices, and manifested delusional thinking. At times she was convinced that her dog had turned against her. She felt that strangers walking on the street were reading her thoughts and were also against her.

Telling her to make an effort to make contact with other people was not successful. Discussion of her fear and paranoia of others did not help. In the course of a birth visualization,[1] she was asked to imagine the baby inside her uterus, with the waters making contact between herself and her baby. Then she was asked to imagine herself as the baby inside the uterus. Suggestions were given for her to imagine herself by a swimming pool and, perhaps, diving in to make contact with the water. Suggestions were again given for her to imagine diving into the water, with much discussion of the pleasure of making contact with the water. The referential index of these images was general enough to symbolize both making contact with her baby and making contact with other people. This was accomplished by discussing the way that she could see, in the pool, other people diving into the water. Milton Erickson's interspersal technique of indirect hypnosis was used to emphasize the idea of making contact with people and making contact with the baby through the image of diving into water. After all, divers must initiate making contact with the water. They can stand beside the water forever and be scared of the water, or they can imagine how good it would feel to take the initiative and just jump into the water. Divers must make the first move toward the water, because the water can't come up to meet them.

The next week, Penny related having "made contact" with two new people and an old acquaintance. Her two new interpersonal contacts had occurred while she looked for furniture and clothing for her baby. For the first time she could remember, Penny had invited an old acquaintance for dinner. Since that time, with continued emotional support during therapy, Penny has reached out into a support group for single mothers which has become a community for her. Her paranoia and voice-hearing has also greatly diminished.

Indirect hypnosis aids in the construction of therapeutic images. Psychological mastery of linguistic principles is a keystone of any successful therapy. With Penny, hypnotic visual images were constructed that paralleled her need to (1) make emotional contact with her baby, (2) prepare her to "dive into" the birth process, and (3) make emotional contact with other people.

Mary was another woman for whom visualization was very helpful. Mary was 36 years old, and had recently given birth to a girl child. Mary had lived in a convent as a nun before going to work for the U.S. Forest Service. Mary, according to her own report, had taken her convent vows so seriously that she had frightened the other nuns. Mary followed every vow and rule very rigidly. She had kept strict silence for four of her seven convent years. She had felt comfortable in that environment, but had been asked to leave by her Mother Superior. After her tenure as a nun, she had worked for the Forest Service in wilderness Oregon. She was stationed alone for months at a time (by her choice) to locate forest fires.

Mary had always lived a life of isolation. She had sexual intercourse once during her Forest Service period, resulting in her only pregnancy. Otherwise she experienced chronic vaginismus. Mary's memories were only of alienation and isolation. She had been sent to live in a Catholic boarding school at age 5, because her mother couldn't handle her and her new sibling. She had grown up in institutions and was moderately paranoid. She eventually ended all her relationships by deciding the other person had turned against her.

Soon after delivery Mary complained of recurrent nightmares of walking into a dark hallway where a black hand was reaching out to grab her. During this time she also believed that an evil man was under her bed at night reaching upwards to grab her. She was breast feeding her daughter and her milk supply was dwindling. Her daughter was not gaining weight. The pediatrician had diagnosed the failure to thrive syndrome and, recognizing the many emotional reasons for Mary's decreased milk production, had referred Mary for visualization. He hoped visualization could help Mary increase her milk supply.

During therapy, visualization was used to guide her through the nightmare to the point at which she always awoke. During this visualization (after an initial induction) Mary was able to confront the hand in her mind's eye and give it a visual image. This object of her fear became a horrid, large, white cockroach. As she was supported and encouraged to continue confronting the image of the cockroach, it slowly resolved into an image of her mother. After discussing the feelings that being a mother aroused within her about her own mother, the nightmare did not recur. On her second visit, after becoming relaxed, she was assisted to imagine the milk in her breast resembling rivers rushing down the mountainsides in the forests she had worked. The image of a forest was developed in detail, and related to Mary's own health and vitality. Great reservoirs of water existed beneath the ground for the trees to reach into and draw up all the water and nutrients they needed to nourish their young branches and buds. Their tissues were full of healthy, life-giving water, all the way to the top, where the water could emerge into the leaves and stems.

Mary's milk supply increased after this visualization, and she was able to continue nursing without a supplemental bottle. Her daughter thrived again.

History of Visualization

Two major psychological disciplines seem to be associated with the recent American increase in use of visualization — behavior therapy and gestalt approaches. Imagery techniques have also been advanced by learning theorists and psychoanalytically trained individuals, interested in overcoming the limitations of analysis, especially its length.

Visualization as a technique had much of its beginnings in Europe in the early 1900's. Tichner represented the then prevalent view that all thinking required imagery. This view was challenged by research from the Würzberg school showing that certain attitudinal sets did not require visual imagery. The Würzberg researchers proceeded to develop into the various behaviorist philosophies of the U.S., Britain, and Russia. Interest was lost in imagery in the U.S. by 1920, but two resources in Europe kept imagery very much alive. One was Carl Jung, with his active imagination techniques for dream interpretation, contrasted to the more passive Freudian association technique. In Jung's approach the dream became an entity of its own. Imagery was a valid experience of itself. The psychotherapist's job was to use imagery to direct and focus the patient into the experience so as to benefit therapeutically.

The other European resource was Desoille, who created the waking dream method with a series of six themes during which the mental imagery journey mirrored the psychotherapy process. The waking dream was constructed of:

1. A theme with swords representing the male, and vessels representing the female, with the purpose of confronting one's own personality characteristics;
2. A descent into the ocean or underground, either of which could represent suppressed characteristics;
3. Coming to terms with one's opposite sexed parent represented by witches in caves or wizards;
4. Coming to terms with one's same sexed parent represented by the reversal of the witch/wizard images;
5. Construction of the social self represented by descent into a cave to confront a monster; and,
6. Resolution of the Oedipal complex using the image of sleeping beauty or a castle in the forest.

These images very obviously are culturally derived from the Zeitgeist of Europe of that time and social class.

Regardless of the usefulness of these specifics, imagery served to do three things:

1. To *diagnose, in a projective manner much as* Thematic Apperception or Rorschach stories
2. To *confront* a created symbol or person, either real or fantasized, and
3. To *re-educate* the patient, with the help of relaxation training, to new patterns of emotional responses.

Diagnosis, confrontation, and re-education are all useful concepts, especially in solving psychophysiological problems (meaning patients with physical symptoms, including ways in which their lifestyle and behavior creates and maintains those symptoms and disorders, as well as ways their attitudes keep them in a physical and mental state of distress.) Re-education with relaxation and imagery helps the patient create new response patterns. Relaxation training begins the re-education process, allowing the person to move from one emotional state to another more readily.

Leurner used imagery in his waking dream method to speed up the psychotherapy process. He felt that the transference became superfluous to the process itself, more direct than just an analysis of the transference relationship of patient to therapist. Leurner focused upon confrontation with real people or with symbols of the fear that limited the person.

The image of a meadow was a major image used by Leurner. Helping patients imagine a meadow educated them to their capability to create visual images, thereby improving self-esteem. The meadow was also used for diagnosis. What kind of meadow would this person create? Would it have lush green vegetation or would it be barren and empty?

Mountain images were also used. Leurner would assess how clients would approach the mountain; whether they would ascend it, stop and go around it, or pick an alternative approach. Leurner also used an image of a stream. The image, symbol, or reality of water has been used for symptom relief for ages. Images of water can be very comforting and provide symptomatic relief, although not necessarily longlasting, unless underlying causes to the symptomatology are approached.

In 1960 in the U.S., the behaviorist, Wolpe, introduced his method of systematic desensitization, creating a kind of marriage between imagery techniques and behavioral research by demonstrating that relaxation training with anxiety-producing imagery was effective therapy. Systematic desensitization combined relaxation and imagery for a person to actually learn new ways of responding to old, fearful situations.

State-dependent learning can help us further understand the usefulness of imagery. State-dependent learning means that learning takes place in a particular emotional state and that, to relearn or unlearn most effectively we may need to be experiencing within that same emotional state. Visualization can be used to transport a patient back to an earlier emotional experience before learning during a crisis resulted in dysfunctional behavior. Descriptions of this earlier period should be concrete, including questions such as "What were you wearing?' What was your father wearing?" This level of concretization helps the patient achieve an emotional state equivalent enough to the original to change state-dependently learned patterns of response.

Visualization and Psychoanalysis

To further an understanding of our use of imagery in psychotherapy, a contrast with imagery as it occurs in psychoanalysis may be helpful.

Kroth found that ease of imagery increased in the reclining position and also increased in states of mild sensory deprivation. In the analytic situation, the patient reclines on the couch, and a state of mild sensory deprivation is created by the patient not looking at the therapist. The patient is thought to be better able to free-associate without seeing the therapist's reactions. The transference neurosis, considered one of the keys of psychoanalysis, may be a function of the setting itself in that the silent response of the analyst to the imagery of the patient's associations creates the situation in which the patient becomes acutely aware that the analyst is listening and evaluating. This lack of relevant environmental feedback really leads to the paranoid consideration reflected in the question "What is the analyst really thinking of me and what I say?" Projections onto the analyst of answers to this question create the transference neurosis. In contrast with my use of imagery, I direct the person with the imagery as the focus (rather than my silence as the focus) and I react to that imagery, focussing projection onto the images instead of the therapist. Transference in the analytic situation is one way to recreate emotional states in which problematic coping styles were learned. Transference helps to achieve an experiential level where the person can re-learn. The analytic transference approach to state-dependent psychotherapy is limited by its lengthiness and expense. Neurotic clients tend to benefit most since they would be expected to be most consciously aware of wondering what the therapist thinks of them. Imagery can be much more helpful with psychotic clients than merely talking, because the psychotic responds to the paranoid question, "What does the therapist think of me?" by escaping into the ozone of non-reality. Visual imagery methods are necessary to follow psychotic clients into their private worlds and help them return in some functional way to the agreed upon mass world of convenience within which we all relate to one another. Psychotic clients cannot be easily trained to focus on their analyst instead of their imagery. For this reason (as well as others) the analytic therapy of psychosis is very lengthy.

I use imagery in some very direct ways. I deal with the client as Leurner did, approaching whatever fears arise through symbolic form. The client is more autonomous than in the analytic situation and can gain self-insight to take back to his or her living situation. The transference exists but is secondary and is addressed as the need arises, but not as the primary mode of therapy. Much of the time I prefer to work below the level of conscious awareness so as to work below the level of defense, since the defenses are primarily a function of the waking consciousness. When therapeutic work occurs on a metaphorical level, resistances initially emerge less often. Imagery occupies the conscious mind to allow the therapy to proceed more effectively. If clients come to the therapy session with preconceived ideas of what we will do, their defenses have already been prepared if we do what they have previously imagined. If they are surprised with a new technique (art therapy, visualization, etc.) their minds are taken off the track of what we were "supposed to do." Resistance has not been prepared for the new, surprising situation. The usefulness of the element of surprise can also be understood in Milton Erickson's sense of engaging conscious ego functions in contemplation of the surprise to such an extent that habitual defenses cannot be activated. Without the activation of such defenses (dysfunctional coping styles), resistance does not emerge nearly so quickly or forcibly. Visualization works on a symbolic, metaphorical level beneath the usual waking level of consciousness. This is a deeper level of consciousness, not always commonly accessible to the waking level. It has been called the Inner Self, Higher Self, Unconscious, or Transcendental Ego.

Other techniques that occupy the conscious mind include story telling and the double-ear technique. In the double-ear technique, once the client is relaxed, one therapist talks into the left ear and the other, into the right ear. Clients experience difficulty consciously listening to both therapists simultaneously. They tend to listen consciously to one or another, letting the non-attended message reach the deeper levels at which visualization operates.

The conscious ego can also be occupied during the imagery of gestalt dialogue because the client becomes so involved in the dramatiza-tion of a certain event or process that his or her usual intellectual view of reality is suspended. The conscious ego is distracted and emotions are expressed that the conscious ego would ordinarily inhibit, allowing the therapist access to previously hidden material.

All these ways of occupying the conscious ego are subtle forms of hypnosis. Much change occurs beneath the level of conscious, waking thinking. Much of what is done with visualization and mental imagery techniques utilizes basic hypnotic principles. Almost all therapists use principles of hypnosis to help the client achieve an altered state of consciousness and engage in the therapeutic process. The use of visuali-zation to reach deeper levels of consciousness helps the client to partially regress to earlier, pre-verbal, predominantly visual levels of learning ages from birth to 3½. Piaget believes that this predominantly visual mode of learning explains why many adults have few memories of events before age 3½. Memory of these ages is stored in pictures, yet the person searches for memory stored with language. Such searches are inevitably fruitless, since the search occurs in the wrong brain area. Visualization often allows the client access to very early memory, since it is available in the visual storage areas of the brain which are activated during visualization.

Visualization and Resistance

Another important use of imagery in psychotherapy is to avoid or by-pass resistance. Sometimes in the therapeutic situation, the client develops such resistance to the process of therapy that change cannot occur. Therapy then becomes a slow-moving process. Sometimes the mere mention of certain key words and phrases will trigger resistance, and the client will disengage even further from the therapist. Visualization, or metaphorical psychotherapy, allows for verbal-level resistance to be bypassed, since the conscious ego does not pay as close attention to the symbolic level. Then, charged memories or feelings can filter upwards toward consciousness, either during the session or afterwards in dreams or spontaneous insights. Therapy can proceed successfully even if these memories never rise to conscious awareness.

Milton Erickson often gave his clients permission to forget the events of the therapy session. The same suggestion can be helpful during visualization and mental imagery therapy. One subtle, very useful suggestion is that, if something is too difficult now, it won't be remembered after the session but can appear in a dream, now or later, perhaps while walking down the street at 7 p.m. tomorrow night, or even later, perhaps on a Saturday evening.

The following example illustrates the use of visualization to resolve resistance to the continuation of therapy. Mandy was a 31 year old, self-proclaimed gay, feminist therapist who came to see me for psychophysiological psychotherapy for symptom relief from chronic ear problems and constant tiredness.

Mandy was aware of my work and felt that her problems were psychophysiological and would be best handled through visualization and mental imagery techniques. She was reluctant to have therapy with a man, given her gay, feminist orientation. She decided to utilize me anyway since she felt that I might have skills she could learn and use in her own work. The only significant relationship that she had with a male when she began therapy was with her teenage son.

Previous relationships with men had been unrewarding and problematic. Usually Mandy thought a great deal and ruminated about life events. Under stress however, she could be emotionally labile and could fit the description commonly given as "hysterical personality."[2] During stress, she coped entirely emotionally without seeming to allow herself access to her logical faculties, even though inside herself she was thinking constantly, increasingly escalating her anxiety-provoking internal dialogue (even though the more she did so, the more an outside observer might have labelled her hysterical). Her behavior (in contrast to her inner process) gave her the appearance of having incorporated the training given women to use only their right brain (intuitive, non-rational, artistic, emotional aspects), and not the left brain (logical, rational, systematic, analytic aspects). Mandy tended to pair herself in relationships with "obsessive" men or women, completing what has been called the classic "obsessive-hysteric dyad," (one thinks, the other feels) even though her emotionality was present seemingly because her partner was so much more so obsessive then she. In her last relationship with a man, she had spent 5 years with a very obsessive man who seemed to vanish whenever she expressed emotions.

I began using visualization with her to help her discover why she was always so tired. As usual, I began by helping her become very relaxed. Then I assisted her in talking to her tiredness and her ears in a gestalt dialogue format. The therapy quickly moved in the direction of focusing upon issues of how to deal with the men in her life, a likely issue to surface considering I was male and she a lesbian-feminist. As the therapy continued, we developed an improved rapport, although parts of Mandy resisted allowing that rapport to develop. Painful memories of early experiences of being ignored or rejected by her father began to surface. That memories of her father were surfacing was particularly frightening for her, since such material seemed too classically Freudian. Sometimes she thought she associated to memories of her father because of my "sexism." She thought I was putting unacceptable Freudian ideas "into her head." This position came from a part of her that believed women shouldn't do therapy with male therapists. Men would always direct the therapy in a Freudian, sexist direction. Sometimes Mandy thought she couldn't learn from her therapy with me because of my sexism. Even more frightening to her was the possibility of becoming emotionally dependent upon me as a therapist. Could she allow herself to become more intimate and to work on improving a relationship with a man?

By the twelfth session, Mandy had tentatively begun a heterosexual love relationship with a previously gay man. He lived two hours away by car so that they saw each other only on weekends. She seemed to be wading into the waters of relationships with men.[3] Her lover was a very expressive artist, quite the opposite of former lovers of either sex.

In the sixteenth sesson Mandy announced upon arrival that I was an incorrigible sexist and no hope existed for further gain from therapy with me. This session was to be our last. She had decided conclusively that the memories and feelings about her father, and the associations she was making between those and her current life problems were entirely the result of my male-stereotypical projections onto her. I was even a worse sexist because I couldn't or wouldn't recognize my own sexism. To interpret her behavior as resistance or fear of intimacy would be to deny my sexism even further. I did not choose to make that interpretation. For several minutes I foundered in the quicksand I had suddenly stumbled into. When I was up to my waist and getting nowhere, I realized visualization might help. In the past we had used visualization to help Mandy achieve a feeling, kinesthetic level of awareness in which rational thinking was not too important. This helped her to turn off her internal mental ruminations. Under stress, Mandy tended to obsess when attention to her feelings could help her or to attend only to her feelings when she needed to think out answers to problems.

I suggested exploration of her feelings through visualization. If her perceptions were accurate, if the beliefs just expressed came from heart-felt feelings, visualization would provide further clarity. We would know with certainty if work with me was impossible. Our closing session would clarify the wishes of her heart. I further suggested beginning at a safe environment that would exclude my energy penetrating. I suggested she imagine constructing a white glow around that safe place to keep me out. I wanted her to feel no interference from me in her important journey toward self-discovery in matters of the heart. I could observe from a safe distance, entering her experience only as she chose to allow me that liberty, and certainly not for some time into the session. Mandy agreed and we began with relaxation.

Relaxation Approaches

Relaxation was the first step toward helping Mandy accomplish the agreed-upon visualization. Relaxation can be accomplished in any number of ways. Simple progressive muscular relaxation as that of Bernstein can be used. Many combinations of techniques can be incorporated, including bioenergetic techniques of deep breathing and release of energy flow. I began by asking Mandy to begin to slow down her breathing. I wanted to help her establish a slow, deep breathing pattern. Then I began to encourage her to imagine she could breathe deeply into the various parts of her body (scalp, forehead, cheeks, mouth and chin, neck, depth of her lungs, chest, arms and hands, back, pelvis, thighs, knees, lower legs, ankles, and feet), and to begin to sense a feeling of warmth and relaxation. I like to link that flow of relaxation into various mental images, including (for Mandy) a mountain spring that comes up from the depths of the earth to become a small stream high in the Sierra, flowing down the mountain and washing away tension from the side of its banks. I mixed metaphors during the relaxation process, including linking the idea of Mandy relaxing her back with the image of a cool, clean mountain stream of relaxing energy flowing down her back. The metaphor of the river flowing down the mountainside and the stream of relaxing energy flowing down the spine was mixed even more by my sometimes using "bone" where properly I should have said "tree stump" or saying "washing away tension" instead of "washing away dirt."

With Mandy I talked about how she could experience the flow of the river down her spine. This river becomes larger and more powerful, becomes bigger and calmer as it goes further down the mountainside. Eventually it reaches the foothills of the knees and becomes more and more deep and powerful as it flows down and out of the mountains, more slowly onward toward the central valley. I included indirect hypnotic suggestions for her level of relaxation (trance level) to go deeper down as she experienced the river going deeper down. "As the river becomes deeper, the flow is more relaxing: it's slower now . . . slowing down . . . it's becoming a slow process of going down deeply, down toward the ocean, down toward the bay. Finally that river flows out into the bay and on into the ocean, carrying with it all the tension of the land that it's washed away from its banks."

Another effective technique I've found is the use of an image of a fountain for relaxing the head. I asked Mandy to visualize water coming up through the center of a fountain, how it comes up into a head and then reaches the top of the fountain and spreads out, cascading down over the forehead where it can flow all the way down the face, washing away any tension that might be present. Imagining that cascading down-flow of water going all the way down to the base of the fountain (neck) was very effective in helping Mandy to relax her forehead, her jaw, her nose, eyes, mouth, and neck.

Another good approach I used with Mandy was the image of a tropical waterfall. Mandy had been to Hawaii and knew what tropical waterfalls look like. I asked Mandy to imagine herself standing beneath a tropical waterfall, feeling the warm, clear water washing away more and more of the tension from her body. That waterfall can be just the right height to feel comfortable — not too cold, not too warm. She could, if she wished, feel the waterfall beginning to wash away more and more of the tensions of the day, flowing all the way down into the stream that flows away from the waterfall.

With less resistant or very experienced clients, the relaxation phase of visualization can be by-passed altogether. Clients capable of bypassing the relaxation phase are usually already very good at relaxing. They can relax almost immediately, an ability usually requiring some previous practice. During the first few visualization sessions, I often spend as much as half the session just on relaxation techniques. While helping the client relax, the therapist can create indirect suggestions embedded in the relaxation process to help the client reach the goals of therapy and instructions are given to relax and go deeper down towards the Inner Self. The goals for this session were emphasized during the relaxation process. I suggested allowing herself to travel down to the level of her heart, to the level of her own true feelings, accomplished by my talking about the river of relaxing energy flowing past the heart of the earth. "Maybe there's a feeling of softening as the water flows by, the sound of a soft wind blowing in the trees as you walk by the riverbank." Many images were linked to the concept of softening, of letting go, and of relaxing. I talked about Mandy allowing herself to imagine herself lying beside the river bank, letting the water flow past and feeling that flow of water going parallel to the flow of wind through the trees. "The sound of the water flowing, the wind blowing can feel so comfortable, so relaxing" to all her parts, her muscles, her bones, *her heart* and lungs.

Once Mandy was relaxed, I suggested that she imagine herself in a very safe place. She could find a special, safe place only for her, either a place she'd been before or a place she could conjure up in her mind as being very safe. It should be a place where she could protect herself from me if I were going to try to "put any ideas into her head;" a very safe place where she could feel her own power and strength. Mandy experienced a high, mountain meadow surrounded by snow-covered peaks, just as one might see in the Sierra Nevada. A gentle stream flowed through the lush, grassy meadow. A male, white deer with large antlers stood in the forest at the edge of the meadow. It didn't enter the meadow, only stood at the edge. She related thinking that the deer represented me asking to be allowed to enter her confidence, but having not yet been granted permission. White, to me, suggested a positive image of pure motives and intentions, implying that Mandy at a deeper level believed me to be non-threatening.

I asked Mandy to visualize herself lying on the grass in the meadow (if she wanted to), feeling herself breathe the cool, clear mountain air;

sensing it go down into her lungs; and begin to imagine the feeling of that protective white light she could surround herself with. (Mandy believed that white light served as a kind of spiritual screen that would keep her safe and secure.) Mandy saw herself lying in the meadow with white light radiating around her like protective armor. Nothing evil could enter. She could feel very safe. Wherever she would go from there, if anything was too intense for her or too frightening she could know that she could return immediately to the meadow. Anything disagreeing with her could be pushed out of the meadow including any image or emotion that she wasn't yet able to process.

Mandy's Journey

I asked Mandy to see an image of her heart if she wished, and then to begin to let herself see herself comforting herself, nurturing herself. She imagined herself as a little girl, aged 6 or 7. She experienced the feeling of being cradled and rocked with her eyes closed. This experience was entirely kinesthetic. I asked Mandy to open her mind's eye to see what the person holding her looked like. She was shocked to see a man with blonde hair and very loving eyes. At first she was very frightened at being held by a man and began to fight the image.

I discouraged her saying, "This image is coming from you; it's your image, this is someone you created; it's not from me. Just let yourself flow with the image. You're protected, you're safe. Look at the person's face, look at the eyes. You can tell if he means you any harm by looking at his eyes."

Mandy relaxed more and appeared more comfortable. She was beginning to let go of some of her chronic body tension. As Mandy relaxed, sometimes she would show a series of quick muscular jerks. Such jerks sometimes occur with clients who have been very tense. As they relax their muscles, perhaps because of the chronic tightness, a kind of quick spasm and contraction precedes lengthening and loosening. When that happens, I usually say, "That's right, good," because it means the patient is relaxing even more and letting go of more tension. This mild reinforcement was very effective for Mandy. I encouraged her beginning to talk to the man in her image. He said he was there to help her and protect her. He could be a guide for her, someone she could draw strength from in her journeys. Then a dark cloud began to pass before the sun, obscuring the horizon in darkness. An angry woman appeared in the cloud, admonishing Mandy to get out of the man's arms and stop allowing herself to be held and nurtured by him. He was only going to hurt her. He was going to take advantage of her, just going to take advantage of her just like all men always did. She should run for her life, come quickly with the woman and run away to safety. Mandy felt herself in conflict. She felt her heart tightening. She felt scared and tense. I asked her to look closely at the two faces, relaxing and allowing the white light to protect her so she could compare and contrast their appearances and demeanors. Who had the more natural face? Who seemed more safe to be with? "Don't listen to words, look at the face. Who do you want to be with? Who would you rather be a part of? Who has more meaning to you?" In her mind's eye she looked at the woman and she looked at the man. She said she wanted to be like the man. The woman was too angry, too frightening and she was becoming scared just looking at her. I asked her to dialogue with the woman.

She said, "No, I'm not going with you; I'm going to stay here. I'm being taken care of, I'm being nurtured. I don't want to go with you."

Then the woman changed into a little girl and the little girl began to cry. Mandy recognized that she was the little girl. She had a spontaneous image of herself as a child pulling on her father's pants leg, asking him to give her attention, saying, "I want you to do something with me. I want you to look at my dress. Please come play with me."

He said, "No, no, no, go talk to your mother. I don't have time, I'm too busy. I can't help you. Go talk to your mother."

She saw more examples of her father ignoring her and directing her to women. She saw herself physically and symbolically pulling on her father's pants leg, trying to get contact with him, but being ignored.

Mandy began to move toward a higher level of consciousness, more akin to her waking level. She related realizing that she believed that she could only receive love from women, because in her past it was only women who consistently gave her love. Her father, brothers, and other men were never reliable or emotionally available to her. I helped her return to her waking level of consciousness and we discussed how working with me had resulted in her experiencing those old frightening feelings of men never being trustworthy. She related realizing how important it was to continue working with those feelings to learn how they affected her life in the present. The session just described was a turning point in helping Mandy to have the courage and strength to look within herself, ready to discover and embrace what lived within. Continuing on the level of the waking, talking ego would not have helped us beyond the sexism impasse. The use of visualization helped us bypass Mandy's resistance. It allowed her to recognize my lack of villainy and sexism. By giving her my permission to see me as a villain in her visualization, I encouraged her to gain access to her inner feelings safely. By this point her ear problems and tiredness had also resolved.

General Issues of Using Visualization

I suggest clients close their eyes during visualization in order to create the state of mild sensory deprivation that helps the client to turn his/her attention inward. During the relaxation phase I do most or all of the talking, guiding the client through relaxation of the body. As the client becomes sufficiently relaxed, I begin serving as a guide to help the exploration of his or her inner world. I might say, "And as you find yourself arriving there you can, if you wish, begin to tell me about that place." The client's beginning description of his or her own safe place is similar to exploring and mapping a newly discovered continent. Initially, we could begin with satellite photos for an overall impression. Then we could decrease to the level of aerial photos. Finally we land reconnaisance parties at the sites appearing most interesting, exciting, and promising for exploration, from our aerial photos. Anne McCaffrey[4] beautifully describes this process and the ensuing excitement of discovery:

> "All of you, come here!" came the excited voice of the Harper, who had prowled ahead . . . .
>
> As everyone gathered about the two, their glow baskets adding to the illumination, it was clear what had arrested their attention. The walls were covered with maps. In great detail, the familiar contours of Northern Pern and the not-so familiar Southern Continent, all of it in its immensity, had been drawn eradicably on the wall.
>
> With a sound — half moan, half shout — Piemur touched the map, tracing with his forefinger the coast which he had so arduously tramped, but which was only a small portion of the total shoreline. . . .
>
> "Now what would this map represent?" F'nor asked, interrupting Piermur's excited comments. . . .
>
> "Perplexing. I shall have to study this . . . !" [said Robinton]
>
> "Here's one for Master Wanson's eyes," Fandarel said, apparently so engrossed in the section he was studying that he hadn't attended Robinton's words.
>
> "A star map!" the young Harper [Piemur] cried. . . .
>
> "What's this then?" Piemur asked, putting his finger on a dark-colored world on the other side of the sun, away from the other planets and their described lines of orbit.
>
> "And what do these lines mean?" Jaxom asked. . . .
>
> "Fascinating," was all the Master [Fandarel] would allow, rubbing his chin as he stared at the enigmatic drawings.

"I prefer this map," Lessa said, smiling with a great deal of satisfaction at the two continents. . . .

"See this spur of land, where the Dragon Stones are now?" Menolly cried. "My great-grandsire remembers the land falling into the sea. . . ."

"The maps are superb discoveries [Fandarel said]. . . .

If a client has difficulty creating visual images, I sometimes ask he or she to begin by seeing and describing what the feet are wearing. Being helped to imagine parts of the body going upwards from the feet, including clothing further anchors the client into a concrete visual experience. Looking next at the ground beneath the feet helps them discover if the ground is grass, or a desert. Looking further and further into the environment helps anchor the client to a vivid visualization.

Questions can help, including "Look at your feet. What do you see on your feet?" Concrete details help inner images seem more real. The level of relaxation achieved by the client can be judged from observation of muscle tension, breathing patterns, eye movements, and other parameters. As the client becomes more relaxed, visible signs of muscle relaxation are present. Tense muscles may sometimes twitch as relaxation occurs. Softening of tense neck, facial, and shoulder numbers is observable. Shoulders become more sloped. Softening of tight muscle cords in the neck can dramatically change the shape of the neck. Relaxation of facial muscles can change the person's appearance. People often look softer, more gentle, and more attractive when relaxed than during their usual state of tension, especially when chronic tension has persisted for years.

Relaxation is often correlated with small rapid eye movements, similar to those observed in REM sleep. Larger, slower eye movement can be a sign of rising relaxation levels.

When the client is relaxed, breathing is generally slow, easy, and regular, similar to the breathing that occurs during sleep. Watching someone fall asleep can help in learning to recognize breathing changes correlated with deeper stages of relaxation. Breathing becomes progressively deeper, slower, and more regular. During the visualization process, the therapist usually becomes more relaxed as well. If I find myself having difficulty relaxing during a visualization session, it is sometimes true that the client is having difficulty relaxing. The therapist's own level of relaxation can be a monitor for how relaxed the client is.

At the conclusion of a visualization session the relaxed client should not immediately pop up into a normal waking state. Frequently a transition period of stretching and flexing of extended joints occurs.

Some clients who have had a very powerful emotional experience during visualization may verbally express very little about that experience. The more indirect signs are essential in recognizing evidence of an emotionally-charged experience. These patients may have much rapid eye movement and appear very relaxed.

If the client falls asleep, I gradually, progressively increase the volume of my voice louder and *louder* until the person wakes up. I do it gradually so waking will not be abrupt. Then my goal becomes helping the client maintain the transition zone between wakefulness and sleep.

Non-expressive clients having powerful emotional experiences may show tears and unique individual breathing patterns, corresponding to the deeper feelings possibly occurring, even though not expressing those feelings.

Mandy's breathing rate increased and became louder as she experienced internal conflict about allowing the man to hold her. Her body mirrored her experiences expressed in the dialogue. When some level of body reflection of described experienced does not occur (including voice dynamics) the visualization may be on too much of an intellectual level and further efforts need to be made in order to build-in the emotional component. Some patients need to have their images constructed for them by the therapist in the initial phases of therapy. Beginning with the image of a meadow, a mountain stream, or a beach with the ocean waves rolling in helps to educate the client to construct personal images.

Indirect hypnotic suggestions can intensify the learning process.

Storytelling Technique

Storytelling is a more structured approach to visualization in which the client is told a story resembling current problems. The relaxation phase is built into this indirectly. If the client is a follower of Baba Muktananda, a story about searching for one's guru may be best. A Christian might do best with a Biblical story. Children's stories are sometimes best. Asking the client about their favorite childhood stories can help the therapist know what kind of story to tell.

If the client is resistant to therapy or imagery, I may ask them to bring their favorite childhood storybook. The relaxation induction can be done by reading the story with alterations to suit the purpose at hand. Not all the words spoken will be contained in the story. Such visualization using modifications of childhood stories are especially effective with children.

A 6-year-old boy had tremendous trouble relating to other children and adults. His favorite story was *Goldilocks and the Three Bears*. In my revised version, at the end of the story Goldilocks and the little bear became the best of friends. They ran through the woods and had fun while the other bears fixed up the chairs and laughed about the whole situation. With such stories as this, the boy began relating better to his peers. His improved relations were quickly reinforced by his peers and his ability developed rapidly so that therapy progressed much faster than might have otherwise been true. Fourteen weekly sessions completed our work.

All therapy (including storytelling) utilizes psycholinguistic (hypnotic) principles. Sometimes the most effective approach to help a client is an exploratory, feeling, visualization approach in which the person experiences his own inner workings. Through recognition of inner workings, clients begin to develop their own technique for changing themselves in order to suit their individual needs. Relaxation at home with deep breathing, and construction of images for the metaphoric investigation of problems may be incorporated as an ongoing means of making change. Such metaphors may include healing and nurturing images to bolster self-esteem. Direct hypnosis is not as useful as the exploratory visualization process in allowing the therapist to learn about the client's inner landscape. Knowledge of the patient's visualizations can help diagnostically in understanding the dynamics of the patient's problem. Such understanding can guide the verbal therapy.

All therapy techniques can be useful. The more that is known about psycholinguistics, the more any type of therapy can be improved, including visualization. Visualization is the therapeutic use of mental imagery. Hypnotherapy is the therapeutic use of linguistics and communication. Visualization and hypnosis are inextricably linked, because the therapist often uses an auditory mode (the spoken word) to help the client create visual images. The client can visualize without the spoken word, and Erickson has shown that the client can be hypnotized through methods other than the spoken word. For example, to help clients who are having difficulty creating images one could say, "Even as you continue to breathe, because, of course, you never stop breathing, you can begin to see a meadow, now, in your mind's eye." This phrase helps the patient link the idea of seeing a meadow with the continued process of breathing. "As you breathe, you can begin to see a meadow." "You never stop breathing" is a *truism* that few would argue. Having accepted the truism (that they are breathing and will continue breathing), it's easier to go one step further accept the idea to begin "seeing a meadow." Just as breathing will not stop, effective conditioning keeps images continuing. When indirect suggestions are ineffective, the storytelling technique can be used. An example of the use of storytelling when relaxation/visualization is ineffective is provided by a 28 year old mother of two with a postpartum kidney stone. Laura came for visualization for pain control and to help her to imagine the stone passing through her ureter. She was experiencing too much pain to allow herself to relax and visualize. Because she seemed resigned to my inability to help her, I offered to tell her a story to fill our remaining time in the hopes that it could, even in some small way, make her feel better. She followed Baba Muktananda and had turned from her wealthy parents to do so, leading me to construct a story of a young woman, (about her age) who lived with her wealthy Indian family. She was wasting away and in great pain, having no understanding of the meaning of her life. She needed to loosen herself from the enclosing confines of her situation and begin to move forward to a new awakening. In fear and trepidation, she slipped away from the constricted, tight environment of her parents' home without anyone's awareness, journeying toward her desired goal. A train brought her from her home in the Punjabi toward the Himalaya. Near the Himalayan border she would have to disembark and *sleep* for the night to rest before her journey began in earnest.

I continued to talk: "and she was probably feeling very anxious because she'd never been away from her parents like that, and there's a lot of pain involved . . . there's a whole lot of pain involved in being away and *just letting go* of those relationships that you've had that have been so important and yet now you don't need them, and the *pain* there is probably quite severe, and the girl was thinking about that *now*, and she was thinking of perhaps about how to *let go* of her *pain*, just for that night perhaps, maybe for no other night because she *had to sleep* . . . she had to *get some sleep*, and she knew when she reached the end of the line she would *have to sleep to be rested* for her journey the next day. . . . And when the train stopped at the village, she got out. . . . It was very frightening and lonely, and it was very scary. . . . She decided she would *lie down to sleep*; she would lie *down*, and as she laid *down*, her *breathing* began to become *slower* and *deeper*, and her *whole body* now began to *relax* as she breathed *slowly* and *deeply*, much as you may be doing *now* . . . her whole body began to *let go* of more and more tension as she became closer and *closer to sleep*, her whole body began just to *let go of* that *pain* of leaving her family, the *pain* of taking on such a long journey, a long tortuous journey along many narrow passageways that . . . she knew if she persevered, it *could happen* very *successfully*, and she knew that she could *pass through* those treacherous places she needed to go, so she *laid down* and began to *become very sleepy*. Her *eyes* were very *heavy*, it was a long tiring day. And that's how . . . ."

By that point Laura was breathing deeply, no longer moaning. I was encouraged by this breathing change and continued with my idea of creating a symbolic journey paralleling the physical passage of the stone through the ureter to the bladder. Such a journey would go through tortuously narrow passageways, eventually leading Laura into a mountain lake, a lake high in the mountains where she would find a spiritual teaching, thereby feeling *very comfortable* now that she had arrived, successfully completing her journey.

During that first night's sleep, I paced Laura through a visualization of her Indian counterpart dreaming during that deep sleep. A sacred monkey came to visit the woman that night in her dreams. (Anyone listening to Indian guru storytellers knows how monkeys make an appearance in virtually every story.) The monkey brought her a sacred banana that she could use for food even though she wouldn't have food the whole time. Even if she couldn't find any food, she could eat this banana and she could *feel comfortable* . . . *everything inside* her could *feel so comfortable* whenever she imagined herself eating the banana. Then a leopard came, bringing her a coat she could wear in the mountains to keep warm. No matter how cold it was, or how fast the wind blew, or even if the wind made a seering *pain* all the way through her, she knew it *could be gone* whenever she put on the coat. Then an elephant came to give her the strength and wisdom to always know which path to choose in order to reach her destination. I helped Laura imagine the Indian woman awakening and continuing on her journey up into the mountains. She travelled through narrow tunnels with hardly enough room to crawl through. She inched her way along narrow ledges overlooking treacherous precipices. Bandits attempted to bushwack her, but the elephant gave her the strength to overpower them, throwing these uninvited intruders off the path and down the mountainside. When the harsh, sharp, biting winds blew around her, the leopard's coat protected her, helping her remain *comfortable inside*, regardless of the hardships she encountered. Whenever she felt the gnawing pain of hunger deep inside her, she could partake of the sacred banana, dissolving and washing away that inner discomfort. Her journey eventually ended at a lake inside the top of a mountain. Entering through a narrow cave, she came upon a large inner cavern containing the lake (symbolic of the bladder). The monks inside the cavern chanted by torch light as in astonishment she learned that they considered her a guru, believing anyone capable of the journey to the lama's retreat to be superhuman and worthy of worship. They repeated what a wonderful journey she made and how wonderful she could feel at having accomplished such a treacherous spiritual quest. The monks asked her to occupy the lama's chair.

After our visualization, Laura experienced no further pain. An X-ray just before the session had shown the location of the stone at the uretero-pelvic juncture (where the drainage system of the kidney empties into a long narrow tube (ureter), carrying urine to the bladder). A kink in the tube just after the location of the stone led her urologist to believe that the stone would never pass spontaneously. He expected surgery to be necessary. Laura's urologist obtained another X-ray (intravenous pyelogram) following our session and discovered to his amazement that the stone had spontaneously passed into the bladder. That Laura's stone had caused her *no pain* in its passage her doctor had proclaimed a miracle. Naturally, his thinking led him to the other side of the mountains from where Laura's visualization had instructed her body effectively, educating it to her desires. Modern "scientific" doctors tend to believe in the god of Random Chance. If drugs or surgery are not responsible for improvement, Random Chance, like Flip Wilson's devil, takes the credit — not Laura.

The story told to Laura involved frequent metaphorical criscrossing between the Indian woman of the story and, as Laura became more drawn into the story, herself. The criscrossing was done by mixing referential index, using interchangeably the words, "You, her, a woman, the woman, etc." Such mixing of referential index is accomplished by linking something the client is doing (just like you are doing *now*: breathing slowly and deeply) to the behavior of the imagined character of the story.

A knowledge of the cultural background of the client assists the therapist to construct maximally effective images. Indian teachers, including Baba Muktananda, Dr. Rammurta Mishra, and B. Rashneesh often use monkeys in their stories. A good Indian guru story should often include a monkey and one or two other animals. I had learned about monkeys and gurus from a graduate school course in Eastern Psychology, during which I also learned to imitate the accent of the gurus performing for us on audio cassette or in person. As Laura became more and more engrossed in the story, I used a slight Indian accent, allowing it to become thicker as the story progressed. My Eastern Psychology professor wasn't always coherent, speaking with a thick Benares accent, which I then imitated.

With a client of different religious preference and cultural background, other appropriate subject matter should be chosen. On one occasion an obstetrical colleague called me to assist her with a very Jewish-identified woman who had delivered a large child precipitously, sustaining a large tear. She had refused anesthesia for her repair, so her obstetrician was calling in desperation for a hypnotist. I began telling her a story of the time Abraham and the Jews wandered for forty years in the desert. I helped her imagine herself journeying with Abraham, looking for the right place for the Jews to settle. It could be such a hard and painful process to wander through the desert unless one called upon God for succor. A small boy (she had just delivered a baby boy) was lost in the desert. He was wandering about and feeling very badly. He knew God could help if only he would call upon God for relief from his suffering. An angel came down to him on a golden ladder and made a covenant to guide him to safety and security. The angel gave him a multi-colored cloak to keep him warm and comfortable, even during the pain of his travail. During this time, the patient relaxed and the obstetrician remarked that the tissue relaxation was as much as with general anesthesia.

Storytelling is an effective technique for clients who disbelieve their own abilities to visualize.

Visualization for Anxiety

A 32 year old woman, pregnant with her second child, gives us an example of the usefulness of visualization when the client experiences high anxiety levels. Danielle had given birth to her first child at home in Marin County without difficulty. She wanted to have her second child at home also, but was inexplicably terrified each time she anticipated the delivery. She had not experienced such fear and anxiety thinking about delivery during her first pregnancy. Logically, it made little sense that she should be so anxious now, especially when her first delivery had been so normal.

Her son was six years old. She was divorced from her first husband, a musician. Danielle had lived for a year and a half with a man she had met through their following of the same spiritual teacher. Friction existed in their relationship, leading to intermittent visits for couples' counseling, though their commitment to the process seemed minor.

Danielle seemed very anxious about becoming a mother to a second child. She seemed to have a kind of mother-child relationship with her current partner. She described being afraid of the responsibility she would have to the child, and fearing that it would come between her and her new partner. Elucidation of the source of her anxiety could have begun with exploration of her feelings about this new man. We could also have begun with visualization of the impending birth.[5] I could have begun with a diagnostic birth visualization to determine the part of the birth process that Danielle most feared. I began with the tunnel techique after relaxation. The tunnel technique consisted of (after relaxation) asking Danielle to see herself standing before a tunnel, stepping inside of it, and then feeling herself moving back through the tunnel to an earlier time when something important happened that it was important to *become aware of*. The tunnel had grey mist. She could feel herself moving back through the tunnel as fast as she would like to. I knew that she believed in karma and reincarnation. I thought she might use the tunnel technique to return to a past time of symbolic relevance. I instructed her to go back to a time just before an event had happened to her, that would help her to understand why she was so afraid of this birth. I gave her instructions to go back to the place she needed to go back to. I didn't know when that was, but there was a part of her that did. Danielle began to experience herself in labor. She went through the birth process. It wasn't clear which birth she was experiencing, but clearly she was giving birth. She delivered the placenta and began to bleed until she was hemorrhaging severely. She saw the face of her current partner there, saying in a sudden epiphany, "This is a past life and I died, I'm dying, and he's my husband." Danielle became very frightened. She had had a very intense labor and experienced a shock at recognizing that she would die. She became panicky. I helped her relax and realize that the death had already taken place (in her view of reincarnation), so she really had nothing to fear. Her knowledge of that previous life and death could enrich this life. Avoiding that knowledge would only keep her fear and would not change the facts of that life.

A two-place dissociation (watching herself have the experience, as opposed to directly experiencing) reduced much of her anxiety. She was able to grieve her loss — dying so young, leaving her husband and her children, leaving this new baby without a mother. She cried with sadness. I suggested that she imagine holding the new baby in her arms and kissing it good-bye, realizing that she had given it the gift of life and that was enough sometimes. She relaxed and allowed herself to experience dying.

Danielle decided her fear related to her current partner who had been her husband in the previous life when she hemorrhaged and died. She decided to give birth in the hospital alternative birth center so she could allow her man to be more involved. The couples' therapy began to be much more successful after this session. Danielle's fear and anxiety diminished below problem levels. The baby was born at home anyway, because Danielle's labor was too fast for her to travel to the hospital.

The main issues during couples' therapy at that time related to whether or not Danielle could depend on her partner. Was he strong enough? They decided he would do more jobs around the house. Tasks were assigned for him to do for her. Some family tasks were switched so she could feel more supported by him for the birth.

Resolution of Indecision

Visualization can be used to help clients make important decisions. A 26 year old woman with a one year old child was very upset at having just discovered she was pregnant again. She was unsure whether she should terminate the pregnancy or not. She needed to decide quickly in order to have time for an abortion. She came for visualization to help herself resolve what to do. I began by helping her travel in her mind's eye to a safe place (after relaxation). She found herself in a southern forest (she was originally from Alabama) with well-spaced trees. Two separate paths led through the forest: 1) having an abortion, and 2) continuing the pregnancy. I helped her to describe how she felt in her heart about each of these two paths. Then she imagined herself at the end of her life. I asked her to imagine dying and looking back over her life. Two separate lives proceeded from the choice point of today, proceeded toward her through the forest. In one of those lives she'd had the abortion. In the other, she'd had the child. She looked back on each life describing what had happened. Next I asked her to image the paths in color, paying close attention to colors that she could see. She described the abortion path with shades of grey and brown. It was more somber and dark. The "giving birth path" was bright like a rainbow. In many ways it was the harder path, yet also the more satisfying and fulfilling. In evaluating the two lives, she felt as though she would feel the best about her life if she had given birth and had grown with the trials of parenting two small children, rather than capitulate to that challenge (as she saw things). I suggested she could imagine a personal guide appearing to help her understand which life had helped her most to achieve the most personal growth possible from this life. Her guide helped her to realize the work and hardship she would experience, having two children so close together. There would be pain and difficulty. In the abortion she saw an easy alternative with a quick ending. At the end of the life path containing the abortion, though, she felt an unshakeable pain, forever remaining as she focused on the abortion. She felt a solid sense of fulfillment in continuing the pregnancy. She talked with her guide about how continuing would be hard, but she could handle the hardships. Continuing the pregnancy, she saw, was the best decision for her life. The guide helped her realize how important the new child was to the older child. I don't know how much of this session was remembered afterwards, except for a strong sense of having had a very powerful experience and having made a decision. The details of the session were not discussed afterwards. A decision had already been made. I asked her to go home and talk to her husband and call back in two days to let me know how they had resolved the issue. She continued the pregnancy and delivered a healthy baby girl normally.

Belief Systems

Working within the context of the client's beliefs allows for easier mobilization of healing abilities. Images of God would be useful for a devout Christian. Jesus should be allowed to take credit for any improvement. Jesus can be there to help the client long after the therapist. Clients (especially those clients who have relatively idiosyncratic belief systems) feel very supported when the therapist respects that belief system. Helpful therapeutic effects can ensue from the resultant rapport and deepened relationship. The therapist and client form a better working alliance. Guides or imaginary helpers can give the client a sense of safety and security. A guide can help the client brave an experience that might otherwise be traumatic. The guide allows for greater relaxation — a prerequisite to a therapeutic experience.

Acceptance and respect of the client's beliefs and experiences is especially important when working with clients spontaneously re-experiencing past lives, and re-experiencing previous death experiences. One woman seeing me described re-experiencing being hung — very frightening for her. I helped her travel slowly through the experience and put white light (part of her belief system) around it, allowing progress through the experience in a step-by-step fashion. Afterwards, she was much more relaxed and problems were solved in other areas of her life, including the disappearance of a chronic neck pain.

Another woman had amnesia about being raped by her father at age sixteen. She didn't remember this event, although she hated her father and experienced considerable sexual anxiety. She came for a visualization about chronic vaginal infections. After relaxation, I suggested she return to a time before her problems ever began. She returned to age 16. Immediately, she said, "Oh, no, something terrible, something terrible is happening here."

I helped her retreat for a moment to gather her resources. I said, "Okay, whatever it is, your conscious self can only remember as much as you can stand at this time." I again used an image of white light and, of that light strengthening her, as this was a part of her belief system.

I said, "Whatever this is, it's already happened and you can relax and feel comfortable and remember as little or as much as you need to, and we can go forward now, a little bit forward into what's happening, *now*. Just tell me who you see here."

She said, "I see, I see my father. He's coming at me. What's he going to do? Oh, no." She described what was happening. Then she said, "Oh no, I can't think about it; it's too awful."

Then we slowed down again: "Okay, let's slow down, relax again, breathe slowly and deeply. Get in touch with how you're feeling now with your breathing and you can decide if you want to go forward or not once you get that white light all around you again." In addition, I used a two-place dissociation technique in which I instructed her *not* to feel things as though they were happening to her in the here and now, but to step back and to watch what was happening to her as though she were an outside observer. This maneuver kept her in a visual instead of kinesthetic mode. The experience needed to be integrated visually since that was the only modality never used by her in recall or re-experience to that point. This client was able to integrate her traumatic memory and to accept that part of herself that had been molested. Her chronic vaginitis was resolved soon thereafter.

Sometimes clients are unable to travel through an experience. Then I say, "Okay, that's fine; you're not ready for that yet and you shouldn't do this, you should leave it for later on. . . . And little bits and pieces of that may come up later for you. . . . You may begin to remember more and more of that. . . . Maybe in a dream something important will come up . . . or just walking to the store . . . who knows when it can happen, but it can, and will . . . we can deal with it again." Then we go on past that experience. Of course almost anything that we go to next refers back to the previous experience, but indirectly. Later the clients become more ready to deal with the unremembered experience. Some don't ever have to actually remember or experience the repressed material in order to create needed change, which results in symptom relief.

Clients can be helped to alter the affective impact of past experience through teaching. During visualization, the details of the experience can be altered. The client can re-live past traumas and change details. One client had the experience of having been separated from his parents at a young age, which he associated with his separation from them when he went away to college. The issue of choice was significant for him. He needed to know if *he* had control over his life or if his parents did. He remembered past painful feelings of not being in control. He was asked to imagine taking control and staying in control of the situation. He imagined talking to his parents and acting in ways he had not acted in the real past. Then he could face his anxiety about his plans to move back with his own family to the area where his parents lived. With this new awareness he wasn't sure if this was the right decision. Was he moving back to please himself or his parents? He resolved the issue by changing his plans against moving back.

Another client who had high blood pressure was (after relaxation) asked to visualize being inside her heart. She felt the thick walls squeezing her out. There wasn't any room for her. Her heart was cramping down like a large muscle, squeezing her out with the blood flow. At that point she began sobbing, saying she didn't have enough room for herself. There wasn't enough room in her life for her. She associated with certain factors in her own that life contributed to her feeling squeezed out. She felt she was taking on too much work and too many responsibilities. She was pregnant with her second child and was already caring for her husband, working and taking care of her first child. She felt she wasn't getting enough help. She realized she felt guilty whenever she asked for help, thinking she should be the strong member of the family, who could take care of everyone else (the expansive heart-giving person). She didn't have any room for herself. The only way that she was able to get her needed room was with high blood pressure. When her blood pressure was elevated (because she was pregnant) she had to stay in bed, and her husband had to make dinner. Her husband had to take care of their son. She didn't have to go to the La Leche League organizing meetings and take charge of committees. She needed support for expressing what was in her heart so her heart could open up and let go of some of the pressure. She screamed and sobbed into a pillow. After this emotional release, we talked about what she could do to change. She was given support for asking for her needs, for being able to renege on certain responsibilities that she couldn't carry out. She was educated to systems theory, to the fact that people around her expected her to fulfill a certain role. They might not like her new changes. She said she didn't care because she couldn't keep up with what she had been doing. She agreed that some people in her life were going to be upset. She had tried to extricate herself from some of these obligations. She hadn't convinced herself that she could change because others might become upset. In the session she decided that, if she wanted to stay well, she had to decrease her obligations. She did so and her blood pressure fell from 150/94 to 120/82 within several days. Her serum estriol levels had been declining and, after her blood pressure dropped, her estriols began to rise and she felt much better (serum estriols represent a measure of how well the placenta is functioning to nourish the baby).

Group Visualization

Groups can be aided in visualization in the same manner that individuals are. It is usually possible to go deeper with an individual than with a group. Each group member must, to some extent, be his own individual guide to himself. Group visualization can provide a powerful experience for people who are aware of their own inner process. The following is an example of a group visualization with a type of relaxation that emphasizes the body. This was done with a group of psychiatrists at the American Psychiatric Association annual meeting in Chicago (1979).

"You can begin by *closing* your eyes and listening to your breathing . . . *become deeper* than it usually is; feel it *going down* your back. . . . When you breath in, you *can feel* your breath *going down* to your diaphragm. . . . Let your breath *easily* come, and I want you to become aware on a biologic level what's happening when you breathe. . . . As you breathe, you are taking in oxygen that you need for yourself, taking in nutrients for yourself, taking in nutrients for every cell in your body and, as you breathe out, you're *letting go* of things you don't need. . . . You are *letting go* of carbon dioxide and other toxins in the air, filtering them all the way *out* of your *body*. . . . *Now* . . . I would like you to take just a *little deeper*, as you *breathe*, you can feel that you have the right to take in all that you need for yourself . . . the air into each and every cell into your body . . . and, as you breathe out, you can begin to *breathe out* things you don't need — *tension, worry*. . . . You can begin to *let go* with each breath out. With your next breath . . . now . . . if you can imagine breathing out right through your left shoulder . . . you're breathing out from your left shoulder, *breathing out* any *tension* out from that arm all the way *down* through to your arm to your elbow. And then from your elbow, all the way *down* through to your wrist and hand, and then out your fingertips. . . . And that left arm can begin to let go; you *don't need* to hold any *tension* in *that* arm. Then with your next breath, take yourself through to your right shoulder in the same way, breathing out any tension from that shoulder through to your elbow . . . and from your elbow *right down through* to your wrist and hand . . . and right out through your fingertips. . . . And you might begin to imagine what the body looks like on the inside, the blood vessels . . . the nerve networks . . . bones . . . see the muscles *loosening* . . . *relaxing*. . . . *Now*, take yourself *down* through to your left hip in the same way. . . . Imagine breathing . . . you're *breathing out* any *tension* from that left hip, *all the way down* through the thigh to the knee. . . . And then, at the knee, I want you *now* to put any tension in your body right *down* into your knee so that the *tension* in the left knee can begin to build and build, to finally *break* and *wash away*, like a dam breaking, *washing away* any *tension* from you, *down* your lower part of the left leg, *down* through the ankle and foot and out through the toes. . . . So that left leg can begin to *let go.* . . . It doesn't have to hold you up . . . it doesn't have to walk anywhere. . . . It can be supported by the floor. . . . *Now*, take yourself in the same way to the right hip. . . . Begin to *breathe out* any *tension* from that hip all the way *down* through your thighs to your knee, and, just imagining what it might look like on the inside of the thigh . . . the blood network . . . the blood vessels . . . that you can begin to see the tissues *become more* and *more healthy* as you . . . as you breathe. . . . As you take in the air that you need for yourself, you become *more* and *more relaxed* with each breath that you take in. . . . Continue to *breath out* any *tension* from your right knee *all the way down* through to your ankle, to your foot, and right out your toes. . . . You *don't need* that *tension.* . . . *Now*, you can come to your throat. . . . As you breathe, I'd like you to feel the air that comes into your throat, and let the tissue in your throat respond to the air by *yielding*, by *making room* so that your throat can *become more* and *more open*, taking in all that you need for yourself . . . a very open tunnel *going down* into your body . . . and you can even *follow* the air *down* into your lungs, *down* into your chest as your chest rises and *then* as it *falls* . . . and, as it rises, you can feel the air create more space inside of you, more space inside of you for your heart, your lungs, for each internal organ in your body to find its natural healthy position and to *adjust as necessary.* . . . *Now*, with your next breath out, begin to *breathe out* any tension from your stomach. . . . Any knots of tension you can begin to breathe out . . . you don't need them so that the stomach can become much like a calm, peaceful lake, adjusting like it needs to inside of you in order to maintain a state of health, to *adjust* as needed *to.* . . . *Anything* that might be coming up *in* your *own* personal *life.* . . . With your next breath, take yourself *down* through the urethra, breathing *out* any tension from your urethra so it can *begin* to be *loose* and *open*, and for the women, I want you to *take* yourself down through to your vagina and imagine breathing *right out* through your vagina . . . letting your vagina *open* and *relax* and become more *comfortable.* . . . With your next breath imagine breathing right down through the anus as well, letting go of any tension there, very clear and open. And now come to a point on the back of your neck. . . . I want you to imagine breathing through your spinal cord from the top all the way *down* the back, *down* to the center of your back, *slipping down deeper* over each vertebra, right *down* through to your middle back, your *lower* back, and right down through to the tail bone. . . . From that same spot on the back of your neck, let the relaxation spread up your scalp so any tension can fall away from you on the lines of your hair, away from your body, onto the floor, onto the couch, and not moving. . . . Let the relaxation *spread down* over your forehead so that any lines on your forehead can begin to drift further and further apart, *all the way down* through your nose, to your cheeks, to your mouth, the jaw, and right down through to the throat again. . . . Once again you can feel yourself breathing in through your throat, taking all that you need, breathing out any tension so that you can begin to get to know your body very well, through the intimate connection that exists just in breathing. . . . *Now,* I would like you to take yourself through your breathing with your breath, imagine taking yourself to a part of your body that needs attention. . . . Either, maybe a part of your body that's given you a problem in the past, or, something that's bothering you now . . . or just to choose part of your body to go to that will give you some information that you need . . . and as you breathe you're actually taking oxygen into the cells of that part of the body . . . and I would like you now to *focus* on the oxygen that's going *there* to those cells through your bloodstream *right down* to that part of your body, and give yourself the right to create an image of what that part of the body looks like on the inside. . . . You can do this *very quickly* by giving yourself the right to imagine it. . . . You might want to note the color or the shape or maybe just feeling. . . . Give yourself a minute to do that. (one minute silence) Now, what I want you to do is begin to *describe it* to yourself, what it looks like, and *now* what I want you to do is move even a step further, and give yourself the right to imagine . . . begin . . . just that one part of yourself . . . you can put all your attention into that one part of your body right *now* . . . and just let yourself feel what it's like to be that one part of the body, that one part of you. . . . You might even now begin to talk as though you are that part, in the first person, in a way that might assume that *you have a message* to tell yourself. . . . Might just start by describing yourself, what you look like as that part of the body, what you feel like, maybe what you need from the rest of the body, from the mind. . . . And any message you might have, especially if you are a symptom, or something that hurts, or something that you don't feel is quite right in your body, you might *let that part tell you* what it was trying say . . . give yourself the right to imagine. . . . Sometimes the body does give us messages in a non-verbal way. . . . What would it say if it could talk? . . . (silence for two minutes) *Now,* produce a physical *symptom* that *you* want to *heal,* that you want to *create* better *health* in. . . . *Right now,* I want you to *imagine* that part of your body as very, very *healthy,* and at first this might be very difficult, but you can give yourself the right to do it, and very quickly you can imagine what it would look like, if it were *perfectly healthy*, radiantly so, as the oxygen comes into your body, as you *give it what it needs*, what would it look like? . . . What would it feel like? . . . It's very important to imagine what it would feel like *totally healed*. . . . *You have every right* to imagine that. . . . Feel how much you *desire that* for yourself, and that, you only want what is best for you . . . and you can let this image, the healthy part, come to mind in your regular waking activities, to begin to feel what it feels like to *be healthy* (two minute silence). *Right now*, what I would like you to do . . . is give yourself something to look forward to, something good you're going to do for yourself in the next week, something that feels good to you, that feels nurturing, and to enjoy looking forward to that. . . . Promise it to yourself. . . . Now I'd like you to take yourself to a comfortable nature scene . . . perhaps it's the forest, perhaps it's a beach, either one you've been to before, or one that you *go to right now*, that you make up in your mind. . . . And research has shown that as a person takes themselves to a place in their mind that they like, a place that is very relaxing to them, the same neuro-hormones or neuro-chemicals can be released as if they were actually there. Wherever you are, I want you to see *yourself* as radiantly *healthy*, giving yourself every right to the sun if it's there . . . taking in the sun through your skin, enabling you to make vitamin D . . . taking from the air what you need . . . (two minute silence). Now very slowly I'd like you to come back to your breathing, letting that scene fade, knowing that you can go there whenever you need to, whenever you want to . . . that you come back to your breathing right now . . . that you can feel the breathing coming in and going out . . . and *become aware* just by sensing where you are in the room. . . . Without yet opening your eyes, I want you to *become aware* of how far you are from the ceiling, how far it feels, how far you feel from the walls, so that you become very much the center of the room, no matter where you are . . . and as you feel yourself to be the center, you can *become* very *energized*. Very slowly as you've *assimilated whatever you need* from this time, I want you to come comfortably to a sitting position, but moving only what you have to move in order to get there, much like the way that a cat moves, so that you *can relax* each muscle after you use it, and *maintain* a sense of *relaxation* throughout your daily living. Take your time.

When someone falls asleep in a group, that can be avoided in an individual session because someone is right beside them hearing what is happening and can prevent that. Falling asleep is often a protective mechanism in a group visualization, because the person can't or doesn't want to cope alone with what could surface to awareness. Sometimes that night or the next when they go to sleep they will have a dream, and remember that it relates to what they weren't ready for yet. It helps to have such a person talking in order to keep focused. Without focusing there can be a tendency to drift. The therapist keeps the person focused on the imagery. Resistance can be manifested as a tendency to drift, or as tiredness.

The self has a natural protective mechanism. If the client needs help and doesn't have it, certain material will not be accessible. It might be a negative experience to become aware of such feelings alone.

Summary

Visualization is a very helpful technique for general psychotherapy and the psychotherapy of physical illness. Its use requires a basic knowledge of psycholinguistics (indirect hypnosis) and basic psychotherapy skills. Two other techniques will be considered in more detail — applied kinesiology and indirect hypnosis — before the completion of Volume 1.

REFERENCES AND NOTES

[1] See *Birthing Normally* by Gayle Peterson (Mindbody Press, Berkeley, 1981) for a more complete discussion of the birth visualization process. Birth visualization consists of deep relaxation and of guiding the woman through her imagined birth experience using mental imagery techniques.

[2] I believe that what is often labelled hysterical or emotionally labile is, in a sense, representative of a reaction formation by the parts of the self concerned with outward appearances against the obsessive anxiety producing internal dialogue which can be turned off only with difficulty. This is, of course, not always true.

[3] At no time was I judgmental or critical of Mandy's sexual orientation, nor did I encourage a heterosexual relationship as movement toward normalcy.

[4] McCaffrey, Anne. The White Dragon. New York: Ballantine, 1978.

[5] As an interesting aside, we have observed that, if women visualize their labor with an abnormal aspect, this abnormality is usually present in their labor, unless they do further psychophysiological integration. One woman could not visualize the baby's shoulders being born. She would not return for further visualization and her baby experienced shoulder dystocia during delivery. Another woman saw a knife coming through her fat, which she saw as the enemy. She had a Cesarean section.

Chapter Nine

Psychotherapy and Applied Kinesiology

Applied kinesiology was originally developed by George Good-heart, a chiropractor in Detroit. He was interested in the relationship between acupuncture and muscles. Dr. Goodheart found that muscle tone (measured by assessing the ability of a muscle to maintain tone against pressure) was related to specific acupuncture meridians. When the muscle tone was poor and the ability to resist against pressure was low, a particular meridian would be judged out of balance by other methods, including pulse diagnosis. Goodheart then discovered areas on the body that could be stimulated by rubbing, to strengthen muscles, improve tone, and balance the meridian. This chapter describes the holistic use of applied kinesiology.

Kinesiology can be used to educate clients about the connection between the body and the mind. I begin by testing the tone of several muscles in order to learn the patterns of strength and weakness. I push firmly but gently on the muscle and ask the client to hold the muscle in the position originally placed. While the point is massaged, the client closes his or her eyes and reports his or her experience in the same way as described for visualization. Combining applied kinesiology with indirect hypnosis, visualization, and psychotherapy creates a very powerful technique. The usual approach to kinesiology is to use it as a balancing process, similar to a tune-up. Chiropractors are the major practitioners of applied kinesiology and approach the technique as a means of re-aligning the body. Usually, little attention is given to the emotional factors and perceptions of life events that would block the flow of energy in a particular meridian. Combining psychotherapy with kinesiology allows for a second-order approach in which the process of rubbing neurolymphatic points helps in the short-term, and the discovery of how energy gets blocked helps in the long-term as the client is helped to change beliefs and therefore, emotional responses to and perceptions of life events.

In using kinesiology the client is usually lying down, and an area corresponding to the weak muscle (called the neuro-lymphatic point) is massaged. During this deep massage, indirect hypnotic instructions are given for the client to become open to whatever experience emerges. The massage of the lymphatic point can be very painful. The client is asked to become aware of any feelings present. With acupuncture, kinesiology, acupressure, and rolfing (and probably any body-oriented therapy), whenever the client imagines an event about which unresolved feelings remain, or experiences opposing feelings, ambivalence, or an inner struggle about expressing or having a feeling about a particular life situation, the physical pain level of the massage or therapy increases. Whatever increases pain during the kinesiology massage seems to contribute to the problem. Solutions to the problem, when imagined, tend to decrease the perception of pain. Clinical examples will unfold shortly to illustrate this phenomenon. The reader can discover this personally, however, by having a friend rub one of the kinesiology or acupressure points while imagining all the factors associated with various unsolved problems and then imagining solutions.

Kinesiology may be very helpful for people who tend to intellectualize and deny emotions. Massaging a part of the body that is connected with a particular problem can also be helpful diagnostically, because not all the person's problems are connected with the symptom of interest. Paying attention to which symptoms worsen the pain of rubbing will help elucidate the problems that need to be worked with.

The following three sessions (with a woman who came for weight loss for 18 sessions and lost 60 pounds) illustrates how kinesiology can be used. The client begins the session. She's talking about wanting improvements in her relationship that came up in the last kinesiology session. I'd given her an assignment to talk to her husband before the next session.

Lewis: Did anything from last time come up for you during the week that you wanted to talk about now?[A]

Adena: I figured out why I kept thinking of my grandmother, because she tried

[A] I always begin a session by giving the client permission to structure the session or to clear up any unfinished business from previous meetings.

really hard not to be a sexual person, and from pictures I saw of her as a young woman, she was a very sexy woman, voluptuous; and she moved out of my grandfather's bedroom after having two kids in 16 months, that kind of nonsense. I think I'm equating being fat with being matronly — not being really *fat*, but being matronly with not being a sexual person, and that's real irritating to me, and it's not helped by the fact that Jerry and I are not having real good sexual relations right now . . . for whatever reasons . . . he's not sure why.[B] Sometimes it really bothers me, sometimes it doesn't. And the fact that he doesn't view me as a sexual person because I'm a mother may have something to do with why I'm not losing as much weight as I want to. That's what I came up with.[C]

Lewis: This sounds like real important stuff.

Adena: It's real hard for me. I was going to call in and cancel our session today. I thought about it and couldn't deal with it.[D]

Lewis: I appreciate how hard it is to come in when there are all those feelings about not wanting to. It's real hard sometimes to come in and continue and keep going.

[B] In my experience, fear of sexuality is a common underlying theme with fat women, but not as common with men. For men, fear of inadequacy or lack of power in relationships seems very common. Obviously as many underlying issues can emerge as there are fat people.

[C] This information emerged into Adena's consciousness during neurolymphatic massage of the point on the large intestine meridian.

[D] Maybe Adena eats when she feels compelled to think about something else, but doesn't want to think. Then she can kick herself for being fat, that taking precedence over the issues she's afraid she can't cope with.

Adena: My sister pushes me. She's a therapist and she goes through all these problems with her clients. It feels good to be able to put my finger on that part of it. I'm thinking that I'm real sensitive. From the waist down I'm real ticklish, and that makes sense.

Lewis: Those are the areas that are thought to be erotic. Tickling is a real good defense against being touched. When you are ticklish, you won't let anyone touch you. . . . Was that hard to say?

Adena: Yes. . . . I've been rehearsing it for the last week to be able to say it.[E]

Lewis: What do you think made it hard to say?

Adena: You don't talk about sex. It's something you keep in the bedroom. Puritan values, and I come from fairly Puritan background.

Lewis: So it's hard just to talk about it with anyone.[F]

Adena: Yes, it's real hard for Jerry and I to talk about it. He comes from the same background.

Lewis: Yes, I can see how that would be real difficult.

Adena: I don't know what to do with it. I'm hoping Doris[G] won't have the same problem.

[E] I've observed that fat is more closely related to body metabolism than to food intake. A tendency to retain feelings and hold them inside seems to slow down the metabolism and cause the person to digest the food too well. The balancing that is brought about with kinesiology can help speed up digestion by releasing the emotional blocks to higher metabolic levels as well as balancing the functioning of the overall system.

[F] Using kinesiology *while we talk* makes it easier for Adena to talk, because in one view, we're not talking and doing psychotherapy as a primary activity; rather we're concretely balancing the muscles. Anxiety is reduced because some of the

Lewis: How will you go about making sure that doesn't happen?

Adena: I don't know. She's only six months old, so I'm not. . . . Jerry and I make a real point to be very affectionate around Doris. We hug and kiss and keep the lines of communication open by talking to her right now. I'm rehearsing; I practice telling her about where babies come from. She thinks that's funny. She thinks most everything is funny.

Lewis: Yeah, I can really understand how that might interfere with your weight loss.[H]

Adena: It's just an excuse.

Lewis: Do you think you are using it?

Adena: I was trying to put all the blame on Jerry, saying "You are not being very responsive to me, and you are not looking at me as a sexual person," but I think I'm not looking at myself that way too. So, you're matronly, and you can't be sexy.

Lewis: Yes. I think I'll point out to you that at some point you and Jerry might want to do some work with Gayle on those issues as a couple[I]

Adena: I'd love to.

Lewis: Jerry might have trouble?

performance element is removed from talking.

[G] Doris is Jerry and Adena's young daughter.

[H] This sentence reframes what will occur in psychotherapy and kinesiology as weight loss. Weight loss will happen and we will concern ourselves with things that might interfere. The usual assumption behind dieting is that weight loss will not occur.

[I] My thinking is that couples' therapy could get directly to some of these issues more quickly than individual therapy, and therefore be more cost

Adena: He really has problems with any kind of therapy.

Lewis: It doesn't really work to do sex therapy with one of the parties. You need to have both partners talking and communicating.

Adena: He says, "Well, I'd be doing it as a favor to you because I don't think we need a third person involved," and I disagree with him completely. I don't see any value in forcing him to do anything.

Lewis: You might set up a session for him doing it as a favor to you, just to see what happens.

Adena: Yeah.

Lewis: He might be real surprised to find out that it's something he'd get a lot from. That happens a lot, when one partner brings in the other partner, who only comes in as a favor. They often discover just what they can really learn. So . . .

Adena: Maybe I'm just resisting too, putting the blame on him.

Lewis: Yes, blaming him for not coming in, when there's a part of you that would be nervous and anxious about his coming in.

Adena: Hmmm. . . . Hit him with it when he's in a real good, receptive mood.

effective. I'm aware that I'm too aligned with Adena to serve as a good couples' therapist for both she and Jerry, so I'm recommending my associate, Gayle Peterson.

Lewis: It sounds like a real problem area for you guys in your relationship.[J]

Adena: It has been for the past couple of years, probably longer than that.

Lewis: It's a common thing that people who are having trouble with their weight are having trouble with it[J] too.

Adena: I always felt skinnier when we are making love.[K] That's how I perceive myself.

Lewis: Do you feel any guilt around . . . sort of . . . making love, and how do you feel afterwards?

Adena: I feel really good. I usually feel really good. It depends on how Jerry is responding.

Lewis: When you don't feel good, how do you feel?

Adena: Just real dissatisfied that Jerry isn't looking at me as a sexual person. He is looking at me as . . . I had the word and I lost it, because I don't want to look at it. I feel used, I feel very used, and so it's like . . . gee . . . "I have this sexual urge and here she is, and I may as well have it." I feel like a hole in the mattress. That's pretty accurate. That's how it's been since Doris was born.

Lewis: Do you feel any guilt around . . . sort of . . . making you feel that way?

[J] I'm mirroring Adena's use of the word "it" for the word "sex," since I don't want to stake myself to one meaning when another may be correct. "It" provides a lack of referential index, since we can't really be sure what "it" refers to, although we can speculate.

[K] Now Adena is defining "it" as "making love." By mirroring her use of the word "it," until she defines the word, I've gotten her meaning. Alternately, I could have used a meta-model[1] approach, and asked her, "What do you mean by "it"? What is "it"?

Adena: I don't. I just get real depressed.

Lewis: And what kinds of things do you do to make yourself feel better when you are depressed?

Adena: Play a lot of music.

Lewis: Anything else you do when you are depressed?

Adena: I don't eat. That's one nice thing about being depressed.

Lewis: That you don't eat?

Adena: I'm usually too upset. I usually bury it and cry a lot. I'm too depressed to be able to eat anything . . . (pauses for several moments).[L] My muscles are fairly solid, so I'm in good shape for being overweight. Old pictures make me feel terrible; looking at my skinny pictures.

Lewis: How does that make you feel?

Adena: Pretty depressed. It is really a bad thing for me to do. And I try to avoid doing it. And I keep thinking about how I took labor one contraction at a time. I should take losing weight one pound at a time, because it might succeed where other systems of dieting haven't.

Lewis: I noticed that you laughed when you said "more depressed looking at those old pictures." How did you feel while you were laughing?

[L]   Adena may be distracting herself by feeling depressed about her body from feeling how dissatisfied she is with her relationship.

Adena: I think it is funny that I torture myself like that. I know that if I look at the pictures I'm going to get depressed about it. I still do. I have them on my bulletin board so I can look at them every once in a while. I have to move things to look at them now. It is just ridiculous to me to put up my pictures and torture myself and yet I do it consistently.

Lewis: Kind of like punishing yourself?

Adena: Bad girl.

Lewis: Do you think it would be helpful to you to talk more or just to go straight into the muscle testing and balancing? Which would help you the most?

Adena: I don't know. There's nothing else right now that's coming up.

Lewis: Maybe we should go ahead. Go ahead and lie down and maybe our work with your muscles will bring up more feelings for you in the next week that we can discuss next time.[M]

Adena: Now that I start thinking, I want to eat, when I know I'm not hungry, I want to eat something. When I start thinking about things that are bothering me emotionally, I'm no longer hungry.

Lewis: That's really good to be aware of.

[M] I'm also giving Adena a suggeston for the kinesiology work to bring up more feelings and issues for us to discuss at a later date.

Adena: Yeah. Should I lie on my back?

Lewis: Yes. Let's begin with the stomach meridian. I'll test your muscle and see if it's strong. Put your arm up like this[N] . . . thumb toward your feet . . . okay . . . ready . . . resist . . . okay . . . that's still somewhat weak. Try the other side . . . okay . . . ready . . . resist. . . . Yeah, also weak. We'll go ahead and work with the stomach meridian. Before we do that let me test the large intestine meridian, the one we worked with last time. Lift your leg[O] . . . good . . . and turn it inward like this . . . okay . . . ready . . . I'm going to push down toward your other leg . . . ready . . . resist. Okay, that's pretty strong . . . good . . . now, let's try the other side. . . . That's real good. A little stronger on the right. Maybe we should just work today with the stomach, then. Okay, I'm going to begin rubbing the point for the stomach meridian,[P] right here. See what comes up for you again, and if any of it takes a form that you can see. Sometimes it's real helpful to talk while you are experiencing, knowing that can make the experience more vivid . . . so that you can describe it as you talk about it, paying attention to the sensation from the point, letting me know what thoughts

[N]   I'm using the standard instructions and positions for the pectoralis major clavicular muscle (stomach meridian) found in reference 2.

[O]   Here I'm using the standard instructions and positions for the tensor fascia lata muscle (large intestine meridian) found in reference 2.

[P]   Again, see reference 2 for the exact location of these points.

or feelings or pictures you're having if the sensation at the point becomes more or less painful. Pay attention as you have done before to what makes the pain connected with my rubbing worse, and what makes the pain better, or what makes it go away.Q

Adena: When the pain really got worse, I was thinking about my mother; she really was a very non-sexual person. She was definitely a mother and not a woman lover. My memories of her were of her being very matronly.

Lewis: It's really important to be aware that your body reacts to thinking that your mother was very matronly. Is there a part of you that believes you can't be skinny after having kids; you have to be a mother and mothers aren't thin?

Adena: (Nods yes) Because all my aunts and my one grandmother were all fairly matronly looking. It's real silly because I have strong memories of them when they were in their mid-thirties. I'm sure that mothers can't be sexual people.

Lewis: So there's a part of you that thinks you can't be a sexy mother?

Adena: Because it was never out in the open. It was kept behind closed doors in the

Q   This sequence of conversation reminds her to pay attention to what we have previously discovered — that thoughts, feelings, or images contributing to the problem will make the rubbing of the point more painful and that thoughts, feelings, or images contributing to solving the problem decrease any pain connected with rubbing the neurolymphatic point. This helps me to center very clearly upon the specific conflicts associated with the problem.

bedroom. It wasn't until I was an adult that I saw my parents actually kissing on the mouth. They'd occasionally peck each other on the cheek, or occasionally he'd put his arm around her, but it was real self-conscious, and that was just the way all of the adults I was around were. My parents started being a little more out-front about being sexual people when we were all grown.

Lewis: Any idea of why you have to be fat to keep sex in the bedroom? Why you can't be thin and still keep sex in the bedroom, too?[R]

Adena: No, but they were embarrassed about appearing sexual. My parents never touched tenderly around us kids. They were never very affectionate.

Lewis: Anything else there for you?

Adena: Huh-uh. I don't think so.

Lewis: I have an idea that you could try if you want to. . . .[S] To just start saying over and over again for a few minutes and see what happens to you, "I have to be fat so I won't be sexual."

Adena: I could cry.

Lewis: Okay. Just see what happens.

[R] Now I'm challenging the linkage that exists in Adena's family and in her mind that she needs to be fat to keep sex in the bedroom. Such a linkage is by no means logical. Thin people can be asexual just as easily as fat people. In fact, some people solve the problem of keeping sex in the bedroom by being so thin as to appear perpetually pre-pubescent.

[S] I never demand that anyone try my suggestions. They always have the choice to refuse.

Adena: It's hard to say. My throat's tightening up. I have to be fat so I won't be sexual . . . That sounds stupid (laughs) . . . I have to be fat so I won't be sexual . . . I have to be fat so I won't be sexual. . . . I should say, I have to be skinny so I can be sexual. . . . I have to be fat so I won't be sexual . . . I have to be fat . . . yaa . . . it's getting hard. . . . It's not right. . . . It's dumb, it's ridiculous.

Lewis: Wonder why it's getting hard to say? Because it's dumb and ridiculous?

Adena: Probably because my gut feeling is that that's the message I've gotten.

Lewis: Even saying it those few times, how did you feel, besides feeling a little silly?

Adena: Besides silly? That's an excuse that I thought was because I'm afraid to be sexual. And that I've always been afraid to be sexual.

Lewis: What's your disaster?[T]

Adena: My disaster if I'm sexual? I have two sisters. One of them is out here, and I have another sister who is two years older than me. And the one that is closest to me in age had a terrible reputation when she was in high school, and she is clearly a very sexual person, and I had a reaction to that and I didn't want to be like her. . . . I didn't

[T] I approach a fear often by asking the person what their worst fantasy or disaster fantasy connected with the fear is.

want to have a reputation. . . . I wanted them to like me because of me, because of the person, not because of the sexual person.

Lewis: I want to be loved for me and not for sex?

Adena: Uh huh.

Lewis: How about if you try saying that?

Adena: I want to be loved for me and not for sex. . . . That's real easy to say.

Lewis: Okay, why don't you try saying it for a while.

Adena: I want to be loved for me and not for sex. . . . I want to be loved for me and not for sex. . . . I want to be loved for me and not for sex. . . . That feels true, that feels okay.

Lewis: How does someone prove that they love you not for sex?

Adena: They don't put any sexual demands on me.

Lewis: I catch the glimpse of some knot that is not unraveled, and I can't get any more than that from what you've just been saying. I catch a glimpse of some place where it all comes together.^U But, I don't know what it is.

Adena: My whole relationship with Jerry was initially non-sexual, and that was one of the

U   I'm reflecting upon a vague feeling I'm having so that Adena can help me by clarifying what's going on, or how the knot will unravel itself.

things I liked about him. That, initially, we liked each other, we were friends, and we didn't become lovers for a couple of years after we met each other. That's a real conflict.

Lewis: Friends and lovers?

Adena: The whole idea that you can be both, that you should be both. It's part of the conflict that I want to have a sexual relationship with Jerry, but at the same time I don't, because then I can feel real used if I do.

Lewis: Used for sex and not loved for yourself?

Adena: Yeah, that's it. That just really freaks me out (laughs). I know I blame my sister, Pat, for putting me through the hassle of having to not be a sexual person because I didn't want to be like her. I hadn't ever thought that I had any of the long term effects.

Lewis: Can you take that any further?

Adena: I think the whole thing is the problem that is probably at the root of the problem that Jerry and I have been having in our relationship. Hmm. I don't know what to do with that.

Lewis: Okay. Let's test your muscle. [V]

Adena: All right. Like this?

[V] The point at which the expression of emotional material begins to slow or stop serves as an indication to me that we need to return to the body. The ore vein of blocked emotions being mined at that particular neurolymphatic point location is becoming sparse enough that our mining operation of the underground of consciousness needs to relocate to continue profitable operation. During the entire time since testing of the last muscle occurred in the transcript, I have been rubbing

Lewis: Right . . . ready . . . resist. Now the other side. . . . Ready . . . resist. . . . Great, both are strong. Now, let's try another muscle . . . the anterior deltoid. Okay . . . let your arm up like this. . . . Okay, I'm going to push down towards the floor. . . . Ready . . . resist . . . okay. . . . That has to do with the gall bladder. My experience has been that that's often where there are feelings that are being held in that aren't being expressed. Mostly I've found anger to be most connected to the gall bladder meridian.

Adena: That's funny you should say that because when you were doing that I was thinking that I really should share all this with Jerry. He gets real upset; he feels real threatened; he takes it real personally when I talk about problems I'm having with sex because that means he has a lot to do with that. I've had problems with it all my life. That *really makes me angry.*

Lewis: And that anger is probably even harder to express than the other stuff. If you can't express the other stuff, you can't express the anger about being unable to express the other stuff.

Adena: Yeah, right.

Lewis: That's a real knot. Let's test the other side . . . okay . . . ready . . . resist . . . good.

the neurolymphatic point with fairly constant pressure. Unlike many "touch for health" instructors and chiropractors, I don't believe it is necessary to test and strengthen all meridians each session. I have observed that balancing one or two meridians during an hour session while the client becomes aware of blocked or repressed feelings and emotions or resolves problems or ambivalences often balances other meridians anyway.

. . . That's weak, too, but a little stronger than the other side. Maybe because you've begun to express that anger.

Adena: I want to put Jerry in a chair and gag him and tie him down. Then I can talk to him. But that doesn't do any good either because then we can't dialogue.

Lewis: Maybe in a setting where you have someone else to mediate?

Adena: I know that. I know that's real important. For some reason I'm afraid he'll get threatened.

Lewis: Maybe you could go see the movie *Wifemistress*.[W] A couple of my male clients made great progress in therapy after seeing that show. Then you could talk about your situation as part of your reaction to the movie.

Adena: I don't know if Jerry would go. Jerry would rather watch *The Creature from the Black Lagoon*.

Lewis: How could you present it to him?

Adena: Right now I think the way I could present it to him is that I'm having problems, and he can help me by talking to me or coming in with me to talk to you. A real pattern is that I bring up something that he feels

[W] The movie *Wifemistress* is probably the best sexually therapeutic movie I have ever seen. This movie played for one year consecutively in Berkeley, and during that time I sent many clients with success, as well as seeing it three times myself. The movie communicates an *attitude* of healthy sexuality, which is in my experience so much more often the problem in the "sexual dysfunctions," rather than a mechanical sense of not "doing it right." I have been disappointed with many sex therapists who approach sex mechanistically without appreciating the need for change in belief and attitude about sexuality.

threatened about and he gets angry, but he doesn't get angry about that [threatening material] but instead gets angry about something else that's really silly and doesn't make any sense.

Lewis: That's a common way that people communicate with each other.

Adena: I figured it out about 2 years ago that he was not really angry about what he was saying he was angry about, but about other things, and that's equally hard too.

Lewis: It sounds like, much as I think that what we are doing is good, it seems more important right now for you and he to meet with Gayle and do some work around your relationship and sexuality. I think that would get you thin much faster than what we are doing.[X]

Adena: I think that's probably real true, and it's just a matter of convincing him.

Lewis: How about if you tell him that I think that in the long run you guys will spend less money by doing it that way?

Adena: (Laughter) That might just hit him in the right place.

Lewis: I think that is true, too.

Adena: I think so. I feel like I need a block of time. He's so busy and I'm so busy that we

[X]   If finances weren't a limitation for Adena, I would have recommended both individual therapy for her and couples' therapy for her and Jerry. My response here is based upon knowledge of her limited resources.

talk on the telephone more than we do in person.

Lewis: That could involve an agreement that you need an hour a week in which you must talk to each other.

Adena: I've been working on that, turning off the TV set and sitting down to talk. It's real hard for us to talk face to face. He calls me from work and we talk for half an hour or 45 minutes.

Lewis: Just like it's hard for you to talk to me here face to face, like you kind of have to rehearse.[Y] It's been getting easier for you as you do it. It would get easier for both of you if you did.

Adena: Maybe it would be helpful if I borrowed this tape at some point and have him listen to it. No, no, I can't do that.

Lewis: No, that wouldn't be real fair.

Adena: I'm looking for the easy way out. We write letters to each other too, especially when we are particularly angry. We have a collection of really angry letters. We used to really communicate with each other only in that way.

Lewis: Where you are getting to is a real common place that couples get to, and in this day, most couples resolve it by

[Y]   Much of our therapy involves actually giving Adena a chance to practice expressing herself, face to face, in a safe situation where she won't be attacked. Such therapy might also be called expressiveness training, and is usually a component of much of my work with clients. Often I observe that clients with physical illness have difficulty expressing their inner feelings both to the active consciousness and to other people.

splitting up, and it is something that once you get on the other side of it, the relationship can really begin to grow and develop and flourish. Other couples resolve it by having separate bedrooms, or whatever they do.

Adena: Or by being miserable. My grandmother spent 55 years being miserable with my grandfather.

Lewis: Luckily, people don't do that anymore in our culture.

Adena: I feel normal living here. It scares me to think about going back there again. [Going back to Indiana]^z

Lewis: You're going back for how long?

Adena: A couple of weeks. My whole family lives back there.

Lewis: It's hard to go back to a place where people still see you as you've been and not as you've become.

Adena: I was considered relatively strange as it was, and I know that Berkeley has had some influence on me so that now I'll seem really weird.

Lewis: For sure. Okay, we'll finish working on this muscle. Let's just test it again. . . . Ready . . . resist. . . . Okay . . . now . . . resist. . . . Ready . . . resist ready . . . resist. Okay, it's still a little weak, but you can see that

^{z} Clients usually experience some type of relapse upon returning home to the environment of their childhood during a course of therapy. Ideally, such a visit should serve as a time for family therapy and emotional reconciliation between family members utilizing the services of the local family therapist. Unfortunately, few families are emotionally able to feel ready for such treatment. I "prescribe the symptoms" to clients returning home for a visit, telling them that there's no question in my mind that they will experience a relapse. What I would like them to do is pay attention to the triggering events or behaviors on the part of other family members, leading them to that relapse. Then, they may "resist" me by not just getting out those feelings has made some other muscles strong. . . . Okay, resist . . . resist. . . . Okay, just let yourself feel, and if you can, you can describe the experiences you are having, which can be helpful, because sometimes that brings up things for you.

Adena: Something about my fear of not having Jerry is there.

Lewis: Like maybe if you expressed all these things to him he would leave?

Adena: Thinking that it's not worth the trouble. But on the other hand, we stuck it out before.[AA] I imagine we either have some sort of masochistic relationship with each other or we've got something worth working out. I prefer to think it is the latter. He's a real good person. I'm real afraid of hurting him, too.

Lewis: Do you think he might have some stuff that might hurt you if he wanted to talk to you?

Adena: Yeah, probably. That may be one of the reasons that we are not talking, that we are afraid of hurting each other. Maintaining the status quo. There's a lot of tension in our relationship, too; just trying to maintain the status quo, trying not to hurt each other.

Lewis: That probably takes a lot out of the part of the relationship that wants to grow.

relapsing, or, if a relapse does occur, it has already been reframed as a temporary occurence.

[AA] The reference to "sticking it out before" suggests that relationship problems are stored in a kinesthetic mode for Adena. Kinesiology is a kinesthetic therapy, and my combining talking with rubbing points gives Adena a model for the transfer of kinesthetic to auditory mode. Use of auditory mode permits better expression and phrasing than remaining stuck in kinesthetic mode.

Adena: Yeah, I think so.

Lewis: Okay . . . resist . . .
okay . . . resist . . . resist . . .
great.

The session continues with work on other muscles. This transcript
gives a sense of how one combines psychotherapy with kinesiology by
massaging the point and encouraging the client to visualize or talk.

The next session was a visualization session which leads into a
kinesiology. Both sessions are presented in order to show the progression through these two techniques.

Adena: I went clothes
shopping Saturday, and it
reinforced this whole thing that
fat people are supposed to look
ridiculous, because all the
clothes are made for people who
weigh five pounds and are six
feet tall. And I'm still depressed
about it. Then I talked to my
brother on Saturday, and I think
I told you about it, he weighed
300 pounds and now he's down
to 187.

Lewis: That's really a big drop.

Adena: Well, yeah. He had
some trauma about it. But that's
real discouraging, and I'm
finding out that you have to
learn about how to be fat; about
how to approach things and feel
good about losing weight and
still feel fat or fatter than he did.
And I've been talking to a friend
of mine who's an ex-fat person. I
just feel like nothing is going to
change.

Lewis: You feel kind of stuck?

Adena: Yeah, I sit back and
look; I've lost ten pounds since

we started doing this. That's something positive, but I *feel* fatter now than I did then.

Lewis: That's something that happens for sure. When people lose weight they start to feel fatter than they did when they were fat. Why? Maybe it has to do with your body image. Maybe your body is trying to get you to eat.

Adena: I've lost my appetite, which is nice in some ways.

Lewis: One thing I would suggest is that we do today instead of doing the muscle work is a visualization to try and find out why you feel fatter when you're less than when you're more.

Adena: (Laughs) Yeah, that might work. I've got to do something to calm down. I went to a thing last night, a private showing of the Dresden exhibit, which was real nice, because there were all these people running around in their costume dresses and looking real skinny, and (laughs). . . .

Lewis: Okay, maybe we should do that then. Do you want to do that?

Adena: Sure, why not.

Lewis: The things that seem to work best are either lying on the floor, or being in the chair with your feet propped up and your head on pillows.

Adena: In the chair.

Lewis: Let me get the pillows.
(Getting set up.)

Visualization:

Lewis: Okay, why don't we begin with just some breathing designed to help you *become more relaxed*, knowing that there is something inside of you that you want to *get in touch*[BB] with around fatness. . . . You can start by breathing *slowly and deeply* . . . okay . . . as you *breathe slowly and deeply* . . . you can begin to breathe into your head, sending the air into that space behind your eyes . . . and just *letting go of* any *tension* that might be there. . . . And breathing into your forehead, *letting go* of the *tension* in your forehead. . . . Breathing into the top of your head and just *letting go* . . . *of* more and more *tension* with each breath. . . . Breathing into the back of your head and *down* your neck, keeping your whole *head more relaxed* . . . feeling how that can feel and . . . breathing in and *letting go* of tension all the way down. . . .[CC] It can be just as the air or a fountain . . . a fountain in which the water comes in and flows up into your head . . . filling up your head . . . rising just as water rises in the fountain, all the way to the top . . . and then *coming down, down,* all over your forehead . . . and *deeper down*

[BB] I'm beginning in a kinesthetic mode because Adena has already related that she *feels* stuck in her fatness. So she needs to *get in touch* with something.

[CC] The use of the phrases "breathing in" and "breathing into" follows the actual rising of Adena's chest during inspiration and expiration.

your temples and ears . . . *further down* over the back of your head, just as water rises to the top of the fountain . . . perhaps real cool and perhaps it's in a container and flows *down* over your nose, cheeks, mouth, chin, neck . . . *all the way down*, back into the water from which you came . . . and as you *breathe, slowly and deeply*, your hands can begin sometime . . . the right time . . . not too soon, if they're not ready . . . to have a warm, tingling feeling at the tips of your fingers, a warm tingling feeling that can begin to grow and expand so that your hands can begin to rise in energy, to have a *feeling of being more full* and *more expanded than they are.* . . . It's just like in the mountains, the water rises from the stream, coming out of the earth, and it begins to *flow down*, first slowly and more shallowly and as it goes down, it begins to *flow more quickly* and *more deeply* — just like that warm feeling can flow *down* into your elbows, can travel all the way *down* through your forearms into your elbows . . . the warm relaxing feeling . . . like watching the water run *down* the mountainside . . . *first* a *small* stream, and *then faster* and bigger and *deeper, traveling down* the mountainside . . . it starts to *go faster* and sometimes there can be waterfalls . . . can be *so comfortable* to sit beside the banks of the river, watching the water run down, *washing the weight* of tension from its banks . . . *running down* from the elbow, running further on into the upper arm — a warm, good feeling, running all the way through. . . .DD The water eventually comes to the foothills. . . . Lying beside the banks . . . breathing slowly and deeply, you can hear the wind whistling in the treetops . . . a *very relaxing* feeling. . . . As the *breathing slows* and becomes *more relaxed*, the water becomes wider, deeper, as it reaches the valley, to go through the valley, . . . just like two streams could come together . . . two arms can join the shoulders, and the force of that relaxed energy can *float down* the spine, *step by step down* the spine, past each bone . . . each vertebrae, one at a time . . . *traveling down* along into a lake of energy. As the bottom of that trunk comes to the bank, a *warm, relaxing* energy can *travel down* the spine, following *all the way down* to the top of the spine and flowing out the place where a lake might let go of its water to flow down a mountainside because *it's full enough.*EE Traveling out to the sea, just as that more relaxing energy can flow on out through the vagina, out of your body, out of the continent, out of the land, into the world. And, as one breathes slowly and deeply, eventually

DD   This imagery can relate also to her weight loss as well as to the relaxation process. Initially her weight loss is slow, and later it can build and go faster and faster and she can be comfortable with that initial slowness. There are also some specific suggestions about "washing the weight" away.

EE   I'm also trying to give the idea that she's full enough and can let go of food on the inside and not keep storing all the nutritional content of her food, but releasing the extra that she doesn't need like extra water would drain away from a lake.

the feet, at some time, can begin
to feel that warm, relaxing feel
of tingling. . . . Perhaps
beginning at your toes, the warm
expanded feeling — just like the
feeling you might have standing
under a tropical waterfall. . . .
Just the right height . . . the
water comes down, splashing
down over your body and your
legs . . . your feet relaxed in the
water . . . the warm feeling . . .
the warm water just directing its
energy downward. . . . The feet
can feel relaxed, especially very
comfortable . . . legs can too.
Breathing into them to relax
them as if to fill them up. . . .
You can let your breath just
flow down into your hands. . . .
So now all the parts of your
body can become more and
more relaxed, and even as you
continue to hear the sound of
my voice you can become more
and more relaxed just as you
breathe, if you want to. And we
might begin with your stomach
by going down to the stomach,
maybe by traveling down inside
through your stomach looking
into it. And if you have a picture
now of what it might look like
inside . . . you can *tell me* . . .
just keeping your eyes closed
and then focused . . . *begin to
describe what you're seeing* . . .
and that can help you go *even
deeper* into the experience,
become more focused.[FF]

Adena: It looks like a very
big, empty cavern.

[FF] The transition from
kinesthetic (fullness, stuckness)
to visual-auditory modes has
been accomplished now.

Lewis: Can you see any linings of the wall?

Adena: Ridges.

Lewis: And what do they look like?

Adena: Pink and white.

Lewis: Now make your stomach look hungry and see what it looks like.

Adena: It does right now from my not having any lunch.

Lewis: Now make it look full and tell me what it looks like.

Adena: Emotional, it's packed.

Lewis: Okay, now can you ask your stomach how it feels about your body being fat? Just let it answer without thinking too much, without your mind saying, without hearing until it's said.

Adena: Uncomfortable, too full. Out of shape.

Lewis: How does it feel about being thin?

Adena: Compact.

Lewis: Can you ask your stomach what part of your body makes you feel like you're fat when you're getting thinner?

Adena: The flab.

Lewis: Does your stomach know what the flab's trip is? The flab . . . .

Adena: The flab's concealing
this thin person, making my
stomach look fat when it's not.
It's an untouchable layer of flab.

Lewis: What's the flab afraid
of? Does the stomach know
what the fear is? Flab, could
you let (tape is changed and some
dialogue is missed) . . . .
Won't you tell what you could
do with flab so it won't stand
in your way?

Adena: (Inaudible)

Lewis: Stomach doesn't know,
though, because when you're
bound to eat and you lose
weight, flab makes you feel
fatter than you are. So stomach
doesn't know how to deal with
flab.

Adena: Almost like it is
pointless to try.

Lewis: Okay, now, would you
like to go back through the tunnel
to find a time in your life when
you learned that . . . when flab
learned its job? Would you like
to *go back?*

Adena: There's a hole. I kept
hearing fat . . . fat . . . that that
was baby fat and that it just
disappeared. . . . And it didn't
just disappear.

Lewis: Can you remember the
first time you heard that?

Adena: No . . . it seems . . .
probably I was nine or ten . . .
when I started becoming real

aware of my body . . . it made it real easy just to ignore and make the whole thing go away.

Lewis: Okay.

Adena: That's sad . . . very much what's happening now. . . . The whole time that I was pregnant I got information not to worry because I was gaining the weight, because after the baby was born it would go away because I was not so fat.

Lewis: And it didn't happen.

Adena: It didn't happen. Now I'm getting the story that when I wean her, it will go away. Just a series of lies, and it's stuff I want to believe.

Lewis: Could you *imagine now* a place where you *could go*, a safe place where *you* could *go* to *undo that*, to meet flab in the flesh and to start some serious negotiation?

Adena: Here?

Lewis: Uh huh. How about *going to a meadow?* Let yourself *see yourself in the meadow. Tell me* about the meadow.

Adena: It's fall and there's tall grass; the flowers have been here before. You know, it's a blue sky and very pretty.

Lewis: Can you remember the last time you were there?

Adena: Right before I found out I was pregnant.

Lewis: And what did you look like then?

Adena: Chunky, but not fat. I thought I was really fat.

Lewis: Uh huh. And while there, stand there in the meadow and in your mind's eye, take off your clothes, and tell me what your body looks like.

Adena: Rubenesque.

Lewis: Okay, tell me about each part of your body, what you see and how you feel about that part.

Adena: My face is a lot thinner . . . I see my cheekbones . . . no double chin. . . . My shoulder bones are sticking apart . . . not real skinny . . . comfortable. . . . Basically no excess fat. . . . Everything's nicely proportioned. . . . I can see my hip bones. . . . My thighs are not touching; the stretch marks are gone . . . pre-baby. . . . Oh no, not too bad.

Lewis: Good . . . now there's a path going through the meadow, and there's something at the end of the path that you need to contact or find. You may not get there today, but you can *start the journey,* if you want to. Somewhere along the path, flab is hiding. You want to run into flab somewhere there, and you need to *deal with flab.* Is flab a he or a she? Can you tell me that? Was there a time you talked before, to flab? Or an it?

Adena: It's an it.

Lewis: It's an it. Somewhere along the path it will be, and it's important for you to recognize any disguises that flab might be carrying. Sometimes flab can be a very cunning, crafty fellow and will disguise himself to make it appear other than it is. If you look around in the meadow, you can find some object that you can carry with you in your journey, to help you recognize flab when you see it. When you find that object, tell me what it is.

Adena: A big club.

Lewis: Okay, ready to *start* on the journey?

Adena: Uh huh.

Lewis: Okay, take your club in hand and just *start out*, and *let me know* what it's like as you walk along the path, where you go and *what you see*.

Adena: Long, tall grass. Higher than my head. Makes it real easy for things to hide. Cake, lots of cake.

Lewis: What does cake say?

Adena: Don't know.

Lewis: And what do you say?

Adena: "Forget it." *Nasty thing;* it makes me really feel sick.

Lewis: Really get in touch
with that nausea. Feel your body
feeling nauseous at the *sight* of
nasty old *cake.* And when you
want to, just bash it with your
club.

Adena: Make it flat.

Lewis: You know when you're
done dealing *with cake.*

Adena: I think I'm done with
it, finally; it's horrible. Every
time I eat it, I hate it.

Lewis: Okay.

Adena: It's real hard to say
no, even though it makes me feel
sick.

Lewis: I'm thinking if you'll
look around now, hiding in the
grass, you can find some
object or figure or being that can
help you in dealing with cake,
that can make it easy to *say no,*
now. Just start looking around
in the tall, waving grass and it
may be very nearby.

Adena: There's a real skinny
being. We were counting
calories. I picked it up and put it
in my hands.

Lewis: Okay, maybe that's a
part of your self that you need
to give you some help, to give
you some feedback, to give you
some strength about what you
can do.

Adena: It says carry a picture
of a skinny me with me . . . that

would help . . . and when people
offer me things like cake and
brownies and all those empty
calories, just pull the picture
out, and say "this is what I want,
not fat."

Lewis: Can you *do that?*

Adena: Yeah.

Lewis: Good. Now is there
anything more to get from that
part of you that you just ran
into?

Adena: An understanding that
I'll probably never get that
skinny again, but it's possible to
get real close to it. I'm not really
stuck this way; it's not really a
hopeless situation.

Lewis: Okay, now find a nice
place to camp and set up your
tent there along the path, and let
me know when you've done
this.

Adena: Okay.

Lewis: Okay, and just lie
down and relax now in your
tent. Being sure that you know
how to get back to the tent, just
let yourself come back to the
room that we started in, at your
own speed, at your own rate,
making sure that your camp is in
good order. Everything is in a
good arrangement to come back
to, to continue whenever you
have the urge to continue.

Adena: I can hardly stay with
that body business and return to
the places where I've been.

Lewis: I'm thinking that you'll need to put this body in your good graces in order to get to that body, and I'm wondering, if *you* could just *give*, perhaps surround this body with white light all around and give it the *acceptance it needs* in the same way that you pitch your tent on the path, to *accept this body* as a stopping point on the way to that body that you want and *settle* down to camp *comfortably* in it.

Adena: How would it be comfortable?

Lewis: You don't have to *get* too *comfortable*, just comfortable enough to rest and take in what you need, and then to get up and continue the journey, just to zero in on a long hike and travel, you need to be comfortable in the place that you rest in.

Adena: I feel like Count Dracula.

Lewis: How is that like Count Dracula?

Adena: I rest and then I can turn into a fat monster.

Lewis: I'm thinking that if you spent a little time each day checking in with that thin part of you, it will be a whole lot easier to *get there* . . . just a few minutes a day . . . a few minutes a day you could see her; could *imagine being her*. She can give you a lot of help, and help you

with the goal of making the
journey to where you need to
go.

Adena: And it's not
something that's useless?

Lewis: No.

Adena: I need to find a zipper.

Lewis: Find where it is then.
Let yourself see the zipper.

Adena: It starts up by my
neck, which makes sense since
this is the first place to start
working on it is in my mouth,
not in my feet. I can't eat from
my stomach — I always begin
with my mouth.

Lewis: Like with cake?

Adena: It's not just with cake.
It's with any kind of food. What
it really boils down to is
knowing that I have the power
to get rid of the fat, to unzip
what I am from the fat. That's
real tricky because I want to be
powerful. I need to be
comfortable with my power in
order to be skinny.

Lewis: And one way to not
get skinny is to believe that you
don't have power until you are
skinny.

Adena: And making excuses.
The other thing is there is a
skinny person inside me, and
that person has the power to
help me be skinny. That's when
I imagine the stomach shrinking.

Just following the first time, I
was always on this tremendous
thing. I'm just a skinny person
with a fat person inside trying to
get out. And now I feel the other
way around; there's a skinny
person inside trying to get out.

A final session toward the end of my work with Adena will provide
a closure on the marriage of kinesiology and psychotherapy.

Adena: I had a really nice talk
with my husband last
Wednesday. I had to go out and
I told him to have a nice big
joint rolled when I came home,
and we talked for three or four
hours, and he doesn't want to
come in and see anyone for
therapy right now. We made a
contract, if things haven't
changed significantly in the next
few months, we're going to re-
evaluate. So that will be July
when we're going to re-evaluate.
That's probably very acceptable
to me, for he gets really scared
about coming for therapy, and I
can't force him to do it. That
was very clear (probably for the
first time in ages) about what I
thought was wrong and what I
wanted to have done in that talk.
He made me really angry and I
wanted to jump up and down on
him, and we talked a lot about
our relationship, when we first
met, and what I wanted out of
that now. Things have changed.
That I didn't feel comfortable
about how the physical
relationship with him was. I also
want a really good intellectual

relationship, and we haven't had
that.

Lewis: Uh-huh.

Adena: So, we're really
working hard on that, starting
reading some books.

Lewis: Okay . . . sounds good.

Adena: Yeah . . . I'm falling in
love with the guy. . . . We'll see.
. . . The last week has been real
good. . . . We'll see what
happens after the honeymoon
runs out.

Lewis: I think that it's a real
important landmark for your
relationship to sit down and talk
like that for three or four hours.

Adena: We've tried before,
but I've been totally inarticulate
about what I needed and how I
was feeling. It wasn't that bad.
He didn't hate me. In fact, I
think he likes me a lot better.

Lewis: Funny how that is. It
usually is the case.

Adena: I should know better.
I should know that . . . I'm
always scared . . . it's kind of
like getting a shot (sigh).

Lewis: Okay, that's great.
How about, was there any of the
other stuff we worked on last
time that you did anything with
during the week?

Adena: No, that was my main
trip.

Lewis: That was pretty major.

Adena: And the realization
that one of the reasons our sex
life is so lousy is because our
intellectual life has been lousy
too. He has to love me for
myself and for my mind, before
he can love me for my body,
and I was not very clear about
that with him until last week.

Lewis: Was that hard for you
to talk about here?

Adena: No, I've been real
excited about coming here all
day.GG In fact I dreamed about
it. I dreamed I came around and
you decided you didn't want to
talk to me, and I had to talk to
somebody I didn't know. I said
that it wasn't really okay, but I
guess I had to go along with
it.HH

Lewis: Was there any more to
the dream than that?

Adena: No, that's all I
remember. I wasn't angry about
it, just kind of disappointed.

Lewis: I'm sure that must have
happened to you once then. You
had an appointment with me
that I wasn't able to keep.

Adena: Yes.

Lewis: Uh huh. Has that ever
happened to you during the time
we've been working here on
your weight problem?

Adena: No.

GG   Adena has now learned to
express herself and can do so
easily in the therapy situation,
and, more importantly, with her
husband.

HH   This dream suggests to me
that Adena is preparing herself
for the termination phase of
therapy.

Lewis: Good. Then maybe it was when we met a year or two ago.

Adena: Yes.

Lewis: Hmm, so maybe there are some feelings left over about that?

Adena: No, I just figured that if people can't be tolerant about sudden changes in schedules and the fact that there are things that come up, maybe we shouldn't be here.[II]

Lewis: Is there any more to talk about? Then let's see what your muscles have to say today. Let's test your stomach muscle [pectoralis major clavicular].[JJ]

Lewis: Ready. Hold your arm up now. I won't try to surprise you. Okay, let's off-balance a little bit now. What you want to do is put your arm right here.[KK]

Lewis: Okay. Ready. This is (pushing) good. See what telling all that stuff to Jerry does?[LL]

Adena: I should have recorded it all, so I could play it back.

Lewis: Really, then you could play it back for him in a month.

Adena: Show him what kind of agreements he made.

Lewis: Put your arm back there.[MM] Okay, I'm going to push down . . . ready . . . this is (pushing) uh huh.

[II] I could have followed up on the feelings about possibly being ready to leave therapy, but I decided to save that discussion for later. I had seen Adena a year previously for a birth visualization during her pregnancy, and had been forced to cancel a session at short notice due to a family emergency. My counter-transference may be emerging, in that my comments indicate I may still feel guilt about having cancelled our session. Adena may also be telling me not to be angry when she cancels me, as that is just one of those events in life that we must learn to tolerate. Maybe she's also saying that her termination of therapy may be somewhat sudden.

[JJ] The client is now lying on her back and raises her arm straight into the air with fingers outstretched and thumb pointed down toward the

Adena: Oh, no.^{NN}

Lewis: That's better than last time, though. Last time both sides were weak and now just one side is. So . . . shall we work that one today? Okay. . . . Now, that?^{OO}

Adena: It hurts.

Lewis: Take some *slow and deep breaths.* . . . *See* what happens. . . *See* what comes into the mind . . . feelings and thoughts . . . maybe something you haven't *expressed* that *you need to.*

Adena: I never really thought about my mother as being not really physical with us. She wasn't real into giving hugs and kisses.

Lewis: When you think about that, what kinds of *memories come up?*

Adena: I wish she had. On one hand, she was real non-demonstrative, and my father was overly demonstrative.

Lewis: Uh huh.

Adena: And, it's kind of sad. It made her sad, I know, but it makes her sad now because her own father was not demonstrative with her, and I guess she just didn't know how.^{PP}

Lewis: Is there anything else that connects with the past?

feet. Testing is done by pushing toward the head and toward the left (45° angle).

^{KK} Every muscle has a point that one massages in order to strengthen it. By having the client put her hand over the point, this will unmask any minor weakness in the muscle. Rubbing the point will strengthen the muscle.

^{LL} Muscles that have always been weak at the beginning of a session are now strong. I'm suggesting that Adena's new found expressiveness has created an internal balancing such that her body will no longer need external balancing by a therapist.

^{MM} Now another muscle is tested.

^{NN} I am testing the anterior deltoid (gall bladder meridian) again.

^{OO} I begin deep massage of the neuro-lymphatic point for the anterior deltoid muscle.

^{PP} As Adena talks and expresses this information, the pain associated with my rubbing the point is progressively diminishing.

Adena: I wish she hadn't had so much moral guilt, and had been more giving with her affection. She had a real hard time with all of us kids, with never having any favorites. And now, I feel real shortchanged, because having to learn to give affection to somebody without any real good role models is tricky. I think in growing up I really needed to perform for her. "See how good I am, mommy? That way she could be proud of me. Basically, since that happened, it's okay. She feels kind of bad about it.

Lewis: How so? Does she feel bad about it?

Adena: She does now. I've talked to her a lot.QQ We talk more now than we would when I was growing up. In more ways, she's more open. She even talks more directly. She says, "my father never hugged me or kissed me unless I asked him to." And he was always real unapproachable and she was the same way, and I think that's her way of saying that she feels bad about what's happened . . . and she's been trying more and more to express her affection and love for all five of us. I feel real bad about that. I guess I would have liked to have been real special to her.

Lewis: You felt you weren't?

Adena: Yeah, one of many.

QQ   Adena used her visit back to Indiana as an opportunity to explore feelings and issues with her family that had never been previously expressed. She did not relapse, but rather established a new position in her family as changed and expressive. My sense was that the entire family benefited from Adena's changes and new-found expressiveness.

Lewis: Did you feel like any of the other kids were more special?

Adena: No, that's probably why it doesn't bother me that much. And I guess it is kind of different because I was my father's favorite, and he's not real good at showing affection.

Lewis: You didn't get a lot of goodies out of being his favorite?

Adena: Oh, I did.

Lewis: What kinds of things did you get?

Adena: He was nicer to me. Kind of hard to believe. He used to go for walks . . . he used to go for walks with us. . . . He was more affectionate, but he felt more comfortable.

Lewis: Why don't you turn over on your stomach and we'll finish up [working the posterior neurolymphatic point]. Okay. Just let your mind continue to wander . . . whatever comes in . . . about your father or mother . . . I know that your mother wasn't that expressive, but see if there's any other things that come up that are important for you to know . . . maybe some feelings that you really *need to express*, but you haven't. . . . Maybe something to do with the visit that you've made to home.

Adena: I'd really like to be angry, but that's not there.

Lewis: At your mother?

Adena: Yes, I think. . . .

Lewis: How about imagining right now, just for fun, that your mother is here and you can get angry with her. You can be angry now and express it, and say the things that you always wanted to say, but didn't or couldn't. Can you do that?

Adena: I don't have very much anger toward her at all.

Lewis: How about the other things you wanted to say?

Adena: Mostly I would like to just put my arms around her and hope that if I did . . . .

Lewis: Then what happens?

Adena: Well, I told her I liked her.

Lewis: It's real hard in your family to say that you love someone?

Adena: Yeah, you say that you like them by doing things.

Lewis: How about imagining that she's here now? You're putting your arms around her and telling her that you love her.

Adena: (Repeats this and cries.)
(inaudible)
Lewis: What? (She's still crying)

Adena: Yeah, I'm sure it is. I can think of all the times that I

wanted to tell her I loved her,
and didn't.

Lewis: Uh huh. . . . Can you
feel your own self and what
happens in your body when you
think about trying to tell her
that you love her?

Adena: Well, my cervix is
tight.

Lewis: What else happens?

Adena: My muscles seem to
be tight across . . . .

Lewis: Across your where?

Adena: Across my shoulders.

Lewis: What else happens to
your body?

Adena: My stomach feels
tight. I think of my grandfather.
I tried to tell him, but I couldn't.
He died a couple of months
later.

Lewis: That's sad. Could you
see yourself doing that now?

Adena: Yes.

Lewis: Now, let's test your
muscle again . . . great . . . that's
better, but it's not strong yet.
There's obviously something
going on around the things
you've already talked about or
described that still needs to be
worked on some more.

Adena: You mean today?

Lewis: Somehow the muscle
just isn't satisfied now. I'll hold

the neurovascular point and see what comes to your mind.

Adena: I think about my father. . . . Yeah, I would really like to yell at my father . . . jump up and down. . . . I might not really want to yell at him. . . . In some ways I would really like to tell him that some of those things that he did and said were very sadistic . . . and the teasing he did was borderline cruelty. . . . Sometimes out and out cruel. . . . He never was like that with me. . . . I'm borderline, but I don't know to what end, what good would it do?[RR]

Lewis: Well, you never know until you do it.

Adena: What it would do is really hurt him a lot.

Lewis: I mean try it here.

Adena: Try it here? I couldn't tell him.

Lewis: You don't have to necessarily tell him in person.

Adena: He couldn't handle it . . . or could he?

Lewis: It sounds like there is a part of you that wants to tell him that you're really angry, and there's a part of you that's afraid to.

Adena: Yeah. . . . I'm afraid of what it will do.

Lewis: Can you imagine him here and let that one part of you

[RR]   Adena is referring to being on the border of expressing her anger at her father.

out now where it's safe, where he can't react wrong?

Adena: Only if I can tie him on a chair and gag him.

Lewis: Okay, why don't you tie him in a chair and gag him?

Adena: I really need a lot of room.

Lewis: Yeah, we've got a lot of room here. (She begins talking to her father)

Adena: "You're a real creep. You were a real creep. . . . You teased too much. . . . You really hurt my feelings. . . . I can't think of anything specific that you really did . . . it's just an overall attitude of games, like if you don't do this, it means that you don't love me. . . . And sarcasm. . . . All I wanted was to (begins crying) . . . .

Lewis: What did you get from that?

Adena: I heard a lot of the same things I say to my husband. It's not a conscious type of program. But it's still there. It still really hurts.

Lewis: How about the way that the emotion that you are feeling now feels in your voice?

Adena: Yeah, I don't sound very angry.

Lewis: Maybe that's just something about your family, because, to me, it didn't match

that much. I heard your voice
even-tempered.

Adena: That's my mother.

Lewis: That way it never goes
up or down.

Adena: Real even keel. . . . In
my life I've seen her get really
angry maybe 5 times.

Lewis: How about you. . . .
Do you get really angry?

Adena: I get angry, but people
don't really know when I am
really angry. I'll go on with
something, but the real issue I
won't really deal with. That
makes me too vulnerable.

Lewis: So, if you were to
really get mad at your father,
how would that make you?

Adena: It might give him a
lever to work with, a chink in
the armor. He's real aware of
that because he's a closed
person. I had 5 minutes when he
actually told me something
about himself . . . that he wasn't
putting on an act . . . he wasn't
trying to protect himself. . . .
That was really nice. . . . I'd
really like to do that again. . . .
But I don't know how to do it.
. . . I have to open up to him
and I have to hope that he
would open up to me. . . . I
really love my father. . . . It's
crazy . . . he's basically a very
good person.

Lewis: Would it help to go
back and try to tell him about
your anger again, put more of it
into your voice?

Adena: I don't know if I can
do it.

The session continues to a conclusion in the same way. Adena
came four more times after this for a total of 18 sessions. Six months
afterwards she had lost 60 pounds. And two and one-half years after
terminating our therapy, she is 70 pounds lighter than when she began
therapy. Her relationship with Jerry is much improved without their
ever having to go for couples' therapy.

Other Unique Aspects of Kinesiology

Mindbody Education

Clients can be educated to the mind-body connection using a very
simple kinesiology technique. The client is asked to hold the arm out
from the side at a 45° angle in order to test the supraspinatus muscle
(see Reference 2 for exact details of how to test muscles). The muscle is
tested to determine its baseline strength. If it is not entirely strong, it is
strengthened. Then the client is asked to imagine something very
wonderful that's happened in his or her life. Indirect hypnotic
suggestions are given to help in building the vividness of the experience
by including auditory, kinesthetic and visual detail. Suggestions are
also given not to be distracted from the experience of that image when
the muscle is tested. When the client tells me that the image is clear and
firmly held so that it won't be dislodged by testing, then I test the
strength of the muscle. The muscle is almost always very strong. Next
the client imagines something very negative that's happened about
which he or she is as yet unresolved. Indirect hypnotic instructions are
given again to experience that event in all three sensory modalities and
not be distracted from the imagery process by the muscle testing. The
muscle is now almost always weak. This procedure and sequence can
be repeated several times to help the client experience the very direct
connection between mind and body (so direct that there is no
difference between mind and body).

What if the client is weak for the positive imagery and strong for
the negative image? Some clients thrive on adversity such that personal
power is felt best when imagining turmoil or conflict, but only in
opposition to someone or some situation. When such a reaction

occurs, I do not respond yet, but repeat the sequence with a "good event #2" and a "bad event #2." I've never had to go past "good event #3" and "bad event #3" for the response to become as predicted. Some clients may need time for their imagery process to "warm up" and become vivid enough to connect with their bodies. Some clients may be confused about their life to the extent that an event superficially labelled as "good" may actually lead them away from necessary growth and development. Conversely, an event labelled "bad" may actually be leading the client toward needed growth and development.

Decision Making

Kinesiology can be used to help the client to make decisions. I usually use the supraspinatus or the general activator muscle for such purposes. The client can imagine a question to which a "yes" or "no" answer exists, having been told previously that the muscle will remain strong upon testing if the answer most pleasing to the body is "yes," and will become weak with the "no" answer. A variety of issues can be tested with the body. Examples include:

Should I move to the country?
Should I look for a new job?
Should I leave my current partner?

and so on.

Cerebral Allergy Testing

Kinesiology is used to test for the body's reactions to a variety of substances. This is done by several methods, none of which are mutually exclusive:

1. The client imagines a particular substance while the muscle is tested.
2. The client ingests or holds on his or her tongue a substance while the muscle is tested.
3. The substance is placed in contact with the client's skin while the muscle is tested.
4. The tester imagines the substance while testing, without the client's awareness of what substance is being imagined.
5. The tester imagines the substance while testing, without the client's awareness, while knocking twice or three times on the client's left temporal bone with the tester's

right hand. (Probably other variations exist with which I am unfamiliar.)

I have used each of these five methods and have observed their accuracy relative to each other (the same results occur regardless of which method is used) and compared them with standard skin testing (scratch and patch) methods of allergy testing. The same substances respond to kinesiology testing as to skin testing, although the severity of the response does not seem correlated between these two methods, and kinesiology may be more sensitive because of its identification of a larger number of substances. (Does it have a higher false positive rate?)

We are led by the usefulness of such techniques to question their mechanism of action. I believe three phenomena explain the action of these techniques. First, the body knows what it needs instantaneously, accurately, and better than any doctor or laboratory test. Other mechanisms must exist to explain such instantaneous reactions. Perhaps the d.c. current systems comprising acupuncture meridians will provide one explanation (see the chapter on mechanism of action of acupuncture in Volume II). Of importance is a common distortion of the scientific method. Some individuals trained in science believe they cannot accept the existence of phenomena for which theory is as yet inadequate to explain. The existence and clinical usefulness of kinesiology is independent of the lack of adequate theory to explain its mechanism of action.

Secondly, the person holds belief systems that affect the body. People who *believe* strongly that sugar is a metabolic poison will test differently to sugar than people who hold no opinion on the subject. One day at a workshop, I tested 20 people who strongly believed sugar was a metabolic poison. All tested very weak to sugar. Twenty other people held no opinion. Four tested weak, 4 showed an intermediate response and 12 were strong. Thus, the needs and desires of the body are modified by the client's belief system. Accurate interpretation of muscle testing results (indeed, of *any* lab test results) is improved with better understanding of the individual's belief systems. Standard, dominant-culture American medicine needs such insights as much as do chiropractors and holistic health practitioners utilizing kinesiology.

Thirdly, the tester's belief system can affect the results, probably through two mechanisms. The tester can directly communicate his or her biases prior to testing. Such communication can influence results, especially if the tester is a dynamic, charismatic person and the client has a tendency to wish to please. Such communication can take place indirectly through the development of an expectancy set for appropriate behavior. Secondly, I believe telepathy plays an important role in affecting kinesiology results. Such a phenomenon can sometimes be dramatically demonstrated with the following procedure:

I ask the client to focus on a pleasant scene or just relax. Then I imagine a "yes" or "no" question and knock with my right hand three times upon the left temple. Then I test the muscle (supraspinatus or general activator) quickly thereafter. This procedure is accurate for me about 75% of the time. Examples of questions I asked during a recent workshop include the following:

	Body Answer	Actual Answer
Were you born in Cincinnati?	No	No
Were you born in California?	Yes	No
Do you live in Palo Alto?	Yes-No	Yes
Is fish your favorite food?	No	No
Do you like camping?	Yes	Yes
Do you like your work?	Yes	Yes

These results show the effect emotions have on the results. The person I was testing had lived in California for many years. Perhaps he lived and behaved *as if* he were a native Californian or, in coming to the state had joined a probable self[3] who was born here. In addition, he was ambivalent about continuing to live in Palo Alto. A strong part of him wished to live in the country and he questioned frequently his continuing to live in Palo Alto.

I believe telepathy is a common phenomenon, *fueled by emotion.* It is so rarely demonstrated in the laboratory, because laboratory scientists have created the distorted belief that all emotion must be removed from a phenomenon in order for proper scientific research to occur. Guessing which playing card another person holds is a relatively meaningless task, with a minimum of emotional fuel, yet this is an example of the major methodology by which telepathy is "scientifically" studied. The definition of science has changed in our society from "a systematic quest for knowledge" to "procedures conducted without emotion."

Freud wrote one of the first papers on telepathy in 1921, called "Psychoanalysis and Telepathy." He said,

It is probable that the study of occult phenomenon will result in the admission that some of these phenomena are real; but it is also likely that a great deal of time will elapse before one will be able to formulate any acceptable theory accounting for these new facts ... my personal attitude towards such material remains one of reluctance and ambivalence.[4]

In another paper Freud wrote that [telepathy]

may be the original archaic method by which individuals understood one another and which has been pushed into the background in the course of phylogenetic (evolutionary) development by the better method of communication by means of signs apprehended by the sense organs. But such older methods may have persisted in the background and may still manifest themselves under certain conditions.[5]

Several writers have reported the occurrence of telepathic dreams and other telepathic communication in psychoanalytic practice.[6] David Shaimberg reports an instance of telepathy in a dream that a patient of his had while in psychoanalysis that is very illustrative of the telepathy process.[7] Shaimberg reports the case of Martin G. who had an ambivalent relationship with his father which Shaimberg described as similar, in some ways, to his own relatioship with his father. Shaimberg's father had developed aphasia[8] and had been found to have subdural hemotomas.[9] During the evening, after the first day that Shaimberg saw Martin, subdural hemotomas had been found and burr holes[10] had been drilled. A blockage had been found in the internal carotid artery going into the brain and further surgery was planned. Shaimberg planned to make a flight to see his father the evening after seeing Martin on the second day. That night Martin reported dreaming the previous night:

I flew somewhere; I seemed to have been there before. There were mountains and woods. I was bringing somebody along, a younger version of myself (Shaimberg was to take his younger brother with him to see their father) maybe my brother or somebody. He needed an operation. You were there. You were to perform the operation on this person. He had to be put in a dentist's chair, and we had to inject something into his head, a mental gas. This person was resisting this operation and went into the other room, closed the door, making threats that he would blow the place up or scream. We decided to use the nurse to lure him out seductively. That is what happened; we finally got him in the dentist's chair, squirting this gas into his head. I seem to remember exposing something, a juncture of a couple blood vessels in a kind of "Y"; there was debris or broken glass in the juncture. We cleaned it out. We sewed him back. The operation was a success.

There was a quality of raw emotion in this dream which I was coming out of when I woke up. It is a raw emotion, a strong kind of emotion, very fearful, very raw and sensitive. Usually when I feel emotion, it is very vague, but here it was electrified. I get the impression that when I came out of the dream it was like I was glad to be away from that part of myself. It was like being in a pressure cooker, all these emotions stewing around, bursting out, frightening.[7]

Shaimberg asked him to say more about his "electrified feelings."

I noticed it in contrast to the muffled feeling that I normally have. I don't know what I feel, so vague emotionally speaking, a non-feeling when I feel, that is always distant, so I notice strength here; it was more urgent, much more.

What is urgent in this dream?

The situation, whatever happened, getting this guy to have this operation seemed very important; he didn't want to cooperate with us, but it was urgent. The nurse seducing him had an urgency — all feeling very direct and strong. I felt her leave to get away, like being urgent all the time was too strong.

What is urgent?

This guy had to get the operation; you and I in the dream had to get him in the chair. To inject this mental gas was important and he wasn't cooperating. Things had to be dealt with. We could not say to hell with it, or avoid it. It seems like one pole with magnet forces pulling around with a very strong possibility something bad might happen.

I was just thinking I had been doing my "mind control" exercise. In the mind control class they tell us to instruct ourselves to have a dream about certain things, to solve a certain problem in dreams. I had instructed myself to have one on the topic of "fear of loss." I don't know if that was the dream.

How is this dream a fear of loss?

I have been afraid to say what I think, to do what I want to do, because I am afraid to lose something.

How do you feel about me in the dream?

All throughout the dream, I didn't want to be there. I had to help you out. You were trying to do this thing, to take care of him; I wasn't enthusiastic about that. I wasn't forced; I had to go along to help you perform the operation. But it wasn't my idea, it was your idea. I seemed to get more involved in this urgent situation because of you. Then the trouble starts when the guy threatens to blow the place up. Because of you, I have to go through with it. Part of the feeling was: boy, am I glad to get out of that; everything seemed to be kind of an emergency.

I keep ending up in these situations. I don't really know what I wanted to do. This is a real life thing for me. I go along. I avoid life and avoid dealing with life. I didn't feel good in the dream; the whole dream bothered me. I was passive, sucked in, forced to deal with a bunch of things that fortunately turned out all right. I wanted just to get away from the situation.

What is that feeling of being sucked in?

Like I don't know what I want; I feel I have to do something, so I allow someone to initiate. I end up somehow involved with them. I follow someone else's lead, go along with them. I have no reason against getting involved, but I don't really want it, and it happens all the time. I find I only go with women where I get some positive indication, a green light, the way they look at me — if I make a pass it would be all right. I pick out somebody neutral. A few months ago I would wait until they asked me out, so this is better. It is applicable in every sphere. It gives me creeps just to think about that. . . .[7]

Shaimberg provides some interesting detail in his discussion of Martin's dream:

Hollios wrote (as quoted by Servadio)[11] that the telepathic message frequently involves material that the analyst is about to repress and that the patient reworks the message to fit his own particular conflicts.

Many investigators have noted that telepathic communication is common when there is sickness or death in the family of the analyst. . . .

In the cases of Martin and myself, the first-born sons of driven, compulsive men, early arousal was structured in relation to the father and became of central importance. We can speculate that when there is arousal in such shared central relationships, the experience can be what we identify as telepathic communication, perhaps what Freud referred to as "the original archaic method by which individuals understood one another.[7]

To Shaimberg's analysis, I would add the important point that the high levels of emotion present in this situation and perhaps Martin's desire to know more about the analyst (again, an emotion) may have provided the fuel for the telepathic communication (presumably some kind of electromagnetic wave phenomena).

In a class at Stanford Medical School, I observed a phenomena involving kinesiology that can be partially explained as a telepathic phenomena. The class was an overview of non-standard approaches to healing and consisted of visiting lecturers discussing their practices and philosophies.[12] A chiropractor demonstrated allergy testing using kinesiology. He gave the students sugar to hold. Every student tested was weak when holding the sugar except for one diabetic student. The chiropractor stated that this particular student was just resistant. In talking to this student later, I learned that he always carried a sugar cube in case of insulin reaction and saw the sugar as a real friend that could save his life. My reasoning was that this student's body felt safe and relaxed around sugar, so much so that this positive feeling about sugar could not be overridden even by his desire to please the lecturer. When I tested several of the same students later with sugar, their response was opposite. The lecturer had not, seemingly, suggested they would be weak to sugar. My belief was that his strong emotional beliefs were communicated telepathically to the students who then responded in accordance with his belief system. These students were similar to Martin in their dependency and desire to please the lecturer as Martin depended upon and wished to please his analyst. In addition, the character of the lecture-demonstration had created a mild trance state for all present similar to the trance state experienced by the patient (such as Martin) during psychotherapy.

Summary

Kinesiology is an excellent technique to use in conjunction with psychotherapy as the case example illustrated. Some of its more esoteric properties may be explained as a combination of telepathy, expectancy sets, and indirect suggestion.

REFERENCES AND NOTES

[1] For an explication of the meta-model, see Cameron-Bandler, Leslie, *And They All Lived Happily Ever After*, Cupertino, California: Meta Publications, 1978.

[2] Thie, J. *Touch for Health*. Pasadena, California: The Enterprises, 1980, 2nd edition. Workshops are available in basic techniques of applied kinesiology through this group and are worth taking.

[3] See Jane Roberts, *Adventures in Consciousness: The Nature of the Psyche*, Englewood Cliffs, N.J.: Prentice-Hall, 1977, for a full discussion of the concept of probable selves and probable events.

[4] Freud, S. Psychoanalysis and Telepathy. In *Standard Edition*, Vol. 18, London: Hogarth Press, 1921.

[5] Freud, S. Dreams and the Occult. In *Standard Edition*, Vol. 22. London: Hogarth Press, 1934.

[6] Ehrenwald, J. *New Dimensions of Depth Analysis*. New York: Grune & Stratton, 1970; Eisenbud, J. *Psi and Psychoanalysis*. New York: Grune & Stratton, 1970, and Ullman, M. *A Nocturnal Approach to Psi*. Proc. Parapsychol. Assoc. 3:35, 1966.

[7] Shaimberg, D. Telepathy and Psychoanalysis: An Instance. *American Journal of Psychotherapy* 30(3):462-472, July, 1976.

[8] Aphasia means being unable to talk.

[9] Subdural hemotoma is a collection of blood underneath the dura, which is the lining of the brain. It causes symptoms due to putting pressure on the brain.

[10] Burr holes are holes in the skull drilled by a neurosurgeon so that blood underneath the dura can drain out and relieve pressure on the brain.

[11] Servadio, E. Psychoanalysis and Telepathy in G. Devereux (ed.) *Psychoanalysis and the Occult*. New York: International University Press, 1953.

[12] Interestingly enough, a great deal of controversy was generated from this class, because high-level officials in the medical school felt it represented anti-science, reasoning that students should not be exposed to such alternatives. The class was cancelled for the next year as a result of this criticism.

Chapter Ten

Hypnosis and Psychophysiological Integration

The therapeutic use of language is clearly integral to healing. Hypnosis, or applied psycholinguistics represents the body of knowledge pertaining to the maximally effective use of language to achieve mutually agreed upon (by client and therapist) specific ends. Legislation of hypnosis is pointless, because *everyone already uses hypnosis*. Hypnosis is ubiquitous. A better goal than regulating its usage is increasing professional awareness of language and suggestion so that suggestion can be used to the client's advantage.

Indirect Hypnosis and Milton Erickson

Milton Erickson is recognized as the major developer of indirect hypnosis. Erickson[1,2] believed that all patients know very well why they are seeking therapy. All patients desire to benefit, and, at one level, come in a receptive state ready to respond to therapy at the first opportunity. Everyone receiving psychotherapy would benefit quickly and easily were it not that within all of us (as within every system[3]) there are tendencies toward inertia (resistance) and tendencies toward growth and change (morphogenesis). The task of the therapist is to engage the inertial elements, thereby altering the balance of the system so that morphogenetic processes are freed to continue their work of growth and change. Hypnosis is one method of engaging those inertial elements. These tendencies toward change and stasis exist in a multi-layered pattern. Sometimes the client exposes the inertial aspects first with statements of hostility and anger; sometimes the morphogenetic elements begin at the fore.

Erickson believed, as I do, that if the client did not truly desire change *on some level*, the therapeutic situation would not have been entered. To facilitate this process of therapeutic change, we should give recognition to the readiness with which the therapist's unconscious mind accepts clues and information about the client. We may dislike someone at first sight and not become consciously aware of the obvious and apparent reasons for such dislike for weeks, months, even a year or more. Respectful awareness of the capacity of the patient's unconscious to perceive meaning in the therpist's own unconscious behavior and feelings is an important principle in psychotherapy, as the client can quickly and accurately perceive the therapist's basic, underlying feelings and intentions.

In addition, the therapist needs be aware of those presenting inertial elements of the client's personal bio-eco-system so as to effectively engage those elements to allow for other parts of the client to initiate growth and change.

Techniques of Trance

An awareness of some of the major techniques of indirect hypnosis is useful. Discussion will follow the categories and terms created by Bandler and Grinder to describe Erickson.[2,12]

1. Pacing

In their analysis of Erickson's technique for inducing and maintaining a hypnotic trance, Bandler and Grinder[2] note that Erickson began by *pacing* the client's experiences.

Pacing refers to leading the client at the proper speed toward some future goal. Pacing can be physiological — using the words "breathing in" and "breathing out" to verbally match the client's actual breathing rate, slowly increasing the verbal length of "breathing in" and "breathing out," noticing the client's breathing rate adjusting to match the therapist's verbal rate. Pacing involves watching the client closely and describing observed changes, reinforcing these changes by therapist feedback, and recreating these changes by presupposing verbally that they have already occurred.

The therapist using pacing techniques makes full use of the basic processes of human linguistic modeling — deletion, distortion, and generalization.[2]

2. Engaging the client's attention

Describing what he already knew to be true about the client, Erickson would get the client's full attention by picking a subject of interest to the client. A farmer would naturally be interested in plants. A physiologist might respond better to a discussion of change in oxygen-carbon dioxide tension during the relaxation process. The subject matter of indirect hypnosis should fit within the client's interests.

3. *Implied causatives*

Obviously true statements ("Standing up causes gravity to press the baby's head harder against the cervix") are linked to statements we wish the client to accept and believe ("So, walking will use that force to push the baby's head down through the cervix"). "So" is often used as the *linkage conjunction*, the word linking truism to phrase to be accepted. Series of factual statements which the client immediately accepts as correct are linked by words such as "so" to a behavior the therapist hopes to elicit from the client.

4. *Meta-communication*

The message to the client is implied "between the lines" of ongoing verbal communication. Erickson might have told the pain therapy client that he wouldn't be talking about flowers and then proceed to discuss flowers. He has warned the client that he will be saying something more important than the content of his discussion of flowers. The client should listen closely for what this message will be. Erickson believed that people have the ability to learn the things they need to know when given an opportunity.

5. *Conversational postulates*

Erickson often began a trance induction with a sentence such as, "I'm wondering if you will *uncross your legs* and *lie down?*" On the surface, this is not a command. Superficially, Erickson was just wondering if the client would uncross his or her legs and lie down. Nevertheless the client may receive this as a request for the client to uncross the legs and lie down. Part of the success of this technique is found in the use of the *interspersal technique*. When many conversational postulates follow one introduction ("I'm wondering") ambiguity arises and the client needs to decide whether conversational postulates continue or whether the succeeding linked messages are actually commands. Conversational postulates disguise forcible commands.

6. Interspersal technique

The beauty of this technique of word emphasis lies in its power. Through a subtle increase in loudness, enunciation, and emphasis or through spacing and verbal pauses, certain words in a sentence are demarcated from others. In the aforementioned sentence, a slight increase in loudness of certain words creates a second sentence: "*Uncross your legs* and *lie down.*" The word "and" does not even have to be emphasized very much for the mind to include it. "And" is the logical connector. The therapist merely says "uncross," "legs," "lie," and "down" louder and more forcibly and a new sentence is created within the structure of the old: "I'm wondering if you'll *uncross* your *legs* (and) *lie down.* The parentheses around "and" indicate that it does not even require emphasis to be included in this new sentence. Examples of the interspersal technique can be found in the underlined words of the visualizations reproduced in earlier chapters.

7. Compressing several requests into one

When separate activities are described so as to seem to need to be done together, the probability increases that all will be done. For example, the sentence, "Would you put away your bicycle while you're taking out the garbage," combines two requests into one. People are more likely to say "No" to one of two separate requests than to two requests combined into one.

8. Deletions

Deletions are used to make sentences acceptably referent to the client as in "Now there is no need to talk," which deletes reference to who talks about what to whom.

9. Nominalizations

Nominalizations make nouns out of verbs and abstractions. A good noun can be carried in a large enough crate. If not, the word used as a noun is a nominalization. Nominalizations carry less information than is available in a good noun. Nominalization represents a linguistic process of presenting a process as an event.

10. Use of ungrammatical sequences to emphasize instructions

11. *Lesser included structures*

Lesser included structures include examples such as "hear me," in phrases as "Your unconscious mind will *hear me.*" Such a phrase presupposes that the client's unconscious mind exists and can hear Erickson. A conversational postulate can include a lesser structure with the opposite intent of the content of the conversational postulate.

12. *Syntactic ambiguity*

Syntactic ambiguity refers to a sentence in which two meanings are possible, whether the sentence is read aloud and listened to or read silently without an internal auditory presentation. A sentence or surface structure is called ambiguous if it is a linguistic representation of more than one distinct experience or, in linguistic terms, if it is a linguistic representation of more than one distinct deep structure. Another type of ambiguity is phonological or sound ambiguity in which under conditions of normal speech most listeners will be unable to distinguish between two visually presented distinguishable versions of the same sentence. The phonological presentation is completely ambiguous.

13. *Selectional restriction*

Selectional restriction is the juxtaposition of one word modifying another in a way that usually violates the norms of our language.[4,5] The transformational linguistic explanation for this phenomenon goes as follows: "Each predicate in a language system is the name of some process or relationship. In the world of human experience certain processes or relationships are restricted in that they can accord with certain classes of people or things. Erickson's use of the phrase 'impossible actuality' violates this selectional restriction."[2]

14. *Fuzzy Functions*

Bandler and Grinder[2] report that in their work with certain processes such as stuttering they encounter what they call "fuzzy functions." A "fuzzy function" represents a method of receiving a message in one input channel (e.g., visual or auditory), and, rather than experiencing or storing that information or message in the same representational system, it is acted upon in another sensory modality. For example, one client experienced asthma attacks whenever he heard the word "kill," or any other word associated with interpersonal violence. Another client flew into an uncontrollable rage whenever she heard the word "dolly." Clients whose model of the world specifies that they should behave as though they had no choice about their kinesthetic experience (asthma) in response to a particular sound sequence (the word "kill") are displaying the "fuzzy function" called "hear-feel." Accepting a model of the world in which they have no control over such fuzzy functions reduces choices for types of coping. If each time the client hears a certain word, an automatic feeling response occurs, there is no longer the ability to creatively respond to the situation. A conditioned habitual response has developed. The client perceives the responsibility for this experience as outside rather than inside. The locus of control is conditioned to be external.

The reader interested in indirect hypnosis can use these categories to analyze the visualization sessions of previous chapters. Even better understanding will be gained from reading the work of Milton Erickson[1,6] or Richard Bandler and John Grinder.[2]

Perception and Communication

When two individuals interact, they create a shared world which both experience. This co-mapping is probably never total. That is, Joe's perception of George's perception differs in some ways from George's perception. R.D. Laing calls this Joe's meta-perspective. Communication is the mechanism humans use to explore each other's perspectives and to improve the accuracy of that correspondence. If Joe behaves in such a way that what George infers about Joe's perception of George's inner world (especially the world George is experiencing right now) is that Joe understands him accurately, trust and rapport will develop. Such a sense of understanding is essential to the hypnotic process. Additionally, if we understand George's difficulties as a constitutive problem (resulting from the beliefs George uses to perceive the world) then therapy involves a deconstitutive process in which George is enabled to undo a part of his belief structure for more personally advantageous reconstruction. The therapist helps to support the belief structure so that collapse of the edifice does not occur during this constitution-reconstitution, remodelling period.

Erickson[7] stated: "The patient's behavior is part of the problem brought into the office; it constitutes the personal environment in which the therapy must take effect; it may constitute the dominant force of the local patient-doctor relationship. Since whatever the patient brings into the office is in some way both part of him and part of his problem, the patient should be viewed with a sympathetic eye, appraising the totality which confronts the therapist." In the use of hypnosis, Erickson believed the doctor must assist each client to achieve an altered state of consciousness allowing him or her to experience the world in a way radically different from the usual state of consciousness, allowing otherwise difficult procedures to be effective and the patient to be cared for properly.

The effectiveness of indirect hypnosis allows us several insights. The client can enter phenomenal worlds where the pain from a dental or medical procedure is not a dominant element of that world. When the ego is completely cathected to "my body" in a particular segment of space-time and assault takes place, severe pain is experienced. That de-cathexis relates to therapist and client deciding together to change the perception of "painful assaultive procedure" to "beneficial necessary procedure." Then the ego may step aside in the service of the greater good and may ignore the pain.

Language plays an important role in the constitution of beliefs. In the altered, focused state of consciousness characteristic of hypnosis, the patient may regain control and direction of body processes to avoid surgical or medical procedures and obtain proper care. Common to the learning occurring during focused hypnotic awareness is the client's learning to control portions of experience usually represented as outside personal control. The client learns to work in conjunction and cooperation with portions of the nervous system usually considered beyond conscious control, including the autonomic nervous system. The client can also succeed in gaining operational control over the development and change of belief systems. With this developing evaluative ability of his or her own belief system, the client has new resources to restructure the constitutional process of beliefs about the body.

Representational Systems

Erickson has been studied and has been found to systematically select cues or signals from the client's most highly valued representational system to assist the client in entering or re-entering trance states.[2] As previously discussed, these representational systems relate to the various sensory modalities — kinesthetic, auditory, visual, olfactory, etc. The hypnotist gains "hidden" knowledge about the client's internal model of the world or representational system. The client does not recognize how the therapist is "reading his or her inner perceptual mind," but responds with an increasing sense of respect for the ability of the therapist to "know" what the client really feels.

Experientially as the therapist moves into the client's inner landscape, a series of separate, but related, experienced or phenomenal worlds are encountered, any one of which may contain the bulk of the client's experience at any one moment. For example, home and family may represent one of those worlds. While sitting at the desk at work, the client may be completely absorbed in thinking about a home situation. In one very real sense, the client is not in the world of work, but is actually present in the phenomenal (meaning experienced) world of home and family. The world of childhood home and family also exists. Many people behave as though still in their childhood home with their childhood family (in their phenomenal or world of inner experience) even though others would see them in the world of work. Different modes of participating in these various phenomenal worlds help differentiate and separate them. One is visual — participating in a world through the visual sensation of that world; for example, by visualizing oneself at the beach. Participation (being there) can be in an auditory mode — hearing the sound of the waves. It can be a kinesthetic mode — feeling the ocean breeze against the face. Kinesthetic references may be highly effective for one client in helping to create a very focused state, while a fantasized visual image would be more appropriate for another client. Erickson typically arranged signals or cues for post-hypnotic behavior in modalities other than the client's most often used representational system. He believed this allowed for bypassing of the modality most frequently connected with conscious mind activity and for more direct communication with the unconscious portion of the person's mind. Bandler and Grinder[2] have noted a consistent pattern of the emergence of the visual representational system as primary, as the client achieves a deeper state of hypnosis.

Guided fantasy

In the context of therapy, one of the most effective techniques for assisting a client to change his or her world view is by a guided fantasy technique. The client is typically asked to close his or her eyes and visualize a particular experience which will assist change. One of the most immediate and effective ways to assist a client to fully express and integrate seemingly opposite polarities is to ensure that one of the polarities is using a visual representational system and the other either a kinesthetic or auditory representational system.[2] Bandler and Grinder[2] have observed that clients executing post-hypnotic suggestions often shift the representational system of predicate adjective (breezy or quiet) to a visual predicate (clear) as the trance state is re-entered and the post-hypnotic suggestion is executed. They have formalized a technique to help people develop additional maps or representational systems for organizing their experience — specifically, using a lead representational system to develop another representational system by finding a point of overlap or intersection between the two.

Trance

Bandler and Grinder[2] note that one of the more interesting differences in the linguistic behavior of subjects in profound somnambulistic trances as opposed to either normal states of consciousness or to behavior during light to moderate trance states is that people will respond to certain sentences which are in the form of questions as though they were commands. This, of course, forces us to philosophically consider the issue of what is a trance and how to define depth of trance. Experientially, a person "in a trance" does not necessarily have an "ah-ha experience," suddenly recognizing the trance state. In fact, paradoxically, a knowledge of participation in a trance is often furthest from awareness. Rather the client is intensely focused on something, if only upon the act of focusing intensely, or upon focusing upon eliminating all thoughts from awareness, in which case the focus is upon an act of elimination, a process to which consciousness can avail itself. Experientially defining trance means to speak of a progressive channeling or focusing of awareness upon fewer "things" or "cogitata." Deeper is defined as coming closer to focusing on one *cogitatum* or experience or thought. This one *cogitatum* could be an experience of a phenomenal world or a focusing in a self-reflexive manner upon awareness itself. Many Eastern style meditators ascribe a higher value to such self-reflexive focusing than to focusing on a phenomenal world.

Erickson[1,6] believed that the ability of the subject in a profound somnambulistic trance to respond to the literal deep structure meaning of a sentence is an excellent indicator that the subject is in a deep trance. One excellent test for the depth of trance in many subjects will be their ability not to respond to the additional meaning given by a conversational postulate.

Probable Worlds

Bandler and Grinder[2] describe an interaction of Erickson with Aldous Huxley that provides a concrete example of what could be called the *probable self phenomenon*. In this experience Erickson helps Huxley enter a deep trance and experience himself at age 23, realizing that the self of age 23 is also experiencing Huxley at age 52. This provides interesting data from which to consider time and the nature of the ego. Huxley at age 52, in the present time of Erickson, met and experienced a being whom he perceived to be a younger version of himself at age 23. He knew this being had many of the same experiences as he. Huxley also experienced his perceived self-at-age-23 experiencing Huxley-at-age-52, each recognizing their relatedness to each other. This relatedness was recognized in a linear fashion in the sense of the question, "Is that really the way I appeared when I was 23?" "Is that really what I'll be like when I'm 52?" As Erickson notes, "Each was aware of the question in the other's mind. Each found the question of 'extraordinarily fascinating interest' and each tried to determine which was the 'actual reality' and which was the 'mere subjective experience that was projected in hallucinatory form.' "[2] In this sense it becomes clear that the concept of actual reality is actual only in the sense of the perceiver.

This is very interesting data for a philosophical ontology. Huxley-at-23 was as real in the world-of-the-trance as Huxley-who-entered-the-trance and yet both experienced each other as separate, real entities.

Jane Roberts[8,9] has described such phenomena. She terms these separate selves each as *probable selves* of the other. In her terms, there are an infinite number of probable realities (phenomenal worlds), each of equal validity. Medard Boss[10] has demonstrated the validity of the client's phenomenal worlds. In the experienced worlds of the client, *during* the time of the experience, each world exists with as much validity as any other world the client can find or imagine. Of ontological interest is the coalescing of two worlds with two separate entities from those respective separate worlds experiencing each other. The recognition of relatedness is fundamental. In my own experience, in one "hypnotic" experience, I perceived a being whom I felt was related to me in some way. He was sailing into the San Francisco Bay. I felt the wonder at seeing the Bay through his eyes, the buildings and skyline absent, but even more wonder at his seeing the Bay through my 1980 perspective.

The commonly accepted concept of linear movement through time can also be challenged. Was the Huxley-at-age-23 the same Huxley as the Huxley-at-age-52? Was the surprise due to the presence of two separate Huxleys, each with equal paths to that point but with divergent futures? Or had they diverged earlier with only some major similar experiences? The Huxley-of-age-52 and the Huxley-of-age-23 shared a common present at that moment. Is this presence universally in existence, or is this presence a mere subjective experience of the other presence which is outwardly projected in hallucinatory form?

Huxley described each seeing the other across a vestibule. The vestibule for him represented a gateway between experiences. A client described in the visualization chapter had a similar experience. In her deep trance state, she experienced on an emotional level hemorrhaging to death. In a sense arguing real memory or subective experience is meaningless. She experienced this in the most real way possible. Terror in a dream is no less terror. She related that her current, new husband for this second child was the same man who had fathered the child at the time she hemorrhaged. This was her interpretation of the experience. She recognized a kind of relatedness between those two individuals. She-now and she-then dialogued with each other in a way in which each appeared real, separable, and distinct. Experientially neither is the mere subjective experience outwardly projected in hallucinatory form of the other. These experiences raise doubt as to common assumptions made about the nature of reality. In such experiences, both beings recognize a fundamental difference between each other. This can be interpreted in a time context in that the two entities are the same separated by time. Such a time separation theory is a simplistic statement of the usual linear notion of reincarnation in which the woman mentioned would be accessing a hidden memory from a previous life. Usual theories of reincarnation hold to the concept of linear time, even though experimental physics has shown that time is not necessarily directed forward or linear.[11] A linear reincarnational theory cannot adequately explain phenomena such as Huxley-at-23 or my 19th-century-sea-captain's recognition of Huxley-at-52 or me, respectively. This phenomenon demands that any theories of time we hold take into account:

1. We commonly, in our waking state, believe that time is linear.
2. Experientially, even waking time speeds up or slows down.
3. In dreams and in hypnotic experiences, time appears to be more like space, rather than simply linear.

This could result in many modifications of the usual linear theory of reincarnation.

There was an intimate interconnectedness or relatedness between the two Huxleys. A Huxley entity may exist as an integration consisting of a Reimann-like sum of separable, distinct, inviolable $(Huxley)_1$'s to $(Huxley)_n$'s. There may be an infinite number of Huxley's. How this can be determined is unclear, but it may be that as many Huxley's as could be imagined could exist.

Regardless of our theoretical constitution of these phenomena, it can be useful clinically. In deference to the nomenclature of Roberts,[8] I will term such phenomena, *probable self recognition phenomena*. Such phenomena can aid therapy. In contemplating the effects of a decision, it can be useful to hypnotically regress the client to the time just before the decision. The client can then experience possible decisions and follow alternative decisions through their separate existences as though each had occurred in one world. Correctness of this approach is sometimes typified by a sense of grey or indistinctness and then a spontaneous catching onto a version of the client's self. Contemplation of a future choice can be approached in the same manner.

A related phenomenon consists of a client recognizing a relatedness between him or herself in a deep trance level to another entity experienced and perceived in that trance level, who existed within the framework of a different time, culture, or setting. Such occurrences are documented in many writings. The usual interpretation of this is as reincarnational phenomena. Phenomenologically, however, we can merely say that on a level of deep trance, I perceive a separate, inviolable entity which led me to question my actual reality as the only real, inviolable reality and led to the promulgation of the supposition that either of us could be the mere subjective experience outwardly projected of the other, even though a certainty existed that this was not the case, that each of us were real and separable. Regardless, a certain relatedness was found in which I could experience the world from the world view of the other and experience him or her experiencing the world from the world view of me.

As mentioned, in my own experience I have entered on several occasions into the world experience of an Other related to me whose activity involves sailing from London around the coast of South America to San Francisco and back. In my experience of sailing into the Bay, at first I had a sense or feeling of wrongness that I couldn't understand. Then it occurred to me that the Golden Gate Bridge was missing, that there were not nearly so many buildings, that the East Bay was particularly barren. Suddenly, I had the experience of him experiencing the Bay from my view, of seeing the Golden Gate Bridge, of seeing the East Bay hills covered with houses, of seeing Marin County, of seeing the structures which were part of my world and of his becoming incredulous. This was not right from his point of view. In that sense we shared a world view that enriched either of us regardless of our metaphysical nature. Such phenomena cut into the usually dry, staid interpretations of this experience as reincarnational memories. If I were simply the linear projection of myself, I could not experience myself experiencing my own world view in the present of another. It would appear to me that I would of necessity be in that world view of the present, totally, while I am here. To go back and forth at will and to appreciate the separateness and relatedness of the other demands a different constitution. The only course seems to be to divest the phenomena from the presupposition of linearity of time, and to rebuild a fresh constitution without a rigid conception of time. If the concept of time is akin to the concept of space in that time is found to exist multidimensionally as an n-dimensional geometric figure which I may expand and contract to several different dimension (as in a multivariate regression) I am more open to a separate aperception of such an experience. I can speak of separate but related entities whom I and they experience as real, as actual, and as inviolable in themselves.

This experience can be used clinically. Recently I have been working in therapy with a woman who feels herself entirely new to this cultural system. She finds herself drawn to theater, to symbolic representation as opposed to literal interpretiveness, and finds herself drawn toward ritual and symbol as a means of psychic enactment. For her, we have used this experience therapeutically to help her to achieve an experience of a separate Other enmeshed in different cultures. She has experienced a relatedness with an African shaman witch-doctor or tribal symbolist. She has experienced a different reality and world view which has helped her to understand her seeming alienation from this culture. This knowledge has intensely enriched her creativity, and enabled her to work through old emotional blocks. In consensual reality her husband was murdered when her son was three months old. She is now preparing a drama based on these related experiences with tribal-others to symbolize and enact her feelings as a method of integration. The incredible creative potential of this is awe-inspiring.

Edith Fiore has used similar experiences in what she terms past life therapy. Such a term, however, suggests the possibility of a certain limited, rigid interpretative framework which may place a damper on the quality of the experience possible. Whereas the experience of a related self in the same time and cultural context can be spoken of as *probable-self-recognition-phenomena*, the experience of a related other-self in another time-cultural context can be termed *alternate-self-recognition-phenomena*. Time is an important distinguishing concept here. Time, culture, and space relate in intriguing ways. I find it therapeutically useful to postulate a synthesis of all of these alternate and probable selves which can be termed the Source Self or Inner Self. I have found it therapeutically useful for the client to engage in dialogue with the Source Self which, in a guided fantasy technique would be termed the client's guide. In addition, I have found it therapeutically useful to allow myself access to this source self, in the sense of receiving imagery and messages of how to communicate and what language and representational system to use with the client. The therapeutic possibilities of this aspect of the "hypnotizable hypnotist" should not be underplayed, as we continue to delve even deeper into the structure of mind and matter.

The following is the second session in a week done with a 30 year old woman who is pregnant and at term. She faces the immanent possibility of a Cesarean section due to a genital herpes infection. The infection was at its peak intensity at the time of this session. It was gone three days following this session. Subsequent work focused on preparing better for the experience of birth. The induction of the first session was longer than this session. In the second session, since Teresa had responded so deeply and quickly the first time, a somewhat shortened technique was used to allow more time for hypnotherapy of the herpes (visualization in this case). We begin.

"I'm thinking you might want to sit down and let yourself begin to relax. Let yourself, if you will, begin to take some slow and deep breaths (pause and deep breathing). Let yourself continue to breathe slowly and deeply, bringing you more in tune with your body if you will, each time you let go of some of the waste products of the lungs, things that you don't need to hold onto. And also letting yourself let go of more and more tension each time that you breathe out. As you continue to breathe in (timed with inhalation) and breathe out (timed with exhalation), you can if you want let yourself experience how it feels to be rid of things you don't want to have and can begin to feel the tension leaving those parts of your body where it's no longer appropriate to be holding on to those things, including tension that right now it would be nice to let go of. You can begin to feel the right arm beginning to relax and maybe there's a warm comfortable feeling as that takes places. You know, caused by more blood being able to flow easily through that part of your body. You can begin to feel very comfortable and relaxed. And you can turn off some of your thinking (pause) about your right hand or anything else and turn your attention to the left hand

and can allow that same feeling that goes along with relaxation to begin in your left hand. Like the flow of water from a lake when it's filled enough to allow that warm feeling like water to flow down your arm and into your shoulder. All those muscles have been very tired at some time all day long. Maybe today you used them and now they've been wanting to relax, just as your shoulders may want to begin to feel very relaxed. As if someone you love were giving them a warm, gentle massage. And that warm, relaxing energy can begin also to accumulate in the shoulder area as you allow yourself to become more and more relaxed. Just like water flowing effortlessly down the side of a mountain, maybe passing by that place where you've been lying listening to the sounds of that water moving down. Or you might imagine yourself standing beneath a small waterfall somewhere in the tropics, with the warm water comfortably washing over your body. Just the right height to make it feel good but not too strong. There in that image the water could strike your scalp just right and then travel down your forehead, taking away any tension with it, dissolving it, and taking itself on down over your eyes and your cheeks, and over your nose and your mouth, helping your whole head to feel a little more comfortable and relaxed. And allowing you to sink down into the couch more as if you were beginning a deep sleep. You can be relaxed if you want to if your head begins to feel heavier, to sink down into the couch, to let the couch support its weight and allow thoughts not to seem to bother you; your neck can feel more relaxed, breathing slowly, easily, deeply. And that waterfall can continue to flow down over your body, down over your back. Step by step you can feel it passing all along your back, along your spine, along the base of your spine, those large muscles on either side. And you can feel it coming down over your front, flowing over each breast, between, over your abdomen, your uterus, all the way down, flowing over your vagina until it passes onto your hips, down to your legs. A very cleansing feeling, a feeling that can wash away tension, can wash away spots that you don't need to have of tension, any tightness in your body, on your body. Can continue on down your legs, glistening on each muscle group as it flows past, allowing your whole body to be able to become so much more relaxed. As it flows down over your feet, traveling over your feet, allowing your feet to relax, maybe you'll feel a warm, comfortable feeling all over your body. Sensation of perhaps lying in the sun. Maybe feeling drowsy in the warm sun at the beach, maybe something else. If so, allowing yourself to savor and enjoy that feeling of, Teresa, being almost asleep. Sometimes a nice feeling can begin like how you would feel if your muscles were very tired and you were allowing them to rest. And you were lying down at night, at the end of the day ready to take a deep sleep. That relaxed you can be, here and now, just as if you were as relaxed as you would be in a deep sleep. If you want, see yourself in a kind of grey fog, all around, very comforting and relaxing. Before you maybe is the mouth of a tunnel. The fog seems to be coming out of the tunnel, looking like fog does when light shines on it. A kind of white light appears on the fog. And you know that, if you decide to enter the tunnel, you can slowly, comfortably and perhaps more rapidly, as you build up speed, move back, move down into yourself. Any noises that you hear can become a part of the process and you can become even more relaxed as this begins to happen. Perhaps noises from around the tunnel, perhaps noises from the past or the present. And you can see into the tunnel clearly, if you want, noticing the texture of the walls, as you come closer to examine the opening of the tunnel. A very comfortable breeze blowing in, air swirling around; a warm and comfortable feeling. And you can let your inner self move a finger on your right hand if what you want to do is to step into the tunnel right now. Being sure *not to think* about moving the finger, just to focus on the image and let whatever will happen with your finger. . . . That's right. You can feel yourself falling into the tunnel. Very warm and easy and fog as if you were being supported as you step into the fog and it just picks you up and lifts you without you having to do the least bit of effort. A feeling that's so comfortable, as if the fog filled the tunnel as if it were a kind of bouyant just carrying you, supporting you even

as it takes you deeper down into the tunnel. All the way
down you can feel yourself supported by that warm,
white, rolling fog as you move down through the tunnel,
the sensation of moving down, traveling down, deeper
down. You can allow yourself to go all the way down,
going as deeply down as you would like to, as would be
comfortable. All the way down into the depths of the
tunnel. And you can relax; you've gone down very
deeply into the tunnel. (This was apparent from her
breathing and behavior.) You can emerge into a place
that can be very relaxing; a place where you can find
answers to your day-to-day problems; a place where
special friends of yours wait to help you find those
answers, to give you guidance; a very relaxing place. And
you can see yourself now, beginning to emerge out of the
tunnel into that place. First, perhaps, you can see light at
the end of the tunnel and then gradually you can become
aware of the white fog beginning to thin as you focus on
your feet, on what you're standing on, become aware of
the things nearby you, of your surroundings nearby and
of your surroundings further away. And now you can
allow your inner self to speak through your lips, to tell
about that comfortable and relaxing place that you find
yourself in deep down at the end of the tunnel."

At this point Teresa began to describe a landscape that she found
herself in. Her voice was too soft to be audible to the tape recorder. It
was a very visually oriented experience, a "being there" very focused
on that world in which she found herself. Eventually she was sitting
down.

"Stay in the place where you found yourself sitting.
Stay very relaxed. You can now let yourself see herpes
walking toward you, coming up to you to sit down, and you
can tell me if you want, exactly what herpes says."

She had visualized a creature she named "herpes" as a very ugly,
troll-like creature. He was coming up to her to speak.

"Ask Herpes now what he has to teach you. What
do you need to learn from him? You can speak for him
through your own lips now."

Herpes began to speak about Teresa's fear of being a good enough
parent, her fear of birth, and her feelings about a previous abortion she

had that had left her feeling very guilty. She was supposed to learn to let go of that.

"Ask herpes now what you have to change to allow him to go away."

Herpes said for her to accept the ugly, unpleasant parts of herself and to realize that herpes was a part of her. This she did and herpes became herself and she welcomed her.

Now you can let yourself watch herpes going to sleep, becoming part of the landscape. When you've finished you can feel yourself being drawn back up through the tunnel, coming back up at your own speed, coming back up into the room that we started in. You can come back very refreshed, invigorated; a feeling of renewed energy, a feeling of being refreshed and washed clean. And you can begin that now, if you want, or in a few seconds.

"Welcome back."
"Yeah."
"I'm sure that you can easily go back to the place you were in to do any hard work that you need to do with yourself whenever you want to."

REFERENCES AND NOTES

[1] Erickson, M., Rossi, I., and Rossi, E. *Hypnotic Realities.* Huntington, NY: Irvington Press, 1980.

[2] Bandler, R., and Grinder, J. *Patterns of the Hypnotic Techniques of Milton H. Erickson, M.D.*, Volumes 1 and 2. Cupertino, California: Meta Publications, 1975 and 1977.

[3] Laszlo, E. Introduction to *Systems Philosophy.* New York: Harper & Row, 1972; The Systems View of the World. New York: George Braziller, 1972.

[4] Grinder, J. and Elgin, S. *A Guide to Transformational Grammar.* New York: Holt, Rinehart, and Winston, 1973.

[5] Chomsky, N. *Aspects of the Theory of Syntax.* Cambridge, Mass.: MIT Press, 1965.

[6] Rossi, E. (ed.) *The Complete Works of Milton Erickson, Volumes I-IV.* Huntington, NY: Irvington Press, 1980.

[7] Erickson, M. The use of symptoms as an integral part of hypnotherapy. *Amer. J. Clin. Hypn.* 8:14-33, 1965.

[8] Roberts, J. *Psychic Politics.* Englewood Cliffs, N.J.: Prentice Hall & Co., 1976.

[9] Roberts, J. *The Unknown Reality,* Volume I. Englewood Cliffs, N.J.: Prentice Hall, 1977.

[10] Boss, Medard. *Existent Foundations of Medicine and Psychology.* New York: Aronson, 1978.

[11] Capra, F. *The Tao of Physics.* Boulder: Shambala, 1976; Zukav, G. The Dancing Wu Li Masters: An overview of the new physics. New York: Bantam, 1980.

[12] The reader can use these categories to analyze hypnosis and visualization sessions already presented. This section is not meant to fully introduce indirect hypnosis. Rather, it is meant to serve as a quick reference to the reader already familiar with indirect hypnosis. The novice can learn from the works referenced above (1, 2, 6, 7) or from workshops, including those offered by Richard Bandler's group in Santa Cruz, California, or by Gayle Peterson of Psychophysiological Associates in Berkeley, California.

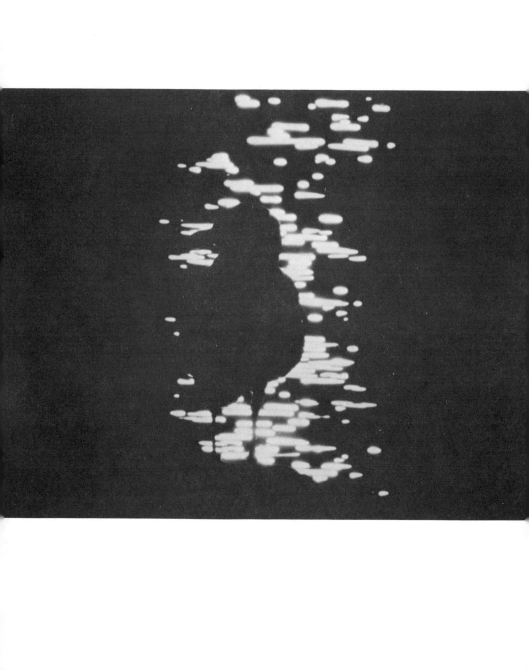

Chapter 11

Conclusions

Mind and Matter has described the application of systems philosophy to the healing of chronic disease. The medicine resulting from applying systems theory is frequently called holistic medicine, and is emerging as *the* new paradigm for conceptualizing health and disease. The holistic or systems model replaces the medical model as the dominant system of thought defining fields of inquiry and theorizing.

The medical model arose within some very specific environmental contexts. The Roman Catholic Church controlled the intellectual world of the Middle Ages until the Renaissance, when the Church's spiritualism had become stale. New thought was needed to break through into yet undiscovered creative realms. Science provided this new milieu.

The world view of the Roman Catholic Church of Europe, even as late as the 16th Century, remained as hard concrete posts supporting the one truth given man by God, set forth in the Old and New Testaments in whatever distorted version each generation happened to receive it. There was no room for creative thought, since all causes were known and were ascribed to God. Science broke through this dogma. The discovery of the microscopic realm brought forth an entirely new world to explore. With the discovery of the association of microbial organisms and disease, another factor related to health and disease, besides punishment or favor from God, was discovered. How liberating to realize that illness was more than just punishment from God! The heretics went even further. Maybe God wasn't involved at all. Maybe illness was just the result of micro-organisms invading the body. God was nowhere in the vicinity of the sick bed — either in cure or in cause. With the lifting of prior beliefs that God's will "caused" everything, new causes were sought. Such causes found a resting place within micro-organisms and specific body organs. The question of why *one particular* human being became ill was defined as outside the paradigm, a position later becoming synonymous with irrelevant.

With new-found freedom from the yoke of the Roman Catholic Church, a new approach to health and disease was able to flourish. Michel Foucault[1] has written eloquently in his book, *The Birth of the Clinic*, about the rise of this new medical paradigm. The autopsy became primary. Illness was defined as existing in the body in a specific location. An autopsy could always reveal the site of the problem.

The concept of the autopsy is closely tied with 17th Century mechanics. Things were as they seemed, nothing more. The planets moved as they were observed to move. A wagon wheel turned as it was observed to turn. When a printing press broke down, it was taken apart, cleaned, and fixed. The same level of attention was turned to human beings. If only we could take apart a human and make repairs as we would a dysfunctional printing press or cannon or firearm. Hence the rise of modern surgery, already so necessary a specialty for a war-like people; and war was certainly not unknown to Europeans.

At first the new paradigm borrowed from early methods of healing which used herbs and other natural remedies. Yet the approach was very different from these earlier, sometimes "pagan" approaches. The approach was that the herb would "fix up" the problem. It was not the case, as in Cherokee medicine, that the herb was related to the whole person and contained spiritual essences. Instead, the herb was disease specific. Further work was done to purify the active substances of herbs into the modern pharmaceuticals of today. We now have synthetic chemistry, allowing science to step aside from even the necessity of beginning with nature's own compounds.

Holistic medicine is slowly emerging with a new set of belief structures. These beliefs have implicitly appeared throughout this book and will now be explicitly summarized.

1. The belief in patient activity

The medical paradigm is characterized by the belief that the ill are victims. This belief was not changed from the Roman Catholic view, but secularized. No longer are the sick victims of God's wrath: they are victims of micro-organisms, chance, or fate. The medical paradigm created a Random God whose aim or wrath was blind. In most 20th

Century medical tracts, the words "wrath of God" could be substituted for "chance" or "random" with no change in meaning. In contrast, holistic medicine views the client as active in promoting health and illness and as *response-able* – capable of responding to life's challenges, including illness.

2. The belief in the interactive nature of life

The medical model freed thinkers from the chains of Catholic mysticism, but created an anti-mystical mysticism in its place. The new mysticism reflected the belief that the elements of nature could be added together, one element replacing the other readily. Through this paradigm, Dalton constructed his atomic table and the beginnings of modern chemistry. Humans were viewed similarly. The various aspects of life were seen as non-interactive. Either a micro-organism *or* a bad diet was the cause. The assumption remained that a cause existed and that, even if an illness had more than one cause, the effects of the two causes could be added together to produce the effect of the illness.

Much of modern medicine still functions on these assumptions. Potentially adverse factors are added together to determine how much at risk a woman is for the complications of childbirth. (Privately, many doctors admit that these risk scores are meaningless except for the most obvious cases.) Epidemiologists continue to figure the relative risk for illness of exposure to various environments and procedures, and statistics are collected on how a group of patients responds to a particular disease. The uniqueness of the individual is ignored as human beings become indistinguishable members of a class and life is reduced to a play of chemicals and electricity. This same paradigm of replacement of interchangeable elements was an important part of the Industrial Revolution, and remains prevalent in much of the business and academic world, where a position is created and a person is found to fill it, replaced readily, moved up, down, or around the company at will.

3. The importance and significance of the individual and of individual uniqueness

The new paradigm places significance upon the individual as the primary unit of study. People are recognized as unique and important *in their own right*. Jay Haley[2] describes one version of this concept of individual uniqueness in a paper entitled "Towards a Theory of Pathological Systems." Haley writes that we can view families as geometric figures with each generation layered below the next. Every corner of the figure (meaning every individual who occupies such a corner) is unique and unrelated to any other corner by virtue of a unique position in space and time. Thus, Haley argues, no two individuals are directly comparable when viewed as a member of a system. The randomization procedures of medical research ignore Haley's insights because randomization of such space-time units is impossible. We should note, however, that such randomization is conceptually similar to removing a heart and attempting to make observations about how a heart functions within a body by observing single heart cells under a microscope.

Medical science recognizes the interaction of systems on a solely biological level in the understanding that hearts become diseased within the body through interaction with other organ systems. For example, high blood pressure in the arteries is associated with the heart having to work harder, with heart muscles becoming thicker, and with other events. The body's metabolic processes, especially those related to calcium and cholesterol, influence the process of atherosclerosis (hardening of the arteries) associated with higher risk of heart attacks. And lung disease, if severe enough, can affect the heart to produce *cor pulmonale,* which can lead to heart failure.

Despite these insights, healing or treatment of the individual is considered without reference to that person's position in a family system, a network of friends and other families, a community system, and even the broader sociocultural system. Issues regarding the broader sociocultural system are especially ignored in most medical model research, since such considerations inevitably reveal that the health care industry, as the largest industry in the United States, has much to gain by people staying or becoming sick and much to lose if prevention were effective. If the population were healthier, medical research and health care institutions would receive less of the current budget than they do now. Even the relationship to illness of a condition as common as poverty is rarely explored, though most clinical research in major teaching hospitals is conducted on the inner-city poor. The forces involved in schizophrenia are similar to the forces of poverty, perhaps explaining economically the observation that schizophrenia is more common among the lower social classes. Medical model explanations of this observation are reminiscent of social Darwinism. The genetic drift hypothesis (still current) maintains that inferior genes (such as those for schizophrenia) drift downward and occupy a larger percentage of the lower classes, but such theorizing does not explain other observations that the families of schizophrenics also frequently show a greater number of highly creative children, as well.

Haley, unfortunately, describes a new kind of determinism, in which individual behavior is largely determined by position in the family system. However, every theoretical perspective is related and provides one view of reality, much as the proverbial blind men describing different aspects of an elephant, and arguing about which is most true. The holistic paradigm represents a synthesis of previous paradigms, giving the blind men sight from which to view a larger reality. Family systems theory needs to be synthesized with individually oriented approaches to present a view in which an individual's behavior is both affected by role and space-time location in a sociocultural-environmental field and the field is also viewed as a gestalt of all the individuals within that field, each person contributing and affecting the field through choices made each day. Regardless of the deterministic elements affecting the perceived desirability of each choice, choices are made, and in that ability to choose, the freedom of the individual is glimpsed.

Victor Frankl,[3] in his book of essays, *Psychotherapy and Existentialism,*writes eloquently about free will and the ability to choose as he describes his experience as an inmate in a Nazi concentration camp during World War II. Frankl describes ultimate choices. Stripped of all other choices, each person was left with the choice of maintaining an active stance of self-integrity and continuing to find meaning from life, or to become a passive victim, dis-integrating from their sense of self-integrity and self-esteem and viewing life as meaningless. Frankl writes that the latter group died very quickly. The former active group either survived insults and the most arduous conditions or died with dignity in spite of the situation.

The holistic paradigm is based upon the significance of the individual. Description leading to theory begins with an understanding of the individual and his or her unique differences from every other human being. Theory construction is systematic, based upon an assessment of which factors affect individual health or upon how health functions within a system for that individual, and not requiring, as does the medical model, that the same factor affect every individual in exactly the same proportions.

A medical model (natural scientific) approach to studying the psychophysiology of asthma would be to construct a hypothesis, for instance, that ambivalent early caretaking of the infant leads to asthma. Evidence for ambivalent early caretaking would be sought in the lives of asthmatics compared to patients with other diseases (diabetes, heart disease). If there were not statistically greater amounts of verifiable ambivalent early caretaking in the asthmatic groups compared to control groups, the hypothesis would be abandoned. A more rigorous extension of this approach would be to randomly assign infants to ambivalent early caretaking to determine if the ambivalently cared for infants had more asthma.

A holistic approach, on the other hand, would begin with description of all possible factors in the life of an individual with asthma, and move toward an understanding of which factors or combinations of factors affect that asthma. Other individuals with asthma would be studied and similarities and differences noted. Theory would begin to develop regarding the many possible individual pathways of development in which asthma is an outcome. The interactive nature of variables is emphasized, rather than the isolation and proof of one effect. Each individual added to the data bank might increase the number of possible pathways to asthma. Common pathways would be sought from analysis of similarities among individuals. Possible pre-disposing or necessary pre-conditions for the development of asthma might be uncovered. A control group would be superfluous to such research, since the emphasis is upon the relationships among events and factors rather than an isolation and comparison of factors. Mathematics would still be relevant, but a different kind of mathematics than the common techniques of chi-square significance testing and linear regression used presently. I envision a mathematical framework which relates to description of interactive effects among variables and to modelling of systems, and probably more tied to differential calculus and the solving of non-linear, simultaneous equations.

4. Emphasis on the meaning of life, especially of a specific individual's life

The holistic paradigm is concerned with the meaning of life for the individual person. Values are defined by the person and are unique to that person. Multiple value systems are tolerated, unlike the emphasis made by the medical model upon length of life and avoidance of risk at all costs. Medical model thinkers may quickly proceed with disfiguring surgery to maximize the chances for cancer recovery without thought to what that surgery will do to the person's quality of life. Breast cancer provides an example of doctors often removing the entire breast and destroying a woman's self-image and body image, when simply removing the lump of cancer (lumpectomy) may be sufficient. The medical model demands *absolute* certainty without reflecting that quality and meaning of life of the individual are relevant considerations.

5. Precedence of observation and description over theory and statistical redundancy

The holistic model is phenomenologically based. It begins with simple description of events and of people. Such description is made without value judgement or premature interpretation. What can be observed receives emphasis, rather than what will fit a currently accepted theory. The medical model's emphasis upon descriptions matching pre-existing theory relegates many important observations to non-existence. The medical model prefers statistical descriptions of the properties of groups well away from the level of the individual, and the medical model scientist responds that case studies never prove anything.

I helped a medical student begin a study of stress and diabetes and in the process learned much about the medical model critique of holistic research. We began with detailed descriptions of the lives of some individual patients with diabetes. We covered every relevent detail − childhood events, stresses preceeding the development of the illness, spiritual beliefs, life events, emotional changes paralleling changes in their illness, and their general world view. Our plan was to map out the emotional and stress factors present for each patient, looking for similarities and differences between patients. We would work therapeutically with those patients, having formulated a theory for each patient of how diabetes functioned within his or her personal system. We would observe if the diabetes changed for each person as factors changed which should, according to our systems perspective, allow the diabetes to improve. The intervention for each patient was different and unique.

A departmental researcher of the university curtailed this research. He argued that the only valid design would be with a matched control group and with each person receiving exactly the same intervention. There should be random assignment of patients into treatment and control group and the intervention should be completely replicable by anyone, not dependent upon the unique world of the patient. I realized then that individual uniqueness was not to be considered as a relevant factor. A meaningful intervention should be expected to help everyone or no one in the medical model. The idea of tailoring the intervention to the patient was heresy. I could not understand why the same intervention was expected to help everyone until I realized that there was an underlying belief that membership in the class of diabetic patients meant that every patient should be the same and should respond the same to a psychophysiological intervention, much as they would be expected to respond the same to insulin. Since I knew each patient had a very different response even to insulin, I was sure that their psyches would differ even more so. The final objection was to our proposal of a different theory for each patient. Here we found that the belief was that the theory should fit the disease and not the patient. The research was viewed as non-scientific and "fluffy." I was, however, grateful for this opportunity to realize the tremendous differences in medical model thinking compared to holistic assessment.

6. Awareness of "whole" and gestalts

"The whole is greater than the sum of the parts" is an expression frequently uttered by holistic thinkers, to which the medical model responds, "The whole is best understood by dividing it into smaller and smaller parts for intensive study of the smallest divisible units." Such differing perspectives illustrate the integrative view versus the reductionist view. Both views are useful, but the medical model has become so enamored with reduction and specialization that the concept of integration has been lost. Unfortunately, many so-called holistic doctors are as reductionistic as their academic, medical center colleagues. Substituting vitamins for drugs and herbs for penicillin does not herald a paradigm change. A paradigm change consists of a second-order change of thinking in which the relationship among patient, treatment, and practitioner changes. Substituting herbs for antibiotics is only a first-order change. The basic relationship of external substance curing internal ailment without patient initiated change remains constant. A second-order change might involve a consideration that the patient's basic lifestyle and beliefs contributing to that lifestyle must change to change the susceptibility to infection. Such awareness does not mean avoiding the benefits of drugs or herbs; it simply places an understanding of their effectiveness within an enlarged perspective. Enlightenment consists of the progressive widening of the context of understanding.

The holistic model does not place itself in opposition to the medical model, but, rather, builds upon the foundations laid by the medical model. While teaching at a medical school, I was confronted by a professor of internal medicine asking how I would treat a patient bleeding to death on the highway with visualization. "On the way to find a surgeon," I replied. I explained that while I thought patients might someday be able to control bleeding through imagery techniques, such a situation was not the one for training and experimenting with a novice patient. David Cheek,[4] an obstetrician-hypnotherapist, has written about incidences of controlling post-partum hemorrhage by telling the woman that she had to stop bleeding with a hypnotic suggestion to do so. Nevertheless, he did so as he prepared his medical armamentarium to intervene as quickly as possible. I have had personal experience with such intervention being successful in the case of postpartum hemorrhage, as have midwifery and obstetrical colleagues. Finally, I tried to reassure my internist colleague that a holistic approach did not intend to throw away all the insights of modern medicine, only to build upon them.

7. Faith in the transcendence of the individual and in innate human potential

The holistic paradigm contains within it the faith that human problems can be solved without any additional biotechnology (even though there is nothing wrong with new and improved biotechnology). The belief remains in the innate ability of human beings to solve problems without more technology. The limits of the human mind to alter structural reality must be determined on a case-to-case basis, those limits being only "experientially and experimentally determined," in the words of John Lilly. This expression translates as "we never know how much we can do until we try." Trying requires believing that success is possible. The medical model world is plagued with doubt and skepticism. Success contingent upon faith is hard to achieve with the medical model. The medical model thinker would believe diabetes cannot be improved except through change of diet, drugs, or exercise. If I had believed so, I would never have taken the opportunity to work with Wanda, described in Chapter Three, who does make tremendous change. I would never have learned what she taught me about the relationships among emotions, beliefs, and diabetes. Doubt, skepticism, and emphasis on theory as primary keeps medical model thinkers from appreciating the possibilities inherent within human potential.

8. Reliance upon process rather than structure

The questions of "how?" and "what?" take precedence over the question of "why?" in the holistic model. "How" is a process question. What events help this patient's asthma to appear or disappear? How does it work within the system comprising that patient's life? The "why is it this way?" question is intrinsically interesting, but not always necessary to answer.

Lastly, we must remember that even a new paradigm eventually becomes outmoded, and holistic thinking is no exception. If we can show wisdom in taking from the medical model what is valuable, perhaps thinkers yet to come, will take from the holistic model in equally wise ways to build even newer ways to think about health and illness.

9. The importance of relationship

Throughout the case histories discussed, the relationship of client and practitioner has been stressed. Relationship is primary, as it provides the container and catalyst for change. Many practitioners and clients do not recognize the primacy of relationship, believing that a particular vitamin or treatment was all important for their cure. But vitamins are given by another caring human being. Techniques such as acupuncture or visualization are administered by another human being. My next book, *Loving and Healing* (with Gayle Peterson) is about the importance of relationship in the healing process. The reader could well benefit from re-examining the preceding case studies from the standpoint of what was the relationship between client and practitioner. *All healing occurs in the context of relationship* — of self to self, with another person, or with a spiritual Source.

Outcomes

The final measure of usefulness of a theory or approach is its usefulness in helping clients. I present here the results I have observed in my clinical practice (with Gayle Peterson, LCSW). Our scale of change is simple:

1 – significant deterioration and/or death
2 – worsening
3 – no change
4 – improvement
5 – no evidence of disease

Our practice began in a community clinic and later became a private practice. With other funding, it would have been interesting to build other measurements into our outcomes, such as speed of change. In a private practice or clinic setting, many factors determine the client's availability for treatment. Our most common frustration was the lack of availability of clients for the intensity or amount of treatment we felt was necessary. Uniformly, clients who did not improve, were not as available for treatment as we wished.

These results do not reflect rigorous research, but merely show that hope is warranted for improvement of chronic disease. More rigorous research would have quantified the amount of improvement, relating it to the severity of the problem when treatment began and ended. Clients who came less than five times are not included in these tables. Why did these people choose not to continue? Rigorous research would address that question. We have now begun a rigorous study of a systems approach to asthma and allergies and hope to answer these questions in the near future. For now, may these results inspire others to begin the healing process and practitioners to work more optimistically toward improvement of chronic disease.

Table 1

Outcomes of chronic disease treatment — 1975 to 1985					
Ailment	# scoring 1	# scoring 2	# scoring 3	# scoring 4	# scoring 5	Total # clients
Diabetes	0	1	2	4	1	8
Uterine fibroids	0	0	1	19	10	30
Undiagnosed pelvic masses	0	0	1	0	4	5
Cancer	4	0	0	6	8	18
Asthma	0	1	5	12	15	33
Allergies	0	1	9	17	3	30
Hypertension	0	4	6	10	19	39
Multiple Sclerosis	0	1	2	2	0	5
Myasthenia gravis	0	1	0	1	0	2
Spastic cerebral palsy	0	1	0	1	0	2
Eye diseases	0	1	2	7	3	13
Ulcers	0	0	2	5	7	14
Intestinal disease	0	1	1	8	7	17
Chronic infections	0	6	10	14	35	59
Amyotrophic lateral selerosis	1	0	0	0	0	1
Back pain	0	3	10	29	24	66
Chronic otitis media (children)	0	2	6	10	26	44
Chronic pain (not back)	0	0	6	33	17	56
Obesity/Eating Disorders	0	0	9	25	10	44
Thyroid disease	0	1	3	5	1	10
Substance use disorders	0	0	7	20	9	36
Schizophrenia	0	0	6	10	3	19
Manic-depressive disorder	0	2	3	5	0	10
Heart disease	0	1	2	4	2	9

Table 2

Outcome — Treatment of birth related conditions 1975-1985					
Condition	# scoring 1	# scoring 2	# scoring 3	# scoring 4	# scoring 5*	Total # clients
Breech presentation	0	0	9	0	78	87
VBAC (vaginal birth after Cesarean)	0	0	11	20**	54	85
Prenatal hypertension/ toxemia	0	1	2	14	41	58
Prenatal and medical complication/ disease	0	0	9	11	33	53
Preparation for normal birth (80-85)	0	21	12	25	143	200

* 5 indicates entirely normal birth.
** 4 indicates vaginal birth with some interventions used.

Renés Descartes and Norman Vincent Peale inspired the title of *Mind and Matter*. Descartes divided the world into the things of the mind *(res cogitans)* and the things of matter *(res extensa)*. Peale introduces the idea of mind over matter. My title implies that mind is matter and matter is mind and therefore consciousness. Neither holds dominion, suppresses or controls the other. Both dance in harmony, as described by the Chinese word for physics, *Wu Li*, which implies that physics is the study of the harmony of nature's dance. So, too, should medicine be the study of the harmony of the dance of mind and matter.

REFERENCES AND NOTES

[1] Foucault, Michel. *Birth of the Clinic: an archaeology of medical perception.* New York: Harper & Row, 1976.

[2] Haley, Jay and Lynn Hoffman. *Techniques of Family Therapy.* New York: Basic Books, 1968.

[3] Frankl, Victor. *Psychotherapy and Existentialism.* New York: Washington Square Press, 1985.

[4] Cheek, David B. and Leslie M. LeChron. *Clinical Hypnotherapy.* Orlando, FL: Grune & Stratton, 1968.

Epilogue

The preceding chapters have focussed on a systems approach to healing chronic illness. Models were developed to explain how illness serves us and the larger groups to which we belong, solving problems that seem to have no other solution. Other world concerns can also be considered from a systems perspective. We must ask the questions: Whom does poverty serve? Whom does war serve? Whom does hunger serve? How do these conditions serve other world dilemnas. The major lessons of a systems approach to medicine can orient us to a systems approach to other world issues:

1. Every patient with any problem represents a unique situation.

2. Diagnosing the illness does not define the proper treatment.

3. A particular illness in a particular patient is solving problems for that patient and for the larger groups to which the patient belongs — the family, the extended kinship system, and the community.

4. Treatment planning must consider every aspect of the patient, including biochemistry, psychophysiology, the family, the community, the patient's belief systems, etc.

5. Healing is a synergistic result of applying technique within the context of relationship.

6. Healing is a process catalyzed by intervention and interaction with other systems, including those of the practitioner(s).

7. There are no causes of the illness or causes of the cure that can

be isolated. Rather, we define the context, note the occurence of the illness, intervene, assess the results of intervention, and plan further intervention in dynamic interaction. Logical cause-and-effect thinking can only hinder our progress.

Appling these lessons to world problems, we may say that:

1. Every problem and every culture is unique. The answers for one culture may not work in another. Successfully solving one problem does not mean we can solve another.

2. Identifying a problem does not define how to solve the problem. These are the insights of a systems view of the world. Jay Forrester of the Massachusetts Institute of Technology, for example, has used a computer model to study the decline of American cities. Forrester discovered that our most humane attempts to save the inner city actually resulted in worsening conditions. He found that large systems respond with behavior that is counter-intuitive.

Intuition might tell us that we can improve depressed urban areas through the creation of low-cost housing, job training programs for low-income workers, and Federal subsidies for the poor and the unemployed. Forrester found that the overall effect of these programs was to draw a low income population to the city and then to trap them in a downward spiral of frustration and discontent.

Low-income housing occupies land that would otherwise be used by industry, thereby creating less jobs for the disadvantaged. Simultaneously, it attracts a higher density of low income residents to the area. This actually drives some existing businesses away. Job training in this context is a sham since it increases skills in an area of decreased opportunities, and increases frustration and depression.Federal subsidies do nothing to correct the underlying difficulties, allowing the problems to grow to the limits of the available funding, while encouraging low incomes so that residents can qualify for special housing.

The result is that cities attract low-income groups and substantially worsen the quality of their lives. People become locked in a system that prevents escape and reduces hope. Forrester's model showed that cities and complex social systems respond counter to individual intuition and to good intentions. Thus identifying a problem may tell us nothing about its solution.

A similar problem exists in medicine. When a person becomes disabled and can no longer work, it is logical for a society to provide that person with money for sustenance until he can work. The problem is that our disability system has no provision for gradual improvement from chronic illness. According to the system, you are either well or you are sick. There is no in-between state. As soon as a person begins to improve and make an income, that income is deducted from disability payments. Disability payments are generally much smaller than the person's former income. For a disabled person to begin to work is a major step, and to receive no reward from society for that effort is very frustrating. Many disabled people decide it is easier not to bother than to go to the great effort to work and to realize no extra income. Additionally, once they begin to work, they are often under pressure to be off disability immediately. Fear begins to operate that they will be called for an evaluation and told they must suddenly work full-time. It seems much safer not to work at all.

Working therapeutically with people receiving disability payments can be very difficult. While our social system is rewarding them for being sick, there are no rewards for the slow improvement that occurs as the disability improves. Many patients never step out of this system that encourages their remaining ill.

The American system of health insurance may contribute to illness in a similar manner. American health insurance may be more accurately called sickness insurance. Insurance pays the cost of being treated for being sick. It does not pay people to remain healthy. The only reward for health is health itself, which is insufficient in some families. To "get your money's worth" from insurance, you must be sick and use it. Otherwise it seems that great sums of money are being paid in premiums for no benefit.

3. A particular problem is always solving another problem on a higher level. Systems tend to aggregrate to form super-systems. Cells aggregate to form an organ; organs aggregate to form a body; bodies aggregate to form a family; families aggregate to form a community, and so on to the level of the entire earth. Components of systems are always attempting to solve problems for the larger group. War, for example, is an attempt to solve an important problem for both capitalist and socialist societies. The United States and the U.S.S.R. argue vituperatively about what is the proper means of production. What neither country allows itself to recognize is that a production orientation itself is becoming antiquated. We are using up all our natural resources in the name of production. Without production, both the United States and the U.S.S.R. could restructure the entire economy to become service oriented and resource renewing. Instead, this production orientation predisposes us for war. War and the threat of war creates a need for production. When the survival of the nation is apparently threatened,

the depletion of natural resources seems a minor matter. The elimination of war will require a change in the goal of both social systems to produce ever more and more. The gross national product must no longer constantly increase in order to indicate national health.

Systems aggregate to form larger wholes whenever a means of communicating information becomes available. With modern communication we live in a global community. The availability of communication has resulted in multi-national corporations and world communities. Amnesty International, the Shell Oil Corporation, and the United Nations are equally examples of this tendency. The values of super-systems may vary tremendously, but the tendency to aggregate is always there. With modern communication and modern weaponry it is essential that we guide the values of our developing super-systems. Thus, in considering any problem, we must look to the larger systems that the problem may be serving.

4. Solving problems requires a consideration of all aspects of the problem − meaning a consideration of all the levels of systems that may be involved. Solving the problem of war may require consideration, on the economic level, of changing a production-based economy to a service-based economy. A change in consciousness of individuals in the society may also be necessary to allow use of non-violent conflict resolution. Beliefs and attitudes must change along with the ways we relate to one another. Each discipline of science and the humanities has something to offer to the potential solution. Similarly, in a healing approach to chronic illness, we integrate the level of the nutritional (molecular), the emotional (brain-mind-body), the familial, and the social.

5. Solving problems requires the creation of relationships. People − not techniques, theories or approaches − solve problems. We cannot apply theories to people, but must work to develop solutions in the context of relationship with the people whom the problem affects.

6. The actual solving of a problem is a process catalyzed by intervention and interaction of systems on all levels, including the systems to which the problem solvers belong.

7. There are no causes that can be isolated. Rather, we define the context of the problem, note its occurence, intervene, assess the results of intervention, and plan further intervention in dynamic interaction. Linear cause-and-effect thinking can only hinder our progress.

To recall Chapter Five, a natural system is a whole with irreducible, even mathematically definable, properties. A system is a complex entity about which it is possible to speak logically and clearly. For example, we say, "the hospital wouldn't let her do what she wanted." When we use the word hospital in this manner we are referring to the hospital as a system. Unconsciously, we frequently refer to systems without understanding the full implications of our use of systems concepts in everyday language.

A system has some formal structure built upon the basis of interdependence among its parts. An important way to understand the structure of a larger system to which we belong is through the use of Plato's technique of the dialectic. When people come together for discussion and learning, by challenging each other and responding to that challenge, we come closer to the truth than we could in isolation. This is because we each experience different aspects of the system we are trying to understand. This concept is crucial to understanding how to apply systems concepts to world problems. *Systems applications require team approaches in which the method of the dialectic can be applied.*

Groups are systems that manifest certain charactertistics by virtue of the task they were formed to complete and the nature of their activities. While individual members in a system may be replaced, the function of these members tend to remain the same. Cells replace each other regularly but the function of the body remains the same. The United States changes Presidents regularly, but many of the policies and functions of the country do not change. It is this invariance that has led some observers to propose that the military-industrial complex originally described and feared by President Eisenhower is actually running the country.

Systems must change with the times. Any system that tries too hard to stay the same becomes an ossified relic of the past. Such systems may be preserved in museums, formal or otherwise, but do not contribute further to the growth of the world around them. For example, Native American culture has tended to ossify in the past, and the culture was slowly dying. Now courageous younger Native Americans are defying tribal traditions of silence and are sharing the Native American heritage with any who care to learn. The result is a resurgence in the power and meaning of the Native American world view for the entire world. We can only regret the loss of knowledge due to earlier prohibitions against teaching outsiders. In contrast, Hindu culture has maintained itself throughout years of invasions by assimilating the invading culture and continuing despite the invasion.

In considering a systems approach to health, we have seen the inter-facing of the emotional brain and other body systems — especially the immune systems, metabolism, the endocrine system, etc. We have considered a method of working with the body that speaks to the way the component systems of the body interact with each other. We have worked on the more subtle levels of energetic interaction to avoid the grosser level interventions of surgery and pharmaceuticals. In the body, uncooperative systems are either rejected or eventually destroy the body and sign the death warrant of the whole. Surgical medicine aims at cutting out these uncooperative systems or structurally forcing them to change. Pharmaceutical medicine attempts to chemically manipulate the lack of cooperation. The healing approaches we have been discussing work to change the style of interaction among the systems and to find ways for uncooperative elements to learn to contribute to the greater good of the body. In studying this problem, we have frequently observed that the uncooperative organ system may be cooperating well with the larger family system or the extended kinship system or community needs. The treatment for chronic illness described in this book almost always contains a prescription for working with the larger family or kinship system to effect change. Changes in the larger system allow the component individual (a lower level in the hierarchy) and the component organs of that individual (an even lower level) to move toward health. In other terms, we can say that energy has been freed that was delegated upwards in the hierarchy.

We can use this same approach to solve world problems. When we consider a systems approach to health care we realize that the field of medicine is not isolated from politics or sociology. When we study the behavior of the larger governmental systems, we are studying one aspect of the forces shaping health, even when we do not name health as a concern. The health of the body cannot be separated from the health of the family, the community, the nation, and the world.

The current academic separation of medicine from political science is another example of the divide and conquer strategy which keeps us from solving our world problems. A new discipline of humanity must be created which will not isolate the various disciplines of the study of humanity in unrelated spheres. A new science of humanity is needed that includes medicine as the study of the relationship of the world and its structures and behaviors to the proper physiological functioning of the human body. We are ready to discard the garage mechanic approach to the body which isolates health from the world.

Most of us are usually concerned with and focused on our individual problems without making a connection to the broader context of how individual problems affect, and are affected by, larger groups. But computer models have begun to show us how beliefs shape institutions and institutions and societies shape beliefs. A systems approach is being used by global modelers to develop computer simulations of world problems which are similar to those described for urban renewal by Professor Forrester. The *Tarrytown Letter* of December, 1982 describes some of these efforts. A computer can simulate a systems approach in which every variable is related to every other variable. Using a computer to do modeling of this sort can remind us that change in one variable changes all other variables.

The message we get from these attempts to model systems is that the world is a complex, interconnected whole. Its problems are not separate, simple, or divisable. Every problem affects every other problem, and we must transcend simple cause-and-effect thinking in order to solve these problems.

Global modelers have come from many different perspectives and original biases, but have eventually come to agree on several main conclusions, listed in the *Tarrytown Letter*. These are:

1. Most thinking about global matters is so limited by regional myopia that it lacks the level of consciousness necessary for useful insights.

This has been the thesis of *Mind and Matter* about chronic illness. The medical system has so myopically restricted itself to laboratory biology that it has failed to appreciate the larger aspects of the problem of chronic illness. Since the biological perspective is, in itself, insufficient, it has been impossible to address problems of the individual client.

In the area of preventing prematurity, most researchers stress better prenatal care, without specifying what must change in prenatal care. Simply taking more blood pressures, measuring more urine, and observing the growth of babies more often will not change prematurity rates. More than just medical variables must be addressed.

2. There's enough food and basic resources to take care of everyone on the planet. Scarcity is not the problem. Politics and values stand in the way.

A similar consideration is true for health care. With the knowledge we now have, and with an approach such as I have described, we can eliminate and improve much chronic illness. Such an approach would be human intensive rather than technology intensive. It would stress relationship rather than laboratory. More money would be spent in salaries, less on hospitals and lab fees. The job market would shift to emphasize human skills rather than technological skills in the health care industry. Only politics and values prevent this from happening. Politics and values prevent medical students from being taught about holistic approaches to chronic illness — few medical schools have any information at all on these subjects in their curriculum.

3. Models increasingly reveal that people and countries are far more interdependent that we imagined. Actions on one part of the globe affect other sectors — but it's currently impossible to pinpoint consequences with accuracy.

In health care, each person's illness affects every other member of a community. I have seen families in which the illness of one member seems to stabilize the health of all other members. When one members improves, other family member(s) become ill, although sometimes it's not possible to predict which member that will be.

4. There's enough to go around today, but tomorrow looks different. Population and resources cannot grow infinitely on a finite planet.

Health care has already reached the limits of expansion. Government agencies call for price reductions. Health Maintainence Organizations are proliferating, but do not provide what their name implies. Most of these facilities provide emergency and sickness care and have minimal or no facilities or funding for prevention or for the long-term treatment of chronic illness in a holistic manner that would allow for improvement. The usual treatment is, "Take these drugs for the rest of your life and see me once a month to adjust the dosage." When the new drugs inevitably fail (see my discussion on asthma drugs from Chapter Four), then different drugs are substituted. All this is done within the framework of a fifteen minute office visit. I worked in one large "HMO" in which I was expected to treat patients with chronic pain in fifteen minute office visits, once every six weeks. When I observed that no one would be helped on this schedule, and suggested that we work more intensively with a smaller group of patients to effectively treat them, I was told that everyone had equal right to our services and other subscribers of the health care plan would complain if they could not have an appointment. The issue was not effective treatment. It was preventing subscribers from complaining about lack of appointments. The solution to the problem actually worked against effective health care.

5. How fast can the world respond to over-production of population and goods? No one knows.

In health care, we continue to ignore the role of over-production of population and goods in affecting illness. In addition, we continue to overproduce health care technology. The most expensive new technology is the artificial heart. The cost of an artificial heart is so great that such a device will probably never be practical. It does not even seem to keep people alive that long, yet there is a fascination   with the technology. The same amount of money would go very far in treating chronic illness patients and in preventing heart disease.

Biomedicine, however, cannot conceptualize prevention because of its medical myopia. Prevention has become eat shellfish or don't eat shellfish. Drink milk or don't drink milk. There is no effort to look at underlying behavior or beliefs particular to our society, or to look at relationships.

6. "Business as usual" will not lead to a desirable future – nor will it even meet our basic human needs. Projections show an ever widening gap between rich and poor, plus problems with raw materials, pollution and worsening economic conditions.

"Business as usual" in health care seems to be benefiting few except for the captains of industry. Doctor's salaries are falling and patients are not getting healthier. Meanwhile pharmaceutical companies are grossing large profits and suppliers of health care technology are making profits. The profits are going to the laboratory/technical side of the health care industry. They are diminishing for the individual practitioner, with the possible exception of certain kinds of surgeons (cardiovascular, especially).

A World Health Organization report shows that the trend in reduction of death from infections began in 1850. The introduction of antibiotics did not grossly change the slope of that decline when streptomycin was introduced in 1948 for wide-spread consumption. Most of the decline had already occurred and continued to occur at its pre-antibiotic rate. In medical school, we heard much about the great role of antibiotics in preventing death. What a shock it was for me to read this!

The World Health Organization has further suggested that most of the technology that money is spent upon in Third World countries has little benefit in improving health care. If that is so, perhaps it is true for developed countries as well.

7. The world's socio-economic systems will undergo a marked transition over the next three decades. Life as we know it will soon be quantitatively and qualitatively very different.

Will the health care system respond? Probably not in a large scale manner until people put pressure upon it.

8. Time is of the essence. A restructuring of the world's social, economic, and political systems seems the only way to save the planet. Technology can, at most, extend the life of the planet for a few decades.

We have already reached the limits of technology to extend human life, given the current social conditions. To continue to pour money into technology is pointless but will probably continue to be done unless we, the people, can prevent it. Pharmaceutical companies will not prevent it. Suppliers of technology will not prevent it. Most doctors will not prevent it, because they would feel naked without technology to use in treatment. Many doctors want very much to feel special. What makes them different from other health practitioners? Their expertise in prescribing drugs, in doing technical procedures to the body, and their ability to do major surgery. Doctors will not relinquish these modalities until medical students are trained to find value in human emotions and relationships.

9. Simple solutions that focus on only one problem at a time are generally counterproductive. Decisions must be made within the broadest possible context, and with models which take the entire system into account.

In medicine, we do not look beyond the simple solution. We treat one patient at a time in short visits, as closely spaced as possible. We try to isolate one factor to treat − one gene, one bacteria, one virus. We treat with medication, not imagining that a family intervention could give us more healing impact than a drug. Physicians are not trained to think about systems any larger than the human body. In fact, after specialty training, most physicians limit the scope of their thought to the particular organ system in which they have specialized.

In summary, not only the health of the body but the health of the world can be served through changing our approaches to problem solving. We need human approaches emphasizing relationship. We need methods of perception that free us from blame and simple cause-and-effect thinking. We need to recognize that we are all part of the problem, and we can all become part of the solution. Only then can we exit the cycle of blame and guilt and begin to achieve a truly inhabitable planet.

Index

P

pacing, 298
pain, 159-161, 189-190, 224-226, 229-230, 279
paradoxical euphoria, 70
parts concept, 54, 102-103
past lives, 33-35, 154, 307-310
pathological-anatomical mode, xii, 166
patient responsiveness, xii, 27
Payne, M., 202
pectoralis major clavicular muscle, 248
Pennington, G.W., 200
Perls, Fritz, 138
permission giving, 172-173
Peterson, Gayle, 17, 201, 237, 244
Petrie, Asineth, 183
phenomenology, xvi-xvii, 33, 152
placebo effect, 180
Platt, J., 200
Podolsky, E., 202
politics, 10, 17
power, 40-41
pregnancy, 174, 176-177, 205-206, 231, 310-314
Pribram, Karl, 201
Probable Worlds, 305-310
P.S.I. Graduate School of Professional Psychology, 203
psychoanalytic views, 174-175, 200, 210-212, 294
psychobiocultural model, 178-179
psychological adjustment, 62-63, 181-182
psychological testing, 122, 175-176
Psychophysiological Associates, 316
psychosomatic view, 74
psychotherapy, 33, 64-65, 176, 260-294

Q

question asking, 220

R

radiation therapy, 11

random chance, 225
rape, 229-230
rational universe, 3
reality, 22
rebirthing, 95
reducers and augmenters, 182-187
reducing mode, 186, 190
reframing, 243
regulation of sensory input, 185
relapse, 258
relaxation, 214-217, 220-224, 232-234
religion, xi, 2
renal blood flow, 198
representational systems, 141, 185-186, 191-192, 303-304
repression, 90, 230-231
research methods, xvi, xviii, 59, 178-179
resistance, 35, 102, 108, 212-214, 297
resolution, 186, 228-229
resolution threshold, 82-83
respect, 144
responsibility, for cancer, 12-13
    of client, 144
Riemann sum, 307
right to refuse, 250
Roberts, Jane, 295, 306, 308
Rogers, Carl, 143-144
Rosenfeld, C.R., 202
Rossi, Ernest, 315
Rothman, D., 200
Rubenstein, 173-174

S

San Francisco Chronicle, 18
Sandler, B., 200-201
Satir, Virginia, 158
Seemans, Mary, 167
selectional restriction, 301
self-esteem, 12-13, 44, 53, 70, 108, 209, 287
self-fulfilling prophecy, 2
Selye, Hans, 182, 201
sensoristat, 183
sensory modalities, 141, 186-187
Servadio, E., 295
sexuality, 45-47, 50, 126, 214, 241, 245, 250
Shaimberg, David, 292-294
Simonton, O. Carl and Stephanie, 19, 26-27, 55
sleep, 104, 220

U

T

V

The Mind and Matter Series

Book 1

Mind and Matter: Healing and Chronic Disease. By Lewis E. Mehl.

Mind and Matter presents a pragmatic and workable approach to the holistic healing of a variety of chronic illnesses, including cancer, asthma, uterine fibroids, and diabetes. Transcripts of session segments with illustrative case material are included, and techniques of visualization, hypnosis and bodywork are discussed at length. The methodologies presented are creative and valuable tools for all health practitioners.

Book 2

Pregnancy as Healing: A Holistic Philosophy for Prenatal Care. Volume 1. By Lewis E. Mehl and Gayle H. Peterson.

Pregnancy as Healing is the first book to definitively describe the postulates of a holistic model, and expand theory into practice. It presents a philosophy of medicine which unites the emotional and spiritual aspects of life with the intimately physical experience of childbearing in a way that reduces complications and trauma during pregnancy and birth. Included is material on holistic prenatal assessment, systems theory, uterine inertia, and birth visualization.

Book 3

Cesarean Birth: Risk and Culture. Volume 2 of Pregnancy as Healing. By Lewis E. Mehl and Gayle H. Peterson.

Cesarean Birth takes the reader through an experience of pregnancy as a time of healing. Holistic prenatal care decreases medical complications through increasing knowledge and understanding of how the elements in a woman's life come together to impact the birthing process. The book addresses issues of vaginal birth after cesarean, family roles and birth complications, grief, and the necessary work of worrying.

Book 4

Birthing Normally: A Personal Growth Approach to Childbirth.
By Gale Peterson. Preface by Michel Odent.

No other birthing book explores the mind-body issue as fully. The author offers simple suggestions to uncover feelings about body image, birth beliefs, and sexuality, and to discover the way these feelings influence the kind of labor a woman has. For the professional, the author suggests ways to affect pregnancy and labor positively through insight, timing, and choice of words. Prospective mothers who use this book as a companion on their inner journey of parenthood will find it yields very positive results.

Also from Mindbody Press:

Professional Training Cassettes by Gayle Peterson and Lewis Mehl.

These tapes are of benefit to both pregnant women and health professionals as an aid to learning visualization skills presented in the Mind and Matter Series of books. Tapes are available on the following topics:

Visualization for first time motherhood

Visualization for second time motherhood

Preparation for Vaginal Birth after Cesarean

Breech visualization

Visualization for Infertility/Insomnia

Visualization for Breastfeeding/High blood pressure

"Creature Feature": exploratory visualization for eczema, asthma, hay fever

Mindbody Press
1749 Vine Street
Berkeley, CA 94703
415-644-8242